TRANSLATING AND
THE COMPUTER 7

Also available from Aslib

Machine Aids for Translators
Translating and the Computer 2

Term Banks for Tomorrow's World
Translating and the Computer 4

Tools for the Trade
Translating and the Computer 5

Translation and Communication
Translating and the Computer 6

TRANSLATING AND THE COMPUTER 7

Edited by
CATRIONA PICKEN

Proceedings of a conference
jointly sponsored by
Aslib, The Association for Information Management
The Aslib Technical Translation Group
The Translators' Guild

14–15 November 1985
CBI Conference Centre, Centre Point, London

First published in 1986
by Aslib, The Association for Information Management,
Information House,
26–27 Boswell Street,
London WC1N 3JZ

© Aslib and contributors, 1986

British Library Cataloguing in Publication Data

International Conference on Translating
  (7th : 1985 : London)
  Translating and the Computer: 7th
  International Conference on Translating.
  1. Machine translating
  I. Title II. Picken, Catriona
  418′.02   P308

  ISBN 0–85142–200–4

Publishing services by Ponting-Green, London and Basingstoke
Photoset by Parker Typesetting Service, Leicester
Typeset in 10 point Plantin
Printed and bound in Great Britain by
The Alden Press, Oxford

CONTENTS

Session II: The impact of machine translation and high technology

Introduction

Catriona Picken

Where two or three translators are gathered together, the talk these days is often of technology; where two or three hundred are gathered together for the 'Translating and the Computer' conference, the talk is mainly of the new technology.

The change that strikes me, and, I expect, other observers, between the early conferences in the series and the most recent ones, is that then – ten years ago – the computer was a mainframe, large organisations had them, and they were attended to by people who had been initiated into the rites and who acted as intermediaries between ordinary mortals and The Machine. Now every other fourteen-year-old is perfectly familiar with computers, either at home or in school, and quite a few parents can grasp them too ... In the remote past of ten years ago, machine translation was something which individual freelance translators, and many staff translators as well, felt they had to know about, without necessarily believing it might impinge on their lives. In 1985, whether or not we approve of its advent, machine-assisted translation is a reality, even to the extent of being used as a teaching tool for the training of students, as Patrick Corness's paper shows.

Readers of these proceedings will soon realise that even the 'first day' papers, where the attention of the conference is focused on the translator as individual, virtually all make some reference to computers, information technology, call it what you like. Everyone is having to come to terms with the new technology, and the first day's three case studies illustrate how this has been done by some. It is indeed gratifying to see that translators are eagerly seizing the opportunities offered. It is certain that those who attend the conference, or would like to, are keen to know what technology can do to help them do their work better, or more easily, or both.

Now that many translators, whether freelance or staff translators, have word-processing facilities, or at the very least an electronic typewriter, they are turning their attention to other developments which could make their lives easier. Quite a few, such as Josette Guédès, now have communications facilities; others, like Commodore Croft, can work while on the move, using portable equipment. What people are now looking for is a collapse in the price barrier for other items, comparable to the way the price of pocket calculators, for instance, has tumbled, followed by home computers and now word processors. Which firm will be the first to launch a really reasonable and efficient small photocopier? Readers will no doubt turn eagerly to Julie Harnett's paper on optical character recognition equipment, but it seems that this is still well beyond the reach of most individuals and quite a lot of firms too. On the other hand, it looks as though the translator surrounded by a mass of information which has to be sorted and organised need despair no longer; software packages for just this purpose have been developed and are now available. Machine translation is, however, still only a reality for large organisations with a high throughput – but this was the case with the earliest computers, so who knows what may happen next?

Perhaps this – I have in front of me a newspaper cutting (source unknown): 'Britain and Japan have agreed to develop jointly an automatic translation telephone which would act as an interpreter between callers, according to an unconfirmed report in the Japanese daily *Nihon Keizei Shimbun*'. Can this be true, I wonder? And would it really help communications in general? I am inclined to think that translators, and interpreters too, need not start to get worried yet. Having said that, maybe one of the papers at the eighth conference, planned for November 1986, will be on the subject of progress in this field!

In the meantime, I should like to take this opportunity of expressing my thanks to all concerned with the conference – my fellow planning committee members, the Aslib conference organisation staff, the CBI, the speakers and all those who chaired or reported on the various sessions. Thanks to the participants, too, for continuing to support this series of conferences in such large numbers. It makes all the efforts well worthwhile.

Session I: The theory and practice of translation

Chaired by Catriona Picken
and Barbara Wilson

Who are the translators? The growing professionalism of translating

Geoffrey Kingscott

Director, Praetorius Ltd, Nottingham, UK

Before we get round to considering where the technology has got to, we ought to make an attempt to fill in the background, the context. Where is translation being carried out? Who is doing the translation? How is it being done?

I have been trying to get to grips with these questions, but it is very difficult to seize on anything very definite. I will be using the phrase 'the translation profession', but in doing so I use it only as a convenient shorthand, because it is evident that while there is a distinguishable mainstream of translation, this stream does not run between clearly defined banks, but at its periphery spreads itself over, and loses itself in, a very wide area of marshland, the extent of which is impossible to survey.

We tend to underestimate the amount of translation work being carried on outside our view; outside the view, that is, of those working in the international institutions with their established structures and developing career patterns, or active in the translator associations, or marketing ourselves to the commercial world. Even in our over-compartmentalised profession, we are in touch with one another, we all know something about ethical codes, about working practices, about new developments.

The one major survey of the world translation market carried out in recent years, that by the Bureau Marcel van Dijk for the Commission of the European Communities,[1] stuck very much to the mainstream.

But I think that the companies selling machine translation systems, with what they have found out by bringing a new drive and a new approach to the marketplace, reaching the places which the rest of us have never reached, will bear out my own impression, that there is a huge volume of translation work being carried on out there by people we have never heard of, and who have never heard of us. A questionnaire survey carried out by John Newton,[2] when he was selling Weidner through The Software Connection, showed to what extent this was the case even among the larger UK companies.

So having made the point, that we often overlook what is going on in the outer marshlands, I will try to get to grips with the amorphous problem of where translation is practised, and by whom.

INTERNATIONAL ORGANISATIONS

Right in the middle of the mainstream, of course, are the international organisations, the United Nations, and the European institutions: the Commission, the Council, the Parliament, the Court of Justice etc. Here we have a structured profession, an established recruitment policy, defined career paths, and ..., something often lacking elsewhere, adequate remuneration; and, perhaps even more important, status.

I am going to have to use a lot of generalisations, and no doubt there are reservations and qualifications – there was, I understand, some form of international translation structure before the Second World War – but to a great extent the profession, as practised at an international level, traces its ancestry, in common with that of conference interpreting, to the Nuremberg tribunals after the war. The profession can be said to have existed since then as a definable entity.

Recruitment to the translation departments of these international bodies is usually by competitive examination, and in certain universities and colleges there are increasingly courses which train translators, terminologists and interpreters to be the sort of employee which these bodies are looking for.

To what extent is a clearly defined translator career path, from the university to the grave, being created by the emergence of translator courses and by the recruitment policies of the international institutions?

In his illuminating chapter entitled specifically 'Who are the translators?' in the Aslib *Translator's Handbook*[3] in 1983, Jeremy Verrinder wrote that many translators only considered translation as a career after graduating. Even that is an advance on the days when you got a job as something else and only afterwards were your language skills brought into use.

I have a feeling that undergraduates choosing courses at universities like Bath, Salford, Bradford or Heriot-Watt in the UK, and similar places on the Continent, may be a bit vague when they start out as to what translation involves, but they are thinking, more and more of them, of translation as career. And a straightforward career, from university to the grave, in translation, is a comparatively new phenomenon which could modify the structure of the profession.

For example, the translator organisations might become more important. In past decades translators have become translators for haphazard reasons; many of the best and most highly organised translators have got into the profession more or less by accident. It is a fact that many well-established translators, the majority, indeed, of the leading freelances in the UK, have never found the need to join any of the translator associations. There are always the public-spirited few, of course, but many translators had found their own way into translation, they are doing well enough, thank you, and now they have not got any time to spare for committees and associations, even when they have heard of them. But young translators entering the profession as a deliberate choice will look round to see what they can do to give weight and depth to their chosen role in life. Provided, that is, they are caught before they enter the cocoon of organisations like the European Commission, where they can feel secure and protected, and above all, valued, without the need for any outside translator body.

The project now being aired, for an Institute of Translation, which will bring together professional translators, the university trainers of future translators, and translation users, is an interesting pointer to what is happening. As far as I know, such a body does not exist in any other country.

To go back to where translation is carried on. I have looked briefly at the international and government organisations. I do not wish to dwell any longer on this activity in centre stream. Important as it is, the way the international institutions recruit, and how they operate, and how the specialist courses in universities and colleges train translators, have been described before.

Moving out from the international associations, there are of course translation departments, large or small, in government ministries, in semi-government organisations, and in other international bodies. They are in touch with one another, and they now meet in a comparatively recent association described by Peter Arthern[4] in an article published in August 1985. They are discussing things like recruitment, and revision procedures, whereas not so long ago such organisations were operating in near-ignorance of one another. Such conferences and associations, once again, represent a definite tendency towards a more clearly defined profession.

INDUSTRY AND COMMERCE

Moving on to the industrial and commercial sphere, there are large companies, particularly multinationals, which have translation departments. In the UK there are surprisingly few of these, but those which do exist tend to be represented, together with government departments, in the Aslib Technical Translation Group. The Shell translation department is quite well known, with its own structures, and has long been very much part of the mainstream, but elsewhere, even in quite large UK companies, translators are often scattered individuals, carrying quite a heavy responsiblility on their shoulders, often for superiors who have little conception of language problems, who may even be reluctant to let them come to conferences.

It is a generalisation again, but in the Federal Republic of Germany and in Switzerland there do seem to be far more in-house translation departments, with translators there enjoying a much higher status than they do in the UK.

Company translation departments and professional translators employed by the larger companies have, partly through this series of conferences, partly through the increasing activity of the translator associations, and partly because of the comparatively recent development of a translation press, become much more aware of what is going on, are much more in touch with fellow translators, than they were a few years ago. So here again there is a movement towards a more professional profession.

It is a story we are coming across again and again. Translators who a few years ago worked in near-isolation are now in touch with one another. Is it because the nature of translation is changing? It does seem more and more that translation is increasingly a task for the specialist, the professional, rather than for the person who happens to be on the spot and who happens to know languages. Is it this which is causing a problem in the Institute of Linguists? The words 'translator' and 'linguist' are no longer synonymous, as many people once thought they were.

Take this particular series of Aslib/TG conferences. They have made their own distinctive contribution towards the promotion of a more cohesive profession, but there was an element of supply and demand; if the conferences had not existed, they would surely have had to be invented.

Returning to our theme, of where translators are to be found. We were looking at industry and commerce. Where do the translators come from?

Some translators in industry have previously had other posts in the company, but once having confessed to language skills, have found themselves doing more and more translation work. The normal method of recruitment, however, seems to be by advertisement, usually in a local newspaper, to a lesser extent in a national newspaper, and to an even lesser extent, in the language press. But times are changing. There is a greater awareness of translation as a profession; light is beginning to dawn, and some advertisements are becoming more specific and there is greater readiness to recruit from within the profession.

One point which will be familiar to many who work in companies is that there is an increasing demand for language training in industry. This is an expanding business. Translation departments are in some cases becoming language departments, providing both translation of documentation and language training for executives. Certainly outside suppliers to industry are aware of the trend. Colleges are more and more marketing their language training services to industry and in one or two cases starting to add – tentatively at the moment – a translation dimension, while translation companies are finding it pays more and more to offer language tuition as well as translation.

Is this trend going to create a demand in industry for more of an all-rounder linguist? Jeremy Verrinder, whom I have already quoted, describes the translator in a small one- or two-person section as being at everybody's beck and call, acting as both translator and interpreter.

I fear that increasingly he or she will be called on to give language tuition to sales executives off to sell in South America, or accountants off to audit the books of the French subsidiary, to provide the 'crash courses' in which so many people still have such touching faith.

But let us now venture out into the unregenerate areas, or the areas untouched by the notion of a translation profession.

In industry and commerce the translation of a document will often be done by a person whose main job is something else, engineer, computer programmer, marketing person, whatever. Sometimes in the past, that person's work has gradually been taken over by his or her acquired translation function, and he or she has become a translator pure and simple. But in many cases this is not so, and the translator reverts to normal duties. Foreign agents for British companies often carry out translation as part of their normal service.

In some cases, of course, the work is being done badly, through ignorance and over-confidence. We in the commercial world have all met cases of this. In John Newton's report, quoted above, he found that 'an alarmingly high proportion of translation is carried out by employees with no relevant training or qualifications, and often into a language other than their mother tongue'.

But also, reluctant though we may be to admit it, the work done in this way, by non-professional linguists, has often been found acceptable. By non-professional in this context I mean not in touch with other translators, not aware of what the mainstream is doing; it does not necessarily mean incompetent.

What is bringing those firms who have used these *ad hoc* methods of translation in the past into the edges of the mainstream – and I think the machine translation companies will again bear out what I say from their own marketing experiences – is not complaints about the quality of the work, or the difficulty in finding the odd linguistic competence: what is causing them problems now is the sheer volume of work to be translated. It is not: 'Help, we do not know how to do translation!', but 'Help, we cannot cope with the amount of translation work now being generated all of a sudden!'.

TRANSLATION COMPANIES AND FREELANCES

The third main area where translation is carried on, international and government institutions and organisations being the first area, and commerce, whether industrial firms, or large firms of solicitors, patent agents etc., being the second, is that of translation companies and freelances. How many of these are there? Well, that is difficult to say as translation companies merge at the smaller end into individual freelances operating under a company-type name – you know the sort of thing: European ... or World ... or Inter-Galactic Translations, Flat 2A, 14 Acacia Drive, East Cheam. And there are some individual freelances who have made themselves into efficient little businesses, with a bigger turnover than some of the so-called companies with pretentious titles.

In the UK, translation companies have always been more prominent than in countries such as the Federal Republic of Germany, the Netherlands, or Switzerland, where more people are familiar with foreign languages. In the UK, foreign languages are something quite alien, and many people in industry are glad for companies to come along and take away the problem. In the Federal Republic of Germany, say, familiarity with language problems means they are more frequently prepared to work directly with individual translators.

How many companies and freelances are there? In 1983 at *Language Monthly* we checked the UK Yellow Pages directories for the whole country, and after eliminating duplications we came up with a figure of 555 individuals with a listed number and 472 translation companies (or individuals with a trading name). But that certainly underestimates the number of individuals earning most of their living from freelance translation.

So how many people, for example, are engaged, for a significant part of their working lives, in translation in all branches? All sorts of figures are bandied about, from the 100,000 said to be working in translation in Japan, to a figure of 13,000 recently quoted for the Federal Republic of Germany (of whom only one-third are said to have the necessary expertise and qualifications). My guess, and it is no more than a guess, is around 3,000 for the UK.

Going back to translation companies and freelances, there are some indications that the leading translation companies in each country are pulling away from the rest, partly because of their superior marketing, and partly because translation is less and less demanded as a separate service; it is increasingly part of a chain, allied to typesetting, computer programming etc. Once upon a time, and that not so long ago, a translation company could be a cottage industry. The odd typewriter, a few dictionaries, a set of index cards and some postal weighing scales were all that was necessary. Now the business is becoming quite capital-intensive, with electronic communications and typesetting and printing equipment.

Translation companies are major users of freelance translator services, and another trend is for nearly every company to use the same freelances. It is not that the freelance pool is shrinking; far from it, the translation companies are deluged with applications from would-be suppliers. But everyone is learning to fish at what we might call the deep end, where the more experienced and more highly organised freelances are concentrated. Because, once again, everyone knows one another more than they did twenty years ago.

International and government institutions, firms large and small, translation companies and freelance translators, these are the three major areas in which translation is carried out. But of course there are other areas. Some of these are quite important in their own right.

One is that of the translation of scientific papers, sometimes cover-to-cover translation of scientific journals. Many of the translators involved do belong to the mainstream, but work directly for publishers.

Another is translation for military defence purposes; a lot of it goes on – there is a whole establishment at Cheltenham beavering away – but unsurprisingly we hear very little about it.

Literary translation is a field on its own where freelances working from home work directly for publishers. And there is Bible translation, quite a little industry in itself, with its own organisations and journals, with a great deal of activity in languages which, though commercially of no great prominence, may have millions of speakers.

Overall, just how much of a translation market is there? In its survey three or four years ago the Bureau van Dijk calculated a 10 per cent per annum growth in the market, on rather tenuous evidence, it seemed to me.

I do not pretend to know how big the potential translation market is, and there are a number of factors which need to be considered.

My own feeling is that the apparent inaccessibility of foreign language material, the delay in translation, and the cost, in that order, do discourage many people in industry and government from having material translated. If translation were a more familiar and less arcane activity, if more people knew how and where it could be done, if material could be translated more easily and more quickly, I feel that the market could expand exponentially. The sky could be the limit.

REFERENCES

1. BUREAU MARCEL VAN DIJK AND PA CONSEILLER DE DIREC-
    TION. *Better translation for better communication*. Pergamon Press for the
    Commission of the European Communities, 1983.
2. NEWTON, John. *Survey on current trends in translation requirements and
    facilities*. For The Software Connection, Fareham, Hampshire (report in
    Language Monthly, (15), December 1984, p.10).
3. PICKEN, Catriona (*ed*.). *The translator's handbook*. London: Aslib, 1983.
4. ARTHERN, Peter. Government translation services compare notes. *Lan-
    guage Monthly*, (23), August 1985, pp.11–14.

AUTHOR

Geoffrey Kingscott, Director, Praetorius Ltd, 5 East Circus Street,
Nottingham NG1 5AH, UK.

Continuing education and training for translators

Jeremy Verrinder

Dean, Faculty of Languages, Polytechnic of Central London, UK

The title of this paper is a very heartening one, since it contains an implicit acceptance that translators have to be trained in the first place. This was not always the case and most active translators with twenty or more years' experience will certainly remember – as I do – the awful 'sink or swim' beginning when we were faced with obscure texts, often without adequate dictionaries or reference material, typewriters which were inevitably 'cast-offs' from the typing pool and, worst of all, people who did not understand and did not want to understand our problems. How we actually coped in those days I do not know, but cope we did in the end in spite of (rather than because of) such an inauspicious beginning. I suppose we always knew that it was not enough to arrive with a piece of paper proclaiming language skills and a lot of good will. There had to be more; there had to be an approach or some kind of method that translators could resort to. But there was no-one to tell us and I suppose we managed in the end with a certain amount of intuition and an even greater slice of good luck.

The problem of training clients as to what they can and cannot expect from a translator is a topic that has been rehearsed on many occasions. Suffice it to say here, however, that the marketplace – for want of a better term – is growing increasingly aware of the status of translators and nowadays actually stipulates that candidates for translator posts have some kind of specialist training as an alternative to a number of years of actual experience.

We have two debts to acknowledge here in my view: firstly to the recent internationalisation of translators themselves. This has really happened as a consequence of developments on the European scene and has opened up a wide range of career possibilities involving working with top-flight translators from other countries. The net result is that our standing as a profession has been considerably enhanced and translators are seen to be playing a full part in high-level international circles instead of being merely useful people to have around to handle foreign language problems. The second debt is the advance of the new technology. New technology has meant a far-reaching change in the working life of translators. It has played a great part in redefining the sort of work that they do and the tools that they have at hand to do it. It has meant higher and more professional standards. It has meant that translators have had to become more thinking and more responsible in their work. They have had to shake themselves out of their earlier apathy and learn to keep up with the ever-changing world around them. In brief, it has made them more professional and aware of standards.

BASIC TRAINING

Today's accepted approach into the profession starts, as before, with the modern language graduate. Modern language degrees, however, are not what they used to be and most universities and polytechnics tend to follow a more 'applied' path in their approach to language teaching. This is so widespread that most students have studied the principles of translation theory and have done practical work with both literary and technical texts by the time they have graduated. This means that the small proportion of modern language graduates who go on to choose a career as a professional translator do so having had first-hand experience of what it is all about. I do not need to point out the difference between this kind of trainee translator and the graduate of a generation before, who more or less stumbled into the profession.

Today's graduates then have to undergo a further course of study to prepare them for their career. I am often asked how I choose a mere handful of candidates from the huge number of hopeful applicants for the postgraduate translator course that we run at the Polytechnic of Central London. Although it is true to say that the individual skills in foreign languages are very important, our first impressions are of the way in which applicants use their own mother tongue. I believe that if people have innate problems in the way they use their own language, they are going to have a lot more problems if they have to make a living in this way. The number and the range of subjects studied – even as far back as O level – can be very indicative of the applicants' range of interests and skills. Clearly most modern arts graduates abandon thoughts of a scientific career at a very early stage in their school lives, but even the remoteness of an occasional O level can be invaluable when preparing trainee translators to come to terms with scientific and engineering texts.

I think it is generally agreed that basic training for translators consists of giving them as many insights as possible in a very limited period of time into the way professional translators work. They have to have first-hand experience of a wide range of technical, commercial, scientific, financial etc. texts, so that they learn how to approach new and sometimes strange subjects. They have to be shown how to follow well-trodden paths of research and cross-referencing. They have to be brought into contact with different registers of English, so that each text can be correctly 'pitched' for the readership and they have to learn not to be satisfied with a standard that falls short of perfection.

FURTHER TRAINING

The question of further training is more complex and differs from basic training inasmuch that candidates for basic training are still working at first principles. At the basic training stage, mechanisms for tackling technical and specialised texts are covered. Very few of the trainees will know at this stage where they will eventually end up or even whether they will get a job at all in today's uncertain climate. Further training on the other hand assumes that the translators are practising translators and that they know that to succeed they have to keep up to date. This may come from the translators themselves, or alternatively, it may come from employers. Many companies are very aware of the need for on-the-job training (not only for translators, I should add) and organise regular training visits or sessions. I am sure that all translators worth their salt will want to become involved in the kind of work that their company does and to familiarise themselves with its products. Good translators have shown themselves to be extremely adept at grasping the bare bones or the underlying principles of even complex technical topics. Employers have a responsibility here too, however. It is a question of mutual advantage for them if their translators are able to assimilate new developments and new jargon, in the same way, for example, as the sales representatives are expected to do.

PROFESSIONAL DEVELOPMENT

Professional translators can be expected to develop in different ways. On the one hand, they must learn to keep abreast with developments on their own immediate working surroundings as far as subject matter is concerned, and on the other hand they may find they are required to widen their portfolio of languages to meet changing market or other requirements. The one-language translator is nowadays a very rare bird indeed and would be an expensive luxury for most employers. On the other hand, the enlargement of the Common Market, for example, and the general increase in international trade and communications, has meant an upsurge in the amount of translation work from other languages, which – with all due respect to them – have not been in very great demand on the commercial scene. Translators are first and foremost professionals. In their employers' eyes, they are the people who actually understand all about languages, and surely there can't be very much difference between French and ... . So the translators develop their skills and very soon learn to adapt their translating techniques to other – perhaps cognate – languages. We accept the fact that translation is essentially a linguistic skill, or even a linguistic exercise and, given adequate knowledge of the source language, for a given text the result should be no different. (Would one really expect to find much difference, for example, between a commercial letter translated from French by an experienced French graduate and a commercial letter from Spanish translated by the French graduate who has in the meantime built up a knowledge of Spanish? I think not. What is important is the technique and the ability to reproduce a 'proper' English business letter.)

The third area of development is coming to terms with the new technology. Outward-looking translators will by now have progressed from the old manual typewriter, the dictating machine and even from the smart new electric – or even electronic – typewriter. They owe it to themselves and to the profession to develop the best in themselves and if this means that every decade they have to start from scratch in order to familiarise themselves with new developments in information technology this is something that they have to take on. Never before have translators had to be so much aware of the changes going on around them. But if they can manage to keep abreast of all these technical developments and at the same time develop their language skills, they will find themselves very valued members of a very respected profession.

AUTHOR

Jeremy Verrinder, Dean, Faculty of Languages, Polytechnic of Central London, UK.

Translators from Amsterdam: an informal history of the translation course at the University of Amsterdam

Eveline Sleebos

Freelance translator and interpreter, The Hague, The Netherlands

Amsterdam's greatest painter, Rembrandt, was insolvent. So was its greatest poet and contemporary of Rembrandt, Joost van den Vondel. He tried to supplement his income by translating.

The subject of this paper is not solvency or, as the case may be, insolvency of translators then and now, but translators from Amsterdam. It was in Amsterdam that the Netherlands Association of Translators (Nederlands Genootschap van Vertalers) was founded in 1956. And it was in Amsterdam that the first academic training course for translators in the Netherlands was established in 1964.

The main points covered are:

- the history of the course
- the degree programme
- personal appraisal
- the new generation of translators.

HISTORY OF THE COURSE

The present training course for translators owes its existence to the initiative taken by the Netherlands Association of Translators (NGV). Together with the University of Amsterdam, NGV established the Translators' and Interpreters' Training Course at the University of Amsterdam in 1964. The training of interpreters never really got off the ground. It was found that the costs involved were not in proportion to the opportunities for employment of interpreters who have Dutch as their mother tongue.

In 1971 the name Instituut voor Vertaalkunde (Translation Training and Research Institute) was adopted. In 1983, following its full integration into the Faculty of Arts of the University of Amsterdam, its name was changed to Instituut voor Vertaalwetenschap (Institute for Translation Studies). This 'evolution' of names at least shows that translators practise what they preach in that no mistake should be made about names!

The original teaching staff of 1964 had made inquiries about the training programmes at various translators' colleges in Europe, e.g. Geneva, Paris, Antwerp, Brussels and Heidelberg. Throughout the years these programmes were put to the test, a process known in educational jargon as curriculum development. It soon became apparent that the theory of translation was indispensable to the practice of translation. Likewise, the need was felt for scientific research in the field of translation.

The training programme gradually began to develop along academic lines. Emphasis was given to translation theory and to working groups studying and reporting on specific translation problems, for example. For the sake of brevity, the Instituut vor Vertaalwetenschap student shall be a 'he' from now on. At the end of my paper I shall give you the exact male/female ratio of the current student population at the Institute and other facts and figures.

The Institute for Translation Studies (head: Professor Dr Raymond van den Broeck) is now fully integrated as a teaching and research department in the Faculty of Arts. It is a three-year course to which students are admitted who have passed their *propaedeuse* examination. This is the preliminary examination a student has to pass when he has successfully completed the first year of any graduate course at a Dutch university. Aspiring translators are required to have passed the preliminary examination of a general language course in English, French or German. The second, although informal, requirement is that the students have Dutch as their mother tongue or language of habitual use.

DEGREE PROGRAMME

The foreign language taken at preliminary level is referred to as the student's first foreign language. On completion of the Translation Studies course, the student graduates in either the Theory or the Practice of Translation. In view of the wide selection of subjects to be studied, the student has to choose between the two orientations on gaining entry to the course.

The basic curriculum during the first two semesters includes advanced study of the first foreign language, translating and translation theory, as well as usage and stylistics of Dutch (the student's mother tongue). Dutch occupies a key position in the degree programme and is a required subject throughout the three years of the course.

In addition, the student starts on his second foreign language. He may choose from one of the three main foreign languages at the Institute – English, French or German – or from Italian, Russian or Spanish, which are also taught as the second foreign language at the Institute. Or, for that matter, he can choose a language that has to be studied in another department of the Faculty of Arts, e.g. Portuguese or a Scandinavian language. The student may even study at another Dutch university, e.g. Indonesian at Leiden University.

After the first two semesters the students are prepared for their graduation in either the Theory or the Practice of Translation. In the practice-oriented programme emphasis is given to the development of translational competence, both into and out of the first foreign language, and out of the second foreign language. The theory-oriented student likewise learns the skill of translating but his programme is mainly aimed at acquiring theoretical knowledge and knowledge of research methods. He may drop his second foreign language but he must choose from general linguistics or text linguistics as his required subject.

For their optional subject students are free to choose from any of the disciplines taught at the University of Amsterdam. On the whole they are advised to take a subject that will enhance their translation ability and their chances of getting a job. Disciplines such as economics, law, political science and environmental studies are currently in favour with student translators. Finally, all students are required to write a thesis on translation, terminology or translation criticism.

PERSONAL APPRAISAL

Before 'bringing on' the new generation of translators I would first like to discuss the old generation of translators from Amsterdam. 'Old' but by no means superannuated translators – I know because I am one of them.

I am one of the Institute's first group of alumni, having completed my studies in 1969. In those days the course had different entry requirements. An open, competitive entrance examination was held each year since only ten places were available for each of the three foreign languages: English, French and German.

The tutorial system was employed. During meetings between a tutor and a student intensive face-to-face teaching and discussion took place, based on translations done by the student. It was a four-year course at the time and the student had to take a special subject during the course, to become a subject specialist. I was lucky to be exempted from acquiring the specialised knowledge. Before I did my course in Amsterdam I had trained and worked as an SRN (State Registered Nurse) in London. So willingly or unwillingly, I was considered an 'instant' medical translator.

When I was a second-year student translator, a major achievement in the medical world gave me an incentive and I started my own medical terminology bank. On 2 December 1967 Professor Christiaan Barnard performed the first heart transplant at Groote Schuur Hospital, Cape Town, South Africa. A new era of spare-part surgery had started and I knew that my modest collection of specialised words and expressions would one day be very useful to me. More recent examples of new medical topics which I now come across as a freelance translator are AIDS (acquired immune deficiency syndrome) and the Björk-Shiley heart valves affair. From the terminological point of view the latest developments in medicine tend to keep medical translators on their toes!

When I was asked to present this paper I was told that, ideally, my subject should essentially be a personal appraisal of my training in Amsterdam. Did it really put me on my feet as a translator when I exchanged my college desk in Amsterdam for an office desk in London?

On completion of my studies in 1969 I started as a technical translator with Shell in its translation division – Foreign Language Services – in Shell Centre, London. I ended up as head of the Dutch Section there. This fact may suggest that my training in Amsterdam paid dividends, but it does not really answer the question whether the course made one a competent staff translator.

In the past, training of translators had largely consisted of on-the-job training. Usually language graduates had entered translation offices and picked up the technical background and translating experience as they went along.

Some form of technical background, ideally a university degree in a science subject or in engineering, is a great asset to the technical translator, who should have specialised knowledge in his subject field. But as with language knowledge, the potential range of the average person is limited. A translator claiming to be an expert in several disciplines should be regarded with suspicion.

The great advantage of team-work in translation – as I experienced when working for Shell – is that a large range of languages and subjects are dealt with adequately. It also allows for a greater degree of specialisation in translation proper. The functions of documentation, establishment of terminology, translating, revising and editing can be shared out.

To my mind my on-the-job training with Shell in London, after my course in Amsterdam, was more in the nature of continuing education (*formation permanente*) in which my training at the Institute proved to be of considerable value to me.

Did the training in Amsterdam correspond to the demands made of its translators by British industry? I can only speak for myself when I answer the question in the affirmative. Did the training in Amsterdam correspond to the demands made of its translators by Dutch industry? Graduates from the Institute for Translation Studies are to be found in institutional translation units such as the Ministry of Foreign Affairs and the Ministry of Agriculture and Fisheries in The Hague, Dutch television and Radio Netherlands International (Radio Nederland Wereldomroep) in Hilversum, and the EEC in Brussels.

My experience as a staff translator in Dutch industry proved extremely useful when I became a freelance three years ago. Having worked for a pharmaceutical company – Gist-Brocades N.V. in Delft – I found that my combined specialisation of medicine and pharmacology aroused the interest, or perhaps curiosity, of a number of drug companies looking for freelance translators.

THE NEW GENERATION OF TRANSLATORS

During my last visit to the Institute in Amsterdam, one fact struck me as a little unusual and I wondered if it was typical of the situation in the Netherlands. I said earlier on that I would let you know the male/female ratio of the student population at the Institute. The present number of students is 212 (academic year 1985/86) and the ratio is 1 male to 9 female student translators.

The overall male/female ratio at the University of Amsterdam, which with its 25,000 students is the largest university in the Netherlands, is 3:2. Has the growing professionalisation of translating raised the threshold for one sex whilst lowering it for the other? I should like to leave the matter open now.

Two male students, Rien Verhoef and Jacques Commandeur, were a great credit to the Institute in 1982. They were awarded the Martinus Nijhoff Prize for their translations into Dutch of Anthony Burgess' *1985* and Saul Bellow's *The adventures of Augie March*. The Nijhoff Prize for literary translations had also been awarded to three tutors at the Institute – James Holmes, Alexander Brotherton and Peter Verstegen – on three separate occasions in previous years.

Although coming at the end, not least in importance is the following fact. Having mentioned the literary prizes awarded to students and tutors, I should like to emphasise that during the course the students' attention is equally focused on literary translation, i.e. fiction, poetry, plays, essays etc., and on technical translation.

It is in a literary vein that I should like to conclude my paper. Having 'brought on' the new generation of translators, I feel I should now quote the very 'old' translator from Amsterdam whom I mentioned at the beginning of my paper: Joost van den Vondel. A contemporary of Shakespeare, Vondel is famous for, among other things, the following quotation:

De weerelt is een schouwtoneel
Elck speelt zijn rol en krijght zijn deel

It is reminiscent of an equally famous quotation from Shakespeare. It is not supposed to be a rendering of Shakespeare since Vondel did not translate from English, but from French, Latin and Greek.

All the world's a stage,
And all the men and women merely players;
They have their exits and their entrances ...

FURTHER READING

Studiegids Vertaalwetenschap. Amsterdam: University of Amsterdam, 1985/86.
PINCHUCK, Isadore. *Scientific and technical translation*. London: André Deutsch, 1977.

AUTHOR

Eveline Sleebos, freelance translator and interpreter, The Hague, The Netherlands.

Legal translators and legal translation: a personal view

Ian Frame

Lawyer-Linguist, Court of Justice of the European Communities, Luxembourg

Since I am a lawyer, let me start with a disclaimer: nothing I shall say is intended to reflect the views of my employers past or present or any professional association to which I may belong. And please don't write any letters – unless they are addressed to me. The reason I start in this fashion is that some years ago, when I had just become a notary, I gave an interview to a charming lady from a careers magazine for schools and somehow allowed her to obtain the impression that all notaries in the United Kingdom earned vast amounts of money. Notaries in, for example, Italy, may earn fortunes but that is not usually the case in the UK. The result was that all the firms of notaries in London (London being the only place in the UK where firms of notaries as such are to be found) were flooded with letters from schoolboys (and their daddies) seeking to become articled clerks. And, by way of punishment, I was given the task of answering them all.

I am a notary. I now work at the Court of Justice of the European Communities in Luxembourg as a translator and reviser – or, to use the description used by the Court, a lawyer-linguist. I believe that in the early days the term used was 'jurist-linguist', being a translation of the French *juriste-linguiste*, but the word 'jurist' sounds pompous when used otherwise than to describe an eminent lawyer with many years' experience and great renown, so the term 'lawyer-linguist' was adopted. There are legal translators of course in the United Nations, and more particularly at the International Court of Justice at The Hague (where they are known as 'legal secretaries' because they are actually involved in the administration of the judicial process and as well as translating they interpret), at the Council of Europe in Strasbourg, in government offices throughout the world, and in many other places. But this paper covers only areas in which I have direct experience, that is to say, the work of London notaries and lawyer-linguists at the Court of Justice of the European Communities.

First of all, notaries. Some readers will know precisely what English notaries are, many will be surprised that they exist, and many will have an inaccurate view of what they are. Anyone from the State of Louisiana in the United States will doubtless be aware that notaries in Louisiana are like French notaries, since the Louisiana system of law is based on French law and notaries there thus differ radically from those of the other forty-nine states, where as a rule they have no legal qualifications. The role of English notaries calls for some clarification. One of the functions of a notary is to translate legal (and other) documents. There are many reasons for this. The notarial profession in England can be divided into two branches. First there are London notaries, or Scriveners, who are members of the Worshipful Company of Scriveners, a City of London Livery Company which celebrated its sixth centenary in 1973 (and therefore all London notaries are freemen of the City of London). Then there are provincial notaries, who are usually solicitors. The London notaries serve five-year articles and take two sets of examinations – the second set includes translation into English from two foreign languages and into one of those languages from English of legal texts. The five-year articles cannot be reduced for any reason whatsoever – unlike solicitors and accountants, notaries are not allowed truncated articles by virtue of having been to university or anywhere else. London notaries are not solicitors (although there is nothing to prevent them from taking the Law Society exams and serving articles with a solicitor after the now compulsory year of pre-articles study). Provincial notaries are solicitors, and are either appointed on application, if it is considered that there is a need for more notaries in the area where they practise as solicitors, or else they serve articles of five years with another notary – but they are not required to take an examination. Thus, they do not take examinations in languages or translation. However, paradoxically, they have the same powers as London notaries and any provincial notary is entitled to certify translations.

London has always been a great commercial centre – perhaps more so in the past than now – and there many bargains are struck every day between parties of many different nationalities. Most countries in which English is the main language have inherited as well the English system of law, the Common Law, in which the notary is unimportant. By contrast, most other European countries and their ex-colonies where English is not spoken have a system of law in which the notary is important. However, notaries existed on both sides of the Channel long before the Code Napoléon was invented.

The notary's office was originally an ecclesiastical one. Even in

England, notaries were appointed by the Pope until Henry VIII decided that the Pope was a bad thing. Since then they have been appointed by the Court of Faculties of the Archbishop of Canterbury. With the development of the Common Law, the notaries' domestic role shrank (although they had a monopoly on conveyancing until 1760, when they lost an action to preserve that monopoly against the professional body of a group of people who called themselves somewhat comically 'Gentlemen Practisers'; they later adopted the equally comical name of 'Solicitors').

As a result of these developments, the London notary exists more to satisfy the requirements of non-English law than to satisfy those of English law. And because of this, in centuries past many London notaries were in fact foreigners, proficient in English as well as in the law of their own countries and, obviously, in their own languages, who prepared documents in various languages and, to comfort the parties involved, attested to the fact that the various versions were true translations of each other. That is why London notaries are still translators today and it may also account for certain peculiar notarial usages which survive to the present day – for example the word 'appearer', which is not a sudden manifestation of ectoplasm but merely a party appearing before a notary, a 'comparant', a 'compareciente', a 'comparente'. Similarly, many English notarial instruments end, or used until recently to end, with the words 'Whereof an act being required I have granted these present to serve and avail as and when need may require'. Here, 'Whereof an act' is clearly a translation of the French *Dont acte* which appears so laconically at the end of French notarial documents. And notaries always say 'at foot of' rather than 'at the foot of', which is probably influenced by the Italian *in calce al documento*.

You may have wondered why in this country we have no equivalent of the *Traducteur Juré* of the Continent. Well, in fact we have one, the notary public. But he or she is a sworn translator more because of custom than anything else. There are rules dealing with translations – for example Rules of Court made under the Foreign Judgements (Reciprocal Enforcement) Act 1933 and the rules of the Supreme Court relating to translations of notices of writ to be served out of the jurisdiction – but in neither case does the notary have a statutory monopoly. In most cases, a translation by a non-notary will be acceptable provided that the translator appears before a notary and swears an affidavit to the effect that the translation is a true translation. So nearly always a notary is involved. Incidentally, the relevant order in the rules of the Supreme Court lays down fees for notarial translations per 100 words of resultant English text, which could lead, or may in fact have already led, to translations which perpetuate expressions containing redundant elements, where three words at least are used instead of one: for example, 'null and void' instead of merely 'void', 'place and stead' instead merely of 'place'. This custom dates back to the days when legal draftsmen were paid by the word and created such phrases to increase their income. Some even used to say 'null and void and of no effect'.

In view of the notary's role it is no coincidence that three of the London translation companies were started by notaries – one started as Walmica (and has changed name several times since then), another is Falcon Translations and the other I shall not name, out of modesty, since I was, over a period of years, sequentially the company secretary and a director of it.

It has always been a matter of great astonishment to me that no-one appears to have challenged the privileged position of notaries with respect to translations. Take a typical notarially certified translation. It bears a red seal and red tape stitching the documents together. The notarial certificate reads as follows:

I the undersigned, Whatshisname, notary public of and practising in the City of London, England, by Royal Authority duly admitted and sworn, do hereby certify and attest: that the document in the English language hereunto annexed is a true and faithful translation of the document in the Spanish language also hereunto annexed. In witness whereof I have hereunto set my hand and affixed my seal of office at London aforesaid, this first day of April one thousand nine hundred and seventy-nine.

I think it is a fairly impressive and pretty document. But there is nothing to prevent anyone from stitching documents together and securing the ends of the ribbon (notaries refer to it as silk) with a big red seal. And the red seal could be impressed with words such as 'Whatshisname, Member of the Translators' Guild' for example. I am sure that in many circumstances such translations would be – or become – acceptable. Admittedly, the translator would not be entitled to use the magic words 'by Royal Authority duly admitted and sworn' but these are mainly ceremonial in any case and some notaries in fact dispense with them.

Another possibility would be for an organised group of translators – and again I am thinking of the Translators' Guild – to apply to the government for an examination procedure to be established in order to create sworn translators, who would have their own seal and would be officially recognised as competent. This would be particularly useful for translations from English being sent abroad, which are often required to be 'legalised'.

Legalisation is the procedure whereby a document going abroad is taken to the consulate of the country of destination and a consular official certifies the authenticity of the document or of a signature and/or seal on it. This is, of course, a cumbersome procedure and fortunately one which has been simplified for most European countries and for many others. The

Hague Convention of 5 October 1961 dispenses with consular legalisation, which is replaced by the affixing to documents of a form of wording called the *Apostille*. Thus in the UK a document can be legalised by the Foreign and Commonwealth Office if it is going, for example, to Spain, Portugal, France, Italy, Yugoslavia, Belgium, Luxembourg, the Netherlands, Japan, the United States, or West Germany. In most other cases the document goes first to the Foreign Office and then to the relevant consulate, which legalises the signature of the Foreign Office official. Thus, if government-accredited sworn translators had their signatures and seals registered with the Foreign Office, documents certified by such translators would probably be acceptable in most countries of the world. I say probably because in some cases local legislation requires a translation to be done locally. This is certainly the case in the United Kingdom. When practising as a notary I spent much time re-translating into English the statutes of Panamanian companies which had already been translated in Panama into slightly incorrect – but in many cases entirely comprehensible – English by Panamanian sworn translators.

The translations that notaries provide are concerned mainly with commerce, property, and birth, marriage, divorce and death. Very nuts-and-bolt type documents, in which accuracy is all-important and style is of secondary importance. And in most cases errors in the original must be reproduced in the translation, since it is not for the translator to make value judgements in legal matters (although of course he will draw attention to errors where he thinks this is appropriate). In very few cases do documents translated by notaries have to be published, and in those cases it is nearly always merely a formality.

In the Communities, however, legal translation is somewhat different. Much of the work translated has to be published and, having been published, is often quoted and referred to again and again. Therefore the translators have a great responsibility, which sometimes weighs heavily upon them. It is as if their final versions were engraved in stone. Many a translator or reviser wakes up in the night in a cold sweat, fearful of having made an error in an important judgement or piece of legislation. And errors in Community documents can be difficult to correct. The classic example is the Italian version of Article 118 of the EEC Treaty which for nearly thirty years has contained an error. *Droit de travail* (labour law) was erroneously translated into Italian as *diritto al lavoro* (entitlement to employment) which is something entirely different. And there seems to be no way of rectifying the error. Likewise, if you examine the French and German versions of the Swiss Code of Obligations (the German was the original) you will find numerous errors in the French version.

But before going on to specific problems of legal translation, a few words about the translations at the Court of Justice of the European

Communities. As far as I know, the Court is the only institution where translators are required to have a formal, non-linguistic qualification as well as a linguistic qualification. They must have a law degree or else be a solicitor, barrister or other recognised legal practitioner. At present, the translators in the Division include solicitors, barristers, a notary, law graduates, and former law lecturers. The documents dealt with are of three main types: judgements of the Court; Opinions of the Advocates General (who are members of the Court who examine each case and state their view as to how it should be resolved); and requests submitted by the national courts for preliminary rulings on the validity or interpretation of Community Law under Article 177 of the EEC Treaty.

The working language of the Court is French, a fact which produces some unusual consequences. Everything has to be translated into French, and all the judges and Advocates General are presumed to know French.

Although each case has a 'language of the case', that being the language of the court from which the case originates or that of the party who commences the proceedings, all judgements are drafted in French and translated into the other languages. Each judge has two legal secretaries who do much of the drafting and their mother-tongue is not necessarily French. Thus, the following situation is quite possible. An English court submits a question to the Court of Justice for a preliminary ruling under Article 177 of the EEC Treaty. The judgement is drafted by a German in French and is then translated into English, the language of the case, by a Welsh, Irish, Scottish or English translator. As you can imagine, there is room for many a misunderstanding along the way, and therefore friendly consultation between the translator and writer is essential. This is one reason why translation at the Court of Justice could never be privatised and placed in the hands of agencies. Another reason is that many of the documents to be translated are very sensitive and must be kept confidential until the appropriate moment. This applies particularly to judgements which have to be translated into the language of the case by, but not made public before, the day on which judgement is to be delivered, and which therefore have to be kept secret. Recently the Court gave judgement in the important case of *Adams* v. *Commission*. That case was viewed by the media as the story of one man's valiant struggle against a large multi-national company and Community bureaucracy, and therefore I don't doubt that many journalists would have loved to see a copy of the judgement before judgement day. None of them did, but had the translation been farmed out security would have been very difficult.

Since I wish to demystify legal translation, let me, before dealing with the difficulties, mention some ways in which legal translation is easy and straightforward, and even pleasurable.

I should like to think that I am being objective when I say that those who have to translate judgements – and please note that the comments which follow are confined to judgements – from English into a foreign language are in a privileged position. One of the differences between the legal system of the Common Law countries and that of the Roman Law countries is the emphasis placed in the Common Law countries upon the oral procedure. Common Law judges are not career judges from the start but are appointed from among senior members of the Bar. Therefore they have had long experience of advocacy and have doubtless on many occasions been ticked off by judges for expressing themselves vaguely or even merely ungrammatically. The following exchange between a judge and counsel is quite conceivable: 'I take it that when you say "compared to" you mean "compared with", I take it that you are highlighting the differences rather than the similarities.' 'Yes my lord, I am most grateful to you for your guidance.' As a result, by the time a barrister becomes a judge he has usually learnt – and had branded into his consciousness – the importance of expressing himself clearly and concisely. Sadly, this is not so in the case of English-speaking lawyers who are not given a public wigging from time to time by judges or lawyers in countries where the oral procedure is less important. Although it is true that *verba volet scripta manet*, written pleadings are not as a rule published and it would be very unusual for a writer of ungrammatical submissions ever to be made aware of his mistakes in a manner as memorable as by rebukes from the bench in open court. As a result, many judgements delivered by courts of Roman Law countries and many documents prepared by English lawyers who are not judges are put together with all the grace and cohesion of a punk rocker's hairdo, are badly reasoned, ungrammatical and disastrously punctuated.

Another advantage of the Common Law system is that in collegiate courts each of the judges gives his own judgement and it is therefore published with his name at the bottom – he feels personally responsible for it. Under the continental system, collegiate courts deliver a single judgement which purports to be the unanimous view of the judges. Although it bears the name of all the judges, any peculiarities in it are attributable to none of them individually – they enjoy a sort of collective anonymity, and their words of wisdom are recorded in a collectively neutral style.

Many parts of translations of judgements are easy because they contain few or no legal terms, as they merely recite the facts of the case. This applies both to Common Law and Napoleonic systems but, once again, I think the Common Law system produces more interesting writing in this respect because the judge (the writer) is identified individually and often feels he is engaged in literary rather than legal writing. Here is an example, from a judgement of Lord Sands of the Scottish Court of Session delivered in 1932:

In this case the local committee have preferred to follow our judgement rather than that of the House of Lords. Now while one may appreciate their patriotism, one regrets that one is unable to support their conclusion. It is quite true that we are a supreme tribunal in valuation matters and our judgements are not subject to review by the House of Lords; and accordingly, in a technical sense the judgements of the House of Lords may not be binding upon us. But there is one thing that is binding upon us and that is the law and the House of Lords is an infallible interpreter of the law. A batsman who, as he said, had been struck on the shoulder by a ball, remonstrated against a ruling of LBW; but the wicket-keeper met his protest by the remark: 'It disna' matter if the ball hit yer neb, if the umpire says yer oot, yer oot'. Accordingly, if the House of Lords says 'This is the proper interpretation of the statute', then it is the proper interpretation. The House of Lords has a perfect legal mind. Learned Lords may come and go but the House of Lords never makes a mistake. That the House of Lords should make a mistake is just as unthinkable as that Colonel Bogey should be bunkered twice and take eight to the hole. Occasionally to some of us decisions of the House of Lords may seem inconsistent. But that is only a seeming. It is our frail vision that is at fault.

On a more practical note, a legal translator working in the commercial world will often find that he or she is asked to do the same work over and over again, with variations. For example, once again if they are working from English, they will often be asked to translate into a foreign language notices of writs to be served out of the jurisdiction where proceedings are started in a UK court against a defendant resident abroad. The document contains a short statement of claim which, like the names of the parties, will be specific to each case, but the bulk of the document will be identical to other notices of writ. And there are several translation agencies in London which have at least French and Spanish versions of notices of writ for service out of the jurisdiction programmed into their word processors so that they can produce a longish document in a remarkably short time, and earn a splendid fee. The same applies to the memoranda and articles of association of English companies which are often based on well-worn precedents. Changing the odd word here and there is what some lawyers call legal drafting. Translating into English, this also applies to the statutes of, for example, the Panamanian companies mentioned earlier, which usually follow a predictable pattern. And, also, the statutes of many French companies reproduce word-for-word large chunks of French company legislation, which the translator may well have translated before or have obtained a reliable translation of.

Those are some of the pleasures. Now for some of the pitfalls and difficulties. People don't, in general, like lawyers as a breed. They are regarded as devious. One reason for this is that they appear in literature and drama more than the members of any other profession. There may have been – but I can't recall any – TV series about chartered surveyors or accountants – but there are many about lawyers: *Perry Mason*, *Rumpole of the Bailey*, A.P. Herbert's *Misleading Cases*. And the works of Dickens are full of lawyers, many of whom are portrayed as devious. And of course many *are* devious – the only consolation is that the majority of the devious ones have become politicians and don't bother us translators too much.

Another reason for their unpopularity, apart from their sometimes exorbitant fees for an intangible product, is their alleged or actual pomposity. People feel that lawyers have created their own mystery and mystique and speak exclusively in juridical jargon. Even the editors of *The Economist* take this view if *The Economist*'s style sheet, part of which was published as an advertisement in *The Sunday Times* colour supplement, is anything to go by. It says, 'Do not be stuffy or pompous. Use the language of everyday speech, not that of spokesmen, lawyers or bureaucrats'. But it is remarkable how many people, including non-lawyer translators faced with a legal text, try to ape lawyers by adopting what they regard as a legal style. When in practice, I occasionally received letters from lay clients which were incomprehensible because of the writer's insistence on peppering them with obsolete legal terms. It is a matter of fact that lawyers' letters to each other are much more straightforward than those written to lawyers by their clients.

One result of this cloak of pomposity is that a translator is often tempted to use a legal-sounding word incorrectly when a simpler word was the correct one. Here is a specific example: a document in Russian issued by a registrar in the Soviet Union certifying the identity of a child's father. A literal translation of its title is 'certificate of affiliation'. However, the English translator, who fell into the sin of pomposity, decided that 'certificate' was not a legalistic enough word and decided to call the document an 'affidavit of paternity'. The error here is that, just as it takes two to tango, it takes two to make an affidavit: the person making the statement and the person who administers the oath to that person to endow the document with the required solemnity. Another specific example is in a decision of the Commission of the European Communities where a German term was translated as 'scheme of arrangement'. The literal and the correct translation of the German term was 'compromise'. The parties to the dispute came to a compromise, as simple as that. However, the translator thought that this sounded too simple and used the grand-sounding term 'scheme of arrangement', which is wholly inappropriate since it is a term of art relating specifically to an arrangement between a debtor and his creditors whereby the creditors obtain some advantage which they would not obtain from bankruptcy or other insolvency proceedings.

The use of appealing ready-made expressions was gently castigated in an Opinion delivered to the Court of Justice of the European Communities by Mr (as he then was) Advocate General Jean-Pierre Warner. He was dealing with a staff case arising from a notice of vacancy issued by the Commission of the European Communities for the post of a lawyer. To quote him:

A third [notice of vacancy ...] required a good knowledge of Dutch law and in addition, rather oddly, knowledge of Anglo-Saxon law, a system which I have always understood became defunct about 900 years ago. Nevertheless, a knowledge, and if possible experience, of this law, was required by a further notice of vacancy.

For me, that alone is good enough reason for rejecting the expression 'Anglo-Saxon'. It is usually used of English-speaking countries or, in a legal context, countries where the Common Law prevails. But in most cases it is wildly inaccurate, particularly since it ignores the waves of Scandinavian, Italian, Chinese, Slav and other immigration to most English-speaking countries.

A further example of pomposity is the excessive use of words such as thereof, whereof, wherefore, thereto, thereunder, therein and thereout. On the other hand, moderate use of such words is useful in cases where the original text makes ambiguous or vague use of words like *ceci, celle-ci, celle-là*, and so on, so that the antecedent is not clearly identified. Sometimes the translator has no alternative but to use a thereof to preserve an ambiguity which he is unable to resolve.

On the other hand, there are occasions when it would be appropriate to be bold and to use slightly unusual legal terms in order to be accurate and to avoid long circumlocutions. Lord Diplock wasn't afraid to do so. Here is a quotation from him:

In the *Hong Kong Fir Shipping* case [...] I was careful to restrict my own observations to synallagmatic contracts. The insertion of this qualifying adjective was widely thought to be a typical example of gratuitous philological exhibitionism; but the present appeal does turn on the difference in legal character between contracts which are synallagmatic (a term which I prefer to bilateral, for there may be more than two parties), and contracts which are not synallagmatic but only unilateral, an expression which, like synallagmatic, I have borrowed from French law (Code Civile, Articles 1102 and 1103).

Similarly, it would have been convenient if, when the UK came into the European Communities, English translators had decided boldly to use the English word, common in Scots law, 'prestation' in certain cases to translate the French word *prestation*. Although initially the word would have sounded strange and would have attracted cynical comment from sections of the press, it would have become accepted in time and would have avoided numerous translation difficulties – after all, we have swallowed words such as 'conjunctural', so why not words such as 'prestation'?

The difficulties described so far arise from characteristics of the translator rather than from the text with which he or she is dealing. But the vast majority of problems arise from the nature of the text. I have already spoken in unglowing terms of documents produced by lawyers and judges within a system which accords very little importance to the oral phase of the procedure. Incidentally, this difference is highlighted linguistically by the fact that in the House of Lords the judgements of the learned Lords are referred to as 'speeches', and by contrast in some Spanish language contexts proceedings are said to be seen (*visto*) rather than heard, even though what is involved is in fact the oral phase of the proceedings. Although I love the Spanish language and nation, I have to say that I believe the Spanish judiciary to be amongst the worst offenders when it comes to writing nearly unintelligible judgements. There appears to be a convention according to which it is bad form to have more than one sentence per paragraph in the recitals to a judgement. Thus you have a series of extremely long sentences beginning with the words *considerando* or *resultando* or *por cuanto*, followed by a main clause onto which are tacked innumerable phrases each containing what Fowler described as an unattached participle, where it is impossible to identify the logical subject of the participle. As often as not this is combined with the vaguest and most ambiguous possible use of *este* and *aquel* (the latter and the former) so that the poor translator is entirely lost unless he or she has been provided with sufficient background information and documentation – which happens in about one case in one hundred.

In the European Communities a number of difficulties arise from the fact that legislation is published in all the official languages and all the versions are supposed to carry the same force. Mistakes are occasionally made in some of the language versions and these may give rise to references to the Court of Justice for interpretation of the provisions in question. In one such instance the following judgement was given: 'De uitdrukking "diens echtgenote" in artikel 10, lid 1, sub b, van verordening nr. 574/72 heeft ook betrekking op de gehuwde man die in een Lid-Staat beroepswerkzaamheden uitoefent', the English translation of which is: 'The expression "whose wife" in Article 10(1)(b) of Regulation No. 574/72 includes a married man who is engaged in a professional or trade activity in a Member State' – truly a case where the female embraces the male.

All lawyers – and thus legal translators as well – are expected to handle Latin maxims with ease. I used to cherish the idea that all the translator needed to do was to translate the surrounding words and leave the Latin phrases in Latin. But now I'm not so sure. It seems that the use of Latin varies from one country to another. When the French use the words *a priori* they are not using them as a term of logic but merely to say 'at first sight'. Similarly, *a posteriori* is often used merely to mean 'subsequently'. If the translator is enamoured of Latin he or she can, in many cases, translate *a priori* as *prima facie* and *a posteriori* as *ex post facto*. A phrase often used in the Court of Justice is *fumus boni iuris* (literally 'the smoke of good law'), which I believe we used in the English translation to leave in the Latin, until we realised that it made people laugh. So it is now translated using words such as 'a *prima facie* case'. And Italian lawyers seem to love the expression *in apicibus* – I've not yet met an English lawyer who knew what it meant. It appears to mean 'on the peaks' and is used by lawyers where a court has touched lightly upon a subject without going into it deeply. It is clearly a case where it is inappropriate to leave the Latin untranslated. Finally, there is the expression *in continenti* often used in Portuguese. It certainly conjures up a splendid image of urgency and in fact is used to mean 'immediately'. It is another phrase which clearly should not be left untranslated.

Fewer difficulties than you might think arise from the difference between the Common Law system and the Continental system of law. After all, it is much less easy to confuse chalk with cheese than to confuse two kinds of cheese. In a lecture given in 1966, when all the legal systems in the Common Market were similar to each other, André Donner, who was the President of the Court of Justice of the European Communities from 1958 to 1966, said the following:

[...] it certainly is true that many fundamental concepts and notions are common to the law of every one of the Six. But in a way that only adds to the misunderstanding. We use the same terms and reason along the same lines, but this seeming identity can intensify the difficulty, because we suppose that in using identical terms we give them identical content. And that is just not correct, for the content of those terms has been developed and modified in the course of six different legal histories. It is not the big differences that are the most irritating. The small and seemingly unimportant ones may be much more so. It would in some way clarify the situation if among the Member States there were at least one with an obviously different system of law, for example England, for then no one could continue to argue as though there were no legal diversity and to presume as a matter of course that every civilised nation has exactly the same notions as his own legal system.

Of course, the UK and Ireland have acceded to the Communities, but whether or not their accession has made life easier for the translators of the original Six I would not presume to say.

Even where the legal systems are radically different, problems may arise where the differences are concealed by linguistic similarity. The case I most often encountered as a notarial translator was that of Argentine *divorcio* proceedings. The obvious temptation is translate *divorcio* as 'divorce'. But divorce does not yet exist in Argentina and it is clearly stated in the Argentine Civil Code that *divorcio* does not dissolve the marriage bond. A result of *divorcio* proceedings is that the parties may be legally separated and terms may be arrived at for the settlement of their property rights. So, a more accurate translation for *divorcio* is 'legal separation'.

I shall mention just a few more difficulties. The first derives from the fact that we do not always see ourselves as others see us and therefore we do not always call ourselves what others call us. Here are just two examples: the first is that Ireland, the southern part of the island between the Irish Sea and the Atlantic, calls itself in Community documents merely Ireland, not the Republic of Ireland. As a general rule, Ireland's wish to be known as Ireland is respected but from time to time someone forgets (a recent example is to be found in the case of *Commission* v. *Ireland* (on co-insurance) now pending before the Court of Justice, where the Commission's Service Juridique refers to *la République d'Irlande*. When this happens, the English translation division courteously truncates the expression to the single word Ireland. I just mentioned the Service Juridique of the Commission. I use the French expression so as not to give away the other example. At an early stage, the English translation division decided that the expression 'Legal Service' was a mis-translation of *Service Juridique* and always refers to it in translation as the Commission's Legal Department, even where in the pleadings the department in question calls itself the Legal Service.

A further difficulty is not strictly a legal one but it arises by operation of law. Under Portuguese law, notarial documents (wills, conveyances and so on, and many certificates of marriage, birth and death) must be written by hand. This would present no problem if the documents were written legibly. But few are. Cacography prevails. It seems mandatory to make what I believe graphologists call garlands and arcades – the peaks and valleys of 'n's and 'u's for example – identical, so that it is impossible to detect the beginning and ending of 'n's and 'm's and 'u's and (in foreign names) 'w's, and with a little imagination, which the writers rarely lack, it is possible to make 'a's look like 'o's and 'p's look like 'q's and to make many other pairs of letters indistinguishable. It is a problem which can be overcome in most cases by guessing what the words ought to be, but the translator is usually stumped where the illegibility occurs in the name of a party or of a small village in Portugal which does not appear on the map.

The last difficulty of legal translation I would like to cover is the lack of good legal dictionaries. I work mainly from Spanish, Portuguese and French, and over the years the only legal dictionary for which I have developed any respect is one that is now out of print, namely the *Legal, commercial and financial dictionary* written by Lewis Sell in two volumes: English/Spanish and Spanish/English. The ones which I find useless I will not name. The main criticism is that they include all the words you know already and none of the words you don't know. In addition, many of them contain erroneous entries. And some contain silly entries. For example, in one dictionary under the French word *fautif*, only one English word is given as a suggested translation: 'faulty'.

Because so much legal work is repetitive – as mentioned earlier much so-called legal drafting consists of changing a word here and there in an old precedent – the legal profession was among the first to invest in word processors. However, they seem to have a childlike trust in whatever is produced by word processors. Many legal documents go through many versions before the final wording is agreed and many times I have seen, faithfully reproduced in the final version, typing errors which occurred in all the previous nineteen versions and should have been removed from the first version.

As regards computer translation (will somebody please tell me why it is called machine translation, when the connotations of a machine are oily cogs and pistons and rattling camshafts?), I must confess that I am among those who are yet to be convinced of its worth. I would like to mention just one aspect, being provoked by an article by James Wilkinson, BBC News Science Correspondent. He referred to a system which 'can translate 1600 words an hour – some five to ten times faster than a person'. I wonder where he got his figures? Those figures indicate that someone somewhere has observed translators at work and decided that they can translate at the rate of 160 to 320 words an hour, that is a maximum of less than one-and-a-half A4 pages with double spacing. And presumably both the computer and the humans whose performance has been monitored are producing raw text.

I made my own observations – not at the Court of Justice but in the commercial world before I joined the Court. For the purpose I divided legal translation into two broad types, which is convenient to call contentious and non-contentious. Contentious, in this context, describes the kind of language used by people who are trying to convince others of a particular view of a situation, as for example in pleadings, opinions and judgements. Non-contentious describes the kind of language used to lay down rules of conduct (legislation, contracts etc.) or to record undisputed facts. I found that the average rate for translation from Spanish into English of contentious material (the more difficult of the two categories) was over 1,000 words per hour raw text dictated, and that for non-contentious material the rate was over 2,000, sometimes as many as 2,500, words per hour raw text dictated – and the non-contentious text needed very little tidying up. The only long-winded part of the operation was the transcribing of tapes. As a legal translator, therefore, I for one would prefer to see money spent on word processors capable of taking dictation, equipped with sophisticated spelling checkers, than on computer translation equipment.

Since I have made frequent references to the differences between the Common Law and Napoleonic Law, let me conclude with a quotation which refers to Napoleon with a mixture of admiration and arrogance on the part of the speaker. It comes from a speech by Lord Brougham to the House of Commons in the nineteenth century, in which he sought help in reforming the law:

The course is clear before us; the race is glorious to run. You have the powers of sending your name down through all times, illustrated by deeds of higher fame, and more useful import, than were ever done within these walls. You saw the greatest warrior of the age – conqueror of Italy – the humbler of Germany – the terror of the north – saw him account all his matchless victories poor, compared with the triumph you are now in a condition to win – saw him condemn the fickleness of fortune, while, in despite of her, he could pronounce his memorable boast 'I shall go down to posterity with the code in my hand'. You have vanquished him in the field; strive now to rival him in the sacred arts of peace! Outstrip him as a law giver, whom in arms you overcame! [...] It was the boast of Augustus that he found Rome of brick and left it of marble [...] But how much nobler will be the Sovereign's boast, when he shall have it to say that he found law dear and left it cheap; found it a sealed book and left it a living letter.

AUTHOR
Ian Frame, lawyer-linguist, Court of Justice of the European Communities, Luxembourg.

Session I:
Summary of discussion 1

(1)   Peter Arthern (Head of the English Translation Division of the Council of the European Communities), commenting on Geoffrey Kingscott's remark about preference given to younger translators in EEC examinations, said that the age limit was forty, but those passing were younger and new recruits in fact were all under thirty. However, this was a matter of chance rather than decision. Questioners from the floor asked about translation courses at undergraduate level, whether any courses included revision of translated texts, and also whether such revision was practised in commercial companies and bureaux. Jeremy Verrinder mentioned the translation module in the PCL's language degree courses, and Professor Benoît Thouin, from the floor, explained that most training programmes in Canada were at undergraduate level, and half at postgraduate level as well. The approach was professional rather than academic, and included revision of both general and specialised texts. Several Canadian programmes included periods of work in a translation company or public organisation, where work was revised and trainees also had to revise the work of others. In recent years courses had been introduced at Ottawa University which involved the translation of texts for the community (not in competition with business firms). This was at fourth-year level, before graduation. To the second part of the question Catriona Picken responded that revision in the Shell translation department was thorough, and from the floor Ms A. Torsvik (Senior Translation Editor, Digital Equipment Corp.) said that revision was built in through the function of editors, who had language competence and scientific qualifications.

(2)   Josephine Bacon, court interpreter, said that she was horrified at the low standard of interpreting and translating she encountered in her work, particularly in criminal matters, and she quoted Lord Hailsham's comment that it didn't matter if an interpreter of Arabic couldn't read or write the language.

Ian Frame agreed that such interpreters and translators should be competent in criminal matters, and suggested that possibly the Lord Chancellor's department should be doing something about providing training. But there was no control over the type of translation work available, and in his experience 98 per cent was civil against 2 per cent criminal, and this was a fact of commercial life.

Geoffrey Kingscott commented that both the Nederlands Genootschap van Vertalers (NGV) and the Bundesverband der Dolmetscher und Übersetzer (BDÜ) had mounted campaigns over the use of unskilled interpreters in court translation of criminal cases, and cited as an example the use in England of community interpreters from police lists who might well speak the wrong dialect. Community interpreting was in its infancy here and elsewhere; it was necessary to spread the idea of a professional approach and convince the police that it was not enough to have an apparent facility in the language. Jeremy Verrinder added that the Nuffield Foundation was thinking of funding a project for community interpreters, and Peter Arthern, from the floor, said that Australia had a developed interpreting system which perhaps should be introduced here.

(3)   Inger Rider (Editor, Esselte Studium, Solna, Sweden) speaking from the floor, asked what advice was given to students about the use of dictionaries. Were they encouraged to pick out mistakes and inform the publishers?

Jeremy Verrinder said that in the PCL Technical and Specialised Translation course the presenter of the topic guided students over the choice of dictionaries, which, he agreed, contained plenty of mistakes. A project was in hand at PCL which involved going page by page through a major German–English dictionary, listing complaints. Nélida Depiante asked if publishers could insert a note asking for mistakes to be notified, to which Inger Rider responded from the floor that they usually did, in the preface which nobody read. Ian Frame commented that in legal translation he never used bilingual dictionaries without at the same time referring to a monolingual dictionary in the source language.

(4)   Lanna Castellano, from the floor, put a question to Geoffrey Kingscott about the organisation of and statistics on literary translators and interpreters.

Geoffrey Kingscott answered that many literary translators were members of the Translators' Association (TA) and therefore in touch with each other, and although many were not, they were in touch with publishers, who had their own network; there was, for instance, a large group of Bible translators. The Association Internationale des Interprètes de Conférence (AIIC) represented interpreters and had a directory listing them. Many remained outside the organisation, but the total number was in any case limited. Most *ad hoc* interpreters were part-timers with other occupations; nobody knew how many there were.

RAPPORTEUR
Anne Napthine, Translator, Shell UK Ltd, Shell Centre,
    London SE1 7NA, UK.

The new technology and the translator: a personal view

Josette Guédès

Legal and technical translator, London, UK

To be of any interest, my appraisal must necessarily reflect my personal experience. However, I have tried to be fair and objective in order to give you some useful pointers.

First of all, my appraisal of the new technology covers essentially the word processor – I use a CPT 8510 – and electronic mail with TEXTNET and my experience of these up to now.

THE WORD PROCESSOR

It would seem that for a translator, the word processor should be the ideal machine. After all, a translator spends most of the day 'processing words' in one way or another. And my word processor is a wonderful tool. I love it, but even after three years, I feel I have yet to find ways really to make the most of its potential.

I am not alone in having misgivings about some aspects of the new technology. The improvement brought about by the WP is linked to the efficiency – or lack of efficiency – of the previous office set-up.

My typing has always been of the multifingered, but unorthodox, variety. For short spells, I can type as fast as my typist, but as I never trained as such, my sustained speed is not impressive. Consequently, since I left the Central Office of Information (where I had worked as technical translator/editor until 1972) to become a full-time freelance translator, I have always dictated my work and had someone else to type it for me.

From 1972 to 1983, I had a French audio-typist working full-time with me. She typed as fast as I could dictate – more or less – and the arrangement was as near-perfect as possible. Until November 1982, I was using

IBM Selectric typewriters with English and French keyboards, plus French golfballs, and Grundig Stenorette equipment. However, with the advent of the word processor, it became clear that one could not stand still and ignore those machines and that I would have to get one and master it.

At the time, I had a very efficient typist but she had set her mind against computers and all the new office machines. Nevertheless, I acquired the WP, thinking it would be easy to find a French audio-typist who would share my enthusiasm for the new technology.

Here, I must say something about the equipment I use now. It is as follows:

> *Current equipment*
> CPT 8510 word processor
> Ricoh VIII printer
> BUZZBOX modem
> DATA LINE
> (plus Grundig Stenorettes and IBM Selectrics)

My dictating set-up has not been altered by the new technology. My WP is a dedicated one. It is a CPT 8510 with one-disk drive, with the French, the maths and the communication programs, and I use it with a Ricoh VIII printer with acoustic hood and a good assortment of daisy wheels.

I occasionally wish that I had a second disk drive but, without it, I can still organise a long job to have the minimum of disruption at the editing stage. It is much more convenient to record the original draft and the corrected version both on the same disk but, with only one disk drive, one must anticipate and keep checking that the draft does not fill the disk beyond the half-way mark, at which point one must switch to a second disk.

The main factors in this choice of set-up were:

1. the white A4-sized screen with black characters, which helps to finalise the lay-out very accurately. The CPT screen seemed to be the best WP screen available, with no flickering, and there is also a brightness control
2. the fact that CPT offers a French program, giving a French keyboard lay-out and the text with accents both on the screen and on the printer
3. that the printer uses daisy wheels and is a serious piece of equipment, giving letter quality in 10, 12 or 15 pitch.

I think it is also what one calls 'user-friendly' and I thought any typist would love it. However, I was mistaken in thinking that, having found a new girl who was very keen and having sent her on the CPT training course, the office would run smoothly ever after.

She was not used to my type of work – I hesitate a little to say that, as practically all my jobs are one-offs, of course – and she just could not cope with getting used to both the work and the WP at the same time, without a lot of help. If one has, for example, a legal text with a lot of sub-paragraphs and indents, it is a very ambitious task to print it with a justified right-hand margin.

Having struggled to understand my tapes and corrected the mistakes, she then spent an inordinate amount of time trying to get a perfect layout, to impress me. As I had not been on the CPT training course then, I could not help her, except with some common sense advice, which must have seemed quite irrelevant to her. I tried to be patient, but deadlines must be kept and things became very difficult for me.

That disastrous experience came to an end after a few weeks; I found myself with a machine which I could not use and without help in the office. I then decided to go on the CPT course myself and I found it extremely well planned and useful. The first part of the training is a two-day course, followed by another two days of 'advanced training' a few months later.

Later on, I also acquired the CPT maths program and went on the special one-day course to use the maths keys. With this program, one can use the computing capacity of the machine and write accountancy pro-grams. For example, I have written a simple one to calculate the balance on an account once the debits and credits have been keyed in. It should also be possible to write one to convert imperial measurements to metric on the screen as one goes along.

Whilst on the subject of programs, I used to be irritated by the default to 10 pitch and the automatic hyphenation *à l'Américaine* that one gets immediately when starting up. Splitting words the American way would not improve my translations. In fact, I prefer not to cut words at all, except on rare occasions. I have therefore included an additional program on my French program disk to give 12 pitch and 'wraparound' (i.e. no hyphenation) and I use it quite regularly instead of going through the Print sequence and changing the type of hyphenation separately. With this new program, it is only necessary to touch the Prog key once to make both changes. But, if it is touched again by mistake, it will naturally do the same operations as before, but from a different starting point. As it was already on 12, it will now give 15 pitch instead. The first inkling I have that something is amiss is when I can't write beyond the right-hand margin any more, the system having defaulted to manual hyphenation. In that case, the only course of action is to go back to the slightly more lengthy Print Sequence and Code + H for the hyphenation.

With the CPT, there is a spelling option in English, and also in French. The English program disk contains a 10,000-word dictionary to which one can add up to 2,000 words of one's own choice. On the French program disk, it is possible to store the same amount of words to give a spelling check as one types, or after a page has been typed.

However, I feel that the amount of work that would be needed to incorporate in the dictionary all the French words I might want to use and all their possible endings would not be cost-effective, as I would still need to check the typist's draft. The bleep which announces any word 'not in the dictionary' would probably not be enough to deter the typist from carrying on without checking. If, however, we were producing a lot of work in English – and as I only translate into French that is unlikely – I would probably make use of the Spelling option. Anyway, it is nice to know it is there.

Once I knew how to operate the machine, I trained several girls to do the keying-in. As they are part-timers, I have made several cards in French to remind them of the routine procedures like starting-up, recording a page, the use of the Insert function for repetitive groups of words, how to do superscripts and subscripts etc. These cards have been very useful. One of them is shown in Figure 1. (They are in French of course, and rather battered by now, but I thought this translation would give you an idea of what I found useful. As the manuals are a bit daunting to the translator, they are even more so to a French typist and I thought I should do something about it.)

TO START A PAGE

– Left-hand margin: code + margin
– Right-hand margin: margin only
– Code + M (with 'tabs' if needed)

TO CENTRE A TITLE

– Type the title normally from the left-hand margin
– Leave the cursor just after the title
– Code + C

Figure 1. Examples of routine procedures on the CPT 8510

The WP also created the need for another type of card. An example is shown in Figure 2. This one enables the typist to know on which cassette I have dictated a particular job, which label to record it under and on which

Job	:	**3088**
Cassettes	:	**H ... 231**
Disk to be used	:	**40**
Label	:	**JIG**
Margins	:	**0-75**
Number of lines/page	:	**60**
lines/inch	:	**6**
Daisywheel	:	**Lettergothic**
Typed by	:	**CD**
Date	:	**6.11.85**
Number of words	:	**1,872**
Remarks/Inserts	:	**See list**

Figure 2.

disk. As the job number at the top is in sequence according to my day-book, I can locate any job easily, provided, that is, I have filled in the card conscientiously in the first place!

Now for a comparison of the two systems. The main advantage of the WP is that it makes it a lot easier to do corrections.

In the old days, I used to dictate all my work and concentrate on producing a version as close as possible to the final one in one go. However, it sometimes happens that some explanation towards the end of a text will put a different slant on something which recurs throughout twenty or maybe thirty pages. In those days, the correcting key was mainly useful to the typist when she was doing the first typed version, as she could correct her mistakes as she went along.

If I wanted to make changes later, I was always aware of the boredom of the poor typist having to retype page after page of text in which she had not the slightest interest and, also, of my own boredom at having to recheck those newly retyped pages. Besides, it was also very wasteful.

We became very good at putting the paper back in the machine to make it fall just right, to use the correcting key facility yet again. These kinds of problems generated a feeling of team-work and 'give and take' and I must admit that, once or twice, I did not have the heart to get something retyped yet again.

With the WP, one could use the Search & Replace function to cope with a repetitive change, but I probably would use Insert since, in French, as you know, a change often means several changes in fact, unless the swap involves words of the same gender and both in the singular or both in the plural.

But – and it is a big but – human nature being what it is, it has adapted very quickly to the WP. The ease of editing means that, when dictating a very lengthy legal sentence, for example, if I get interrupted by the telephone, I will sometimes indicate in pencil on the original that this is a point that I shall have to look at very closely at the editing stage and I just carry on.

As for the typist, since she does not do the corrections any more, she also becomes more relaxed about leaving mistakes, all the more readily, as she thinks that correcting is no longer a problem. And it really is not a problem, but it is time-consuming and therefore wasteful.

Up to now, I have done all the editing and printing myself, as so many little things can go wrong, like a line being skipped inadvertently, and a good translation is very much a matter of attention to detail (after one has dealt with the not unimportant matter of meaning, of course!).

Since I do the editing, I need fewer hours from the typist. This would go into the category of economic advantages, if one were to forget about the high cost of leasing the equipment in the first place. Whereas I used to have on average 150 hours of typing help per month, I reckon I now use about half that amount. But no help with answering the door or the telephone, making the coffee, and no little chats either!

But, I have come to realise that mistakes at the editing stage can't be totally avoided and that one should allow for another complete proof-reading. In that case, one has to allow yet more time from the typist and from the translator. Thus, on a run-of-the-mill job, the economic advantage of the WP vanishes.

The efficiency of the office is firmly in the hands of the translator and the typist. If both are efficient and conscientious, the WP should, theoretically, give more productivity than the typewriter. And the quality of the presentation is definitely much improved.

There are not many jobs where one is asked specifically to produce the work on a WP, and even fewer jobs where the client is prepared to pay extra for it. I suspect, though, that both agencies and clients are very pleased to get a camera-ready job at the standard rate. If generating goodwill is important – and I believe it is – then there the WP scores.

With the WP, one will sometimes get asked to keep some special jobs on disk for future amendments. Making amendments is not the most fulfilling type of work there is, but one does learn from them and, at least, the WP's advanced functions are being used and the client is appreciative.

As a translator, one is nearly always dealing with one-offs. But the WP can eliminate some tedious jobs like complicated tables. If a particular client comes back regularly with the same spreadsheet to up-date, it can be kept on disk and the job can be done much more easily – and with much better results – than on a typewriter. One can also, in such a case, take advantage of the 15-pitch option to get more text into the same space, which is a definite plus point, as the French text tends naturally to be longer.

ELECTRONIC MAIL

Now for a few words about electronic mail. My experience is limited and probably affected by all the practical difficulties of establishing a working system in the first place. But I am sure this must be a lot easier in 1985 than it was even a year ago, and I look forward with great interest to Nélida Depiante's paper on this same subject.

I have been a member of TEXTNET for about twelve months now and my feeling is that the paperless office is not a likely development for a long while yet. TEXTNET is a brilliant concept; I think Robert Rooke had a wonderful idea when he thought of using the technology to link the translators to their would-be clients and agencies. His French program is excellent and one can easily transmit and receive texts in French with all the accents.

I feel at present that several aspects are not yet fully developed but that, in the future, it will become a real possibility.

Initially, I liked the futuristic aspect, the idea of worldwide links straight from the keyboard and the use of a mainframe as a clearing-house for messages. What put me off were the repeated failures of the equipment, the costly and lengthy debugging and the unreliability of payments for work done over the telephone. If speed – both in the reception of the original and in the transmission of the translation – is to be the main advantage, then the financial aspect of the transaction must follow suit.

I could only work 'on trust' for people in this country that I know already or through personal recommendation. Otherwise, the only way I can feel reassured about starting a job is with an order form on headed paper. Very old-fashioned maybe, but still essential to my mind even in 1985. If one insists on an order on paper, then the job itself might as well come by post or be brought by a messenger.

Between people who have a long-established working relationship, electronic mail does away with messengers for urgent jobs and can transmit telexes and give a word count, provided the job is available on a word processor and can be sent to the mainframe in the first place.

The use of WPs and modems is not widespread enough at present to enable electronic mail really to take off yet. Although some of my major clients are also on TEXTNET, the amount of work I do on electronic mail is minimal.

Besides, the equipment I use for communications has been the least satisfactory so far. Even now, though my system is in working order, I sometimes need to dial five or six times to get through to the main computer. When I finally manage it, I might have to repeat my ID and my password so many times that I have been known to give up in despair. So much for time-saving. I must admit I also find the typing 'online' very irritating and I should probably avoid it altogether.

The debugging of the installation has been costly. Many cables were tried and replaced and I even went as far as installing a separate data line, as I was led to believe that my Ambassador telephone system was at fault, but without any positive results. The failure was probably due in fact to a loose connection at the back of the modem.

Having struggled to establish the communication system at great cost in time and money, I must admit to being disappointed. The communication package from CPT includes a connecting cable for the modem, the program disk and also a manual. It does not include any formal training and I can't help feeling that, if CPT were to provide for communications as much assistance as for word processing and maths, some of my discontent would probably vanish.

My conclusion would be that until more offices use WPs and electronic mail, the pioneers will not be reaping the full benefits of their investment in effort and monetary terms. But it is only a matter of time.

Anyway, the new technology is a fascinating field in itself and I, for one, am totally hooked on it. In fact, I keep thinking up new ways of making the most of it.

AUTHOR

Josette Guédès, Legal and Technical Translator, 42 Whitehall Park, Highgate, London N19 3TN, UK

Part-timer's progress

Commodore Christopher Croft

Director, SCANTECH, Winchester, Hampshire, UK

In this paper I will take as my text these few words:

VÆRMELDINGEN
På **Østlandet** blir været mye bedre
imorgen. Snøbyger på **Årdal** og **Æretveit**.

Not that there is anything special about them – in fact some may recognise them as a mini weather forecast – but they encapsulate what I need from my equipment, that is the ability to produce, as neatly and easily as possible, text not only in English but in another language ‹ in this case Norwegian – that requires a number of additional characters. Apart from these extra characters Æ, Ø and Å, I have included underlining and bold print for good measure and, to save getting lost on the way, I propose to return to this as a sort of benchmark when describing my progress from portable typewriter to word processor.

In the beginning, life was simple and for a small sum my first portable typewriter was supplied modified to include the three Norwegian letters, but at the expense of six other characters. Underlining was no problem of course and bold type had hardly been thought of. Life as a young naval engineer involved a good deal of travel and for twenty years my spare time translation activity required no more than this simple arrangement of modified portable typewriter, carbon paper and a generous supply of Tippex.

That is not to say that technology had been standing still. The electric portable became available but this seemed to offer only a marginal improvement in type quality in exchange for much complexity and potential unreliability. So I decided to do nothing.

Then the golf-ball arrived bringing with it the promise of beautiful presentation, the ability literally to lift off any mistakes, and the possibility of choosing from a wide variety of typestyles and foreign or other special characters. Being more settled by then, and able to consider a piece of proper office equipment, I was tempted, but the high initial cost and the thought of the maintenance problem posed by all that electro-mechanical complexity finally made me decide to do nothing once again.

But the micro seemed to change all that. With nothing mechanical to go wrong – apart from the keyboard, the cassettes or disk drives that might be needed for storing the finished product, and of course the printer – here was inherent reliability combined with editing facilities, special character sets; in fact with 'mod. cons.' of every sort limited only by one's own ingenuity and that of the word-processing software writer.

Now at just about that time my engineering work was bringing me more and more into contact with computers and I could feel a growing need to get to grips with one at first hand. And that is when it all really began.

I ordered a BBC Model B and, although I planned to use it with cassette tape for storage to begin with, I asked for the optional disk interface to be fitted just in case. At the time the BBC microcomputer was only available to order, and after a long wait at that, so I broke what I would call the first rule of computer buying, namely *see the system working, doing exactly what you want it to do,* before you buy it.

As a result, when it finally arrived, it took almost a week of handbook reading, telephone calls and a fifty-mile round trip to the nearest agent before I could get the machine to run. There was nothing wrong; it was just that I was trying to read in from a cassette while the computer (having been fitted with a disk interface) was looking – unless told otherwise – for an input from a disk.

At that early stage there was no word-processing software available and perhaps that was just as well because it takes time to get used to a microcomputer. The handbooks are thick and inevitably contain terminology that is hard to understand unless one has already been initiated. I got as far as writing simple programs in BASIC (the language that most microcomputers use, although their particular dialects vary) and this was to prove useful later.

This initial learning was done using simply the BBC microcomputer with a television set as the display. This was fine but I could see that a higher resolution screen would be needed if eighty characters per line were to be legibly displayed. Even more pressing was the need for a printer, if only needed at this stage to keep a record of what I was learning in the way of programming.

So I acquired a fairly high-definition colour monitor and an Epson dot-matrix printer. The monitor made a big difference and the printer too proved to be ideal. But with the characters being made up from dots selected from a 9 × 7 matrix one could not expect letter quality, or even the so-called 'near letter quality' (NLQ) that many dot-matrix printers can now provide. Nevertheless, by combining three of its print modes (expanded, condensed and emphasised) a very neat semi-bold print could be achieved.

I mention this to illustrate the usefulness of some programming ability if one is using a microcomputer like the BBC model because, in order to set up the printer to produce, say, semi-bold print, one needs to type in three different commands each involving perhaps five or six keystrokes, and then type in three similar commands to revert to normal print. Much time could be saved by writing a short program allocating these sets of commands (and any similar ones for accents, underlining, calling up foreign character sets etc.) to the special function keys that most micros have.

A typical short program sets up the function keys on a BBC microcomputer for my own particular needs: that is a Norwegian character set, a left margin of six spaces, a line length of seventy characters, underlining, underlined enlarged print, emphasised print and so on, ending up with a command to run the Wordwise word-processing software (which had by then become available in the form of a plug-in chip) to make the system ready for use.

Having got that far one might expect plain sailing. But not quite. Going back to the 'mini weather forecast', with the BBC microcomputer in the editing mode, not only do the printer commands appear embedded in the text (Norwegian character set, start underlining, end underlining, start emphasised print, end emphasised print and so on), but various symbols appear in place of the Norwegian characters. This is because each key on the standard computer keyboard has a particular eight-bit signal associated with it and the only way to get the dot-matrix printer to print, say, Norwegian characters is to tell it to translate the standard signal for the key in question, in this case 'close curly bracket', into the special print signal needed to print 'A with circle', and so on for the other special letters required. Not as bad as it sounds and one soon gets used to it and one can simply label the keytops concerned.

By pressing the appropriate key on the BBC microcomputer the text can be previewed *more or less* as it will be printed. All of these embedded editing commands disappear and the formatted text alone is displayed. I stress 'more or less' because the underlining is not shown and the Norwegian letters are still shown as symbols (in fact a different set again, due to a quirk of the BBC micro). Never mind, one can get used to it and the result on paper is quite reasonable.

Things then went smoothly for a while until I realised that I really did need a letter-quality printer and that meant a daisy wheel. To cover those odd jobs like forms where one really needs a typewriter (and as a fallback in case any problem arose with the computer) I decided to go for a daisy-wheel typewriter equipped with the necessary electronics built in to allow connection to a computer. There was only one then available, the Olympia ESW 103. Not cheap at about £800 (after bargaining) but very satisfactory.

So now I had (in exchange for the best part of £2,000) a word-processing system with dot-matrix or daisy-wheel output selectable at will. But what about the 'weather forecast' using the daisy-wheel printer? Of course the standard print-wheel had no Norwegian characters but what about more basic facilities like bold print and underlining?

The typewriter had a bold print key but I never did manage to sort out the special commands that the BBC microcomputer would need to send to start and stop bold printing. Underlining was a problem too but in a different way. The ESW 103 has no 'automatic underlining', that is to say underlining is done simply by backspacing and printing the underline letter by letter like one would on a manual machine. So to achieve underlining under computer control, it was necessary to insert as many backspaces as necessary followed by the same number of underlines. This worked well enough but all the extra commands made the display look even less like the finished product and it upset the line length setting since the computer saw a backspace as just another character.

And what about the Norwegian characters? Simply ordering and fitting a Norwegian daisy wheel was not a good answer because such a wheel is designed to match a Norwegian keyboard and this is very different from the usual English keyboard layout. Some twenty keys need to be relabelled and this hardly helps to achieve smooth error-free typing. And it looks even worse on the display which of course knows nothing of what one is doing to the keyboard and printer. I have tried it using a Swedish wheel, which is different again and requires a whole new lot of key labels. The screen display was barely intelligible and very hard work. Definitely not recommended.

One answer to the problem of producing daisy-wheel print in, say, Norwegian, on a system like this is to go back to basics, much as one does with a manual machine, and have a standard daisy-wheel professionally altered by replacing little-used characters by the new special characters required. Not cheap, especially as it is worth using a metal rather than a plastic wheel, but it works well and involves a minimum of key labelling.

Before leaving the BBC microcomputer let me mention the business of storing the finished product. The internal memory is largely taken up by the word-processing software, leaving space for about five pages of text before the system starts to protest. So one has to store text outside the machine (the internal memory is cleared anyway when the microcomputer is switched off). I used cassette tapes but these are cumbersome, slow and not all that reliable, so it really has to be disks.

When I was just about settled with the BBC system, and was considering the purchase of a twin disk drive, two new circumstances arose. The first was that a new job was going to mean less time at home and the second was that an unexpected windfall meant that I could re-equip for convenience and pleasure of use without having to justify it on productivity grounds.

My first move was to look at lap computers that I could use, say, on the train or more generally while travelling, with the intention of dumping the text into the BBC system on return home for final editing and printing. The Tandy Model 100, together with two virtually identical machines from Olivetti and NEC, seemed possible but the forty-character line length was less than ideal and no supplier seemed interested in proving to me that the link-up with the BBC microcomputer really would work.

Then quite by chance I saw the Epson PX-8, beautifully made, with an eighty-character line length and the ability to work with eight different character sets including all three Scandinavian languages. And it was of course designed to be fully compatible with Epson printers so that, simply by selecting a particular language, both the PX-8 display and the printer worked with the appropriate character set.

The supplier also offered to link the PX-8 both to the BBC microcomputer and separately (if needed) to my Olympia daisy-wheel printer. And then a further complication. I happened to see an advertisement for a new Sony Word Processor. It seemed to be beautifully designed and it had a full A4-sized display with the text displayed in black on a pale blue background.

A visit to Sony UK in Staines convinced me that the Series 35 Word Processor outclassed any micro-based system that I had seen. It looked good, it felt good and the more I tried it the more I appreciated the amount of thought that must have gone into the design of the software. The display itself, with very high-definition characters, exactly like a typeface complete with serifs, was an absolute eye-opener after working with, or trying, so many computer displays.

And so the die was cast. I agreed to buy both systems on condition that Epson and Sony suppliers got together to ensure that I could feed work done on the Epson across into the main Sony machine for display, final editing, printing and storage.

The hardware involved comprises the PX-8 (normally on the move in my briefcase), the Sony keyboard and twin 3.5 inch disk drives, the full page display and the Diablo 630 printer. This is the fastest of the range of printers offered as part of the Sony system and I have it on a separate table to isolate the rest of the system from the shaking it would otherwise get from the printer.

Returning to the Epson PX-8, this needed no extra programming since it came with built-in communications software, plenty of internal memory (some fifty pages of text) and a so-called 'portable' version of WordStar. Using WordStar is a story in itself. It certainly offers every facility but it does involve learning a whole lot of coded commands.

So take just one as an example, deletion of a paragraph. With WordStar the sequence is:

> Cursor to start of paragraph – cursor keys
> Mark start of paragraph – Control KB
> Cursor to end of paragraph – cursor keys
> Mark end of paragraph – Control KK
> Delete marked block – Control KY

In contrast the same process on the Sony Series 35 involves simply:

> Position cursor anywhere in paragraph
> Delete – Paragraph – Execute

With the PX-8, I have some of the more difficult-to-remember commands printed on a card where I can see it as I work.

Returning to my original 'mini weather forecast', when typed into the Epson, the Norwegian letters are there, but the liquid crystal display cannot show either bold print or underlining. If I were going to print out directly using an Epson printer, I could achieve both bold print and underlining just by using the appropriate WordStar commands. But since I want to transmit the text to the Sony Word Processor (which does not understand WordStar) I need to find another way.

I have to type in 'less than' and 'greater than' symbols where I want to begin and end underlining, and a rather odd sign (which replaces the dollar sign when the Norwegian character set is being used) to start and stop bold print. I could have used any characters and it was just that these are ones that I rarely need. Having chosen them, it only remains to tell the Sony Word Processor to translate these particular symbols into the appropriate printer instructions when receiving text from the Epson PX-8.

The same sort of translation ensures that a Norwegian 'A with circle' displayed on the Epson (but which is actually transmitted as a bracket symbol) is turned back into an 'A with circle' on the Sony display. It may sound complicated but this is easily incorporated into the Sony Communications System disk and (in my case at least) at no extra cost.

The same applies to coping with different daisy wheels. As any one who has used a variety of daisy wheels can confirm, their sequences – that is which letter is positioned on which petal of the daisy wheel – vary enormously, especially when foreign character sets or scientific symbols have to be included. No problem with the Sony system, though. You just let your supplier know the wheels you want to use and the system disk he supplies you with will do the rest. The result is that you always get exactly what you key in (or transfer across from another machine as I do from the Epson) and the screen will always show exactly what you are going to get on paper.

The 'mini weather forecast' on the Sony display really is just as it will appear in print.

With time so short I will not say any more about the Sony Series 35, apart from briefly mentioning two facilities which I do use quite a lot. There is what Sony call a 'steno' document on which one can enter up to sixty or so words or phrases so that, by depressing any key followed by the steno key, one can call up the appropriate word or phrase. If necessary each key can call up a block of text of any size up to a full A4 page.

For technical translations I find it easiest to keep a separate steno document disc for each different job and, if I cannot remember the steno glossary for the job in hand, that is where the other special facility comes in useful. A single keystroke splits the screen into two half pages, each equivalent to a normal VDU 24-line display.

The working document occupies the top half and any other document (or page of the working document) can be displayed on the bottom half. By keying V and the steno key, I can, for example, enter the entire 'mini weather forecast' complete with underlining, bold type etc. One could equally well display a technical glossary, say, and one can work on either half page and copy or move text from one half page to the other.

AUTHOR

Commodore Christopher Croft, Director, SCANTECH,
  Downlands, Sleepers Hill, Winchester, Hampshire SO22 4NB, UK.

Freelancer on the line

Nélida E. Depiante

Freelance translator, London, UK

In the past I have heard stories of success from people using word processors and from translators who have left employment and now work for their ex-employers on a freelance basis, making twice as much money as they earned before. In such a context, my story is more of 'postponed success', a hopeful misnomer for failure. So let me give you the background.

I had been thinking of going freelance some time in the future, but the opportunity came prematurely when Shell reorganised its Foreign Language Services department. I am a fastidious translator (in the English and Spanish senses of the word!) and I try to translate into a type of Spanish which should be acceptable in a variety of countries at a variety of levels. Often my work is reproduced by photocopying methods and bound into manuals or distributed as periodical bulletins. Soon what I produce will not have to be input again by a typesetter when it is meant for quality printing, but will be used direct from my disk or screen.

This should help explain why I thought I needed the modern technology to mask my shortcomings as a typist and as a translator. I want a word-processing system that is easy and quick to use, and does not require a lot of skill to operate. I want an easy way of dealing with accents, upside-down question and exclamation marks, various typefaces, indentations, mathematical formulae and chemical structures and I want to see everything on screen as I am going to get it on paper. I want all that from equipment which is small enough, smart enough and silent enough to fit comfortably in the flat which constitutes my home and to allow work to be carried out late at night without disturbing the neighbours; equipment that will make communications by modern methods possible. I want it all at an affordable price. I also have the temerity to demand an amber screen against the proven benefits and wide acceptance of a green one in Britain.

Well, I want ... rather I 'wanted' all that. What I have got or am likely to get is another matter.

In January 1984, when I started thinking about the equipment I should get, my experience of modern equipment was limited to two systems and a lot of hearsay; one of the two systems was the IBM electronic typewriter with magnetic cards, which the Foreign Language typists used in Shell, but I had never typed on it myself.

The other system was a dedicated word processor, the Logica VTS 2200, which I had been using for a number of months in Shell Centre (it is the system currently being used in the Foreign Language Services department and it was carefully picked for them). It is terrifically user-friendly: what can be done on this system is enough to set very high standards for any list of requirements. And its keyboard is excellent. However the system is hardware driven, so it works its own software. It only 'talks' to a Ricoh daisy-wheel printer. Stop codes and changes of daisy wheel cannot be used in the same job, which rules out the use of different typefaces. Because it is obsolete, by January 1985 its price had nearly halved; this almost tempted me to buy it. However, in Shell, any job that the word processor cannot handle is handed to the typist to be produced on the IBM machine – a facility I would not have at home.

In February 1984 I heard a most enlightening talk by Commodore Croft and added, among other things, a dot-matrix printer to my list of points to consider. Since then I have seen many systems. My lists of requirements have been all over London, or indeed England; I went for demonstrations and salesmen came to see me at home. Some colleagues kindly showed me their equipment. The story would take days to tell. I ended up not seeing the wood for the trees and getting lost in my own requirements. The main problem was the fact that I was a small customer, trying to buy equipment for foreign languages in Britain. Apparently the choice would be much easier on the Continent.

At first, I intended to follow a gradual progression from a Brother CE70 (to bridge the first gap), through a more powerful electronic typewriter to a word processor when the market was right, probably in 1986. But then I persuaded myself that it would be better to go for a word-processing system in one leap.

However when I went to exhibitions or for *ad hoc* demonstrations, I found that I could not try the things I needed to see, because the machine was not loaded with the Spanish program or was not connected to the right printer, or had just broken down or whatever. Computer salesmen used to tell me, at the time of making the appointment: 'You will be very *impressed* with what we have to offer.' (Are they drilled in that expression?)

Personally, I was getting more and more *depressed*.

The salespersons and programmers seem to have no idea of the fact that foreign languages do not always function like English and that it is no solution to try to take over the foreign language and impose the *pax britannica* (or indeed *pax americana*) on it in order to bring its primitive and unruly structures into the twentieth century.

The printing stage is another difficult issue. And one that computer people tend to dismiss as unimportant. It is possible to find a very good system, on the screen, to which no suitable, affordable printer can be attached. Consider a page which has something on it like Figure 1 (and these are very simple examples).

If the system allows for the use of different printwheels, how many changes of printwheels would be needed each time the user wanted a print-out? The formulae may be done by hand, of course, but then ... so much for modern technology!

I started by assigning up to £7,500 for the purchase of the complete system. But at that level, many of my requirements were not met. (Recently I saw a handy typesetting machine, ideal for journalists, for example, for as little as £1,500. However, I was told I could not have anything for Spanish for under £50,000, or it may have been £15,000 and I misheard it. In any case both figures are equally out of reach for me.)

$$A = (V_f + V_p - V_1) / W \qquad \underline{or}$$

$$P_p = (\gamma d_c^2 N_\gamma + c d_c N_c) (f - 0.363 [f - s] \qquad \underline{or}$$

The growth curves presented here for *D. rotundata* were similar to those obtained for *D. alata* by Campbell *et.al* (1962).

Figure 1.

The state of the market in 1984 seemed to make it possible to go for far less, but new equipment was not being launched as promised. A chunk of my budget went on research and loss of earnings. So I had to lower the maximum sum. The government has tampered with allowances for depreciation, so people can no longer recover the whole of the income tax allowance for their outlay in one year. And it may be relevant to say that while I was getting a computer to work more quickly, my old customers were getting computers to pay more slowly.

I considered the possibility of renting a Logica VTS 2200 for a time; the hiring of equipment is not as easy for a person working on his/her own as it is for a big organisation. Besides, it may be expensive in comparison with the purchase price. I decided that the best thing was to buy something ... anything ... and then see what I could do with it. At best, I might be lucky; at worst, I would be throwing my money away ... on experience. As you know, experience is what you have when you've got nothing else left.

For flexibility, a microcomputer appeared to be the answer. And I went for an Apricot PC and the Vuwriter software. Vuwriter was developed in conjunction with the University of Manchester and it is a very good scientific program, used by universities and technical colleges. A new version, called Arts, has just been released, which handles more languages and uses the equipment more efficiently.

In October 1984, when I was about to send a firm order to a very helpful dealer, Shell told me they wanted to carry out an experiment in having translators working at home, electronically linked to the Shell offices. I was the obvious person to take part in the experiment and this would bridge the gap for me until better things were on the market. I would have liked to have done the experiment on the equipment I would finally have. One of the reasons is that work is kept on disk for future updating and disks from one system do not work in others. But after careful consideration, I agreed to Shell's proposal that I should have at home one of their rented Logicas (for which I would pay a small percentage of the rental) with communications facilities.

It is easy to make machines talk in plain English. But transmitting oddities is another matter. Some people use codes for foreign characters so that the sender indicates in some form that a certain character is '*a*' with tilde, for instance. Then the recipient looks for these codes and edits the document accordingly. This seemed laborious. We wanted to transmit everything as it was to be printed. So big heads were put together to try to work this out. I was given a heavy flat box which was a Racal Milgo 'modem'; this was plugged into both the telephone socket and a power socket. Once we could not achieve communications and it was when I was cleaning the following day that I found a socket tucked at the end of a cable glaring at me from a tangle of cables on the floor. I had missed one connection! I had found that the equipment had to be unplugged completely when I went out; otherwise the telephone-answering machine would switch itself on and run all the tape, disabling itself. Experts could not find a reason for this, but it happened.

The working out of the instructions to transmit and to receive took some time and at the beginning it was found that two steps were transposed in the instructions and we failed to communicate. The learning was a bit stressful and tiring. It would take half an hour or an hour at a time, and could not be done as often as we would have liked. The actual transmission of the document was quick. All the other operations were time-consuming. The connection could be lost through delays, or the telephone lines were engaged, or there was a lot of 'noise' in them and funny characters were produced. As to the time to communicate: near close of business in the evening was easier and there was less noise. Or we had to do it at lunchtime, when the users of the equipment in the office were enjoying their scrumptious meals in Shell Centre and made no claims on the particular machine prepared for communications. But finally we got the idea. We could transmit diacritics in their place, upside-down question/exclamation marks, underlining, text in its right place if it was going to be printed on preprinted company stationery etc.; we lost the discretionary hyphen and the emboldening, for example.

Shell did not send text to me over the phone, because it was not convenient to input it by keying it and they did not have an optical character reader. For the work we tested, it was sufficient if they put the text in the post the previous day (maybe a special messenger could have been used if necessary – or telex, but then document layout would have been a problem).

Before or after the communication we could 'chat' on the screen if we wanted and tell each other how things were going. For some reason, our chatting on the screen was hilarious normally, because of the many mistakes we typed and because if we had started with wrong margins or something, we could have just one letter per line. Or, as happens in conversation, one side would start to type before the other side had finished.

The advantages of having the same equipment were clear in other areas: if I went to the office to check a draft, I could take my disk and do the editing there or leave the work for a staff translator to edit and print. Or I could incorporate work done by somebody else into my work for updating, or I could send disks by post. However, as I have already mentioned, I was not prepared to make the Logica word processor my choice.

In February/March 1985 I went out to look for equipment again, so that I could have it when the experiment ended in May or June. I have already mentioned how frustrating it is to deal with computer people and this is no time to go into a tale of woe. IBM, for instance, were very dismissive because I said I wanted to retain the pound sign and have the dollar sign as well.

Finally, an order was placed at the beginning of July for delivery at the beginning of August. On the day of the delivery, in the morning I was told everything was fine and in the afternoon I found out the dealer could not deliver. Now I had no equipment of any sort. After some more days of frantic searching during which I even condescended to see an IBM Personal Computer, I took an old magazine and rang an Apricot dealer in London, made enquiries and ordered the same equipment I was about to buy in October 1984. It was August 1985. Luckily, this particular dealer turned out to be more efficient and I now have an Apricot PC with 256K RAM, two disk drives ... and an amber screen, a Vuwriter word-processing system and a Toshiba P1351 dot-matrix printer ... and a string of minor teething troubles!

Now the main issue is communications. There would be no problem in communicating all the Greek characters, diacritics, scientific symbols, emboldening etc., between equipment running Vuwriter or between Apricot machines. Communications use seven bits and keep the eighth bit for parity checking. But Vuwriter uses the eighth bit for the strange characters. There was concern about the loss of this parity checking. In fact, Vuwriter is used at the College of Technology in Canterbury and they have communicated successfully between Wales and Canterbury and they intend to have workstations in different parts of the country. Contrary to what I have heard at lectures, Canterbury say that it is cheaper for them to use the public telephone line than to use electronic mail. My main problem however is for my work to be received by the Logica machine in Shell. Translation tables must be devised. This is not impossible, but it is expensive. I am told that it may be two weeks' work and the cost would be several thousand pounds. So I have come this far, now I have to stop and look which way to go.

I am finding it more difficult than I expected to get used to the new system, mainly the operating system of the machine, rather than the software. If something goes wrong, the hardware people tend to blame the software and vice versa. A word-processing system on a microcomputer is much slower than a dedicated word processor. I did not know that not all the memory can be used for storing the document. I almost died of a heart attack when, for my first document, the machine told me I had used up all the memory after two pages. Scientific and foreign characters and heavy editing take a great deal of memory. I intend to buy more memory.

With a microcomputer, I cannot see how you can get to the paperless office of the advertisements. Long documents have to be split. Going back to see what you said previously means getting in and out of documents. This takes time and you only have a bit of the text on the screen at any one time. There is no comparison with having the hard copy in front of you. But then, I am used to paper!

There is a lot being said about computers not being good for the health. I do not believe anybody will die of 'computeritis' but I have experienced a few problems. One is stress, mainly due to not knowing how to operate the system or what to expect of it. I decided to pay for a day's tuition and my trainer was a charming young lady from Manchester University who has given me further on-going support out of her own kindness.

Something funny and annoying happened to me: I found that I could not control certain fingers when using electronic keypads. The harder I tried the worse it was. The medical verdict was that I have an extra rib. I thought I had proved the Bible right. But I am told that men can get it as well. What apparently happens is that some people have some additional 'rib fibres' in the neck region, which can cause pain and slight problems with finger control, shown up by sensitive keypads.

I am very grateful for the new machine aids which allow me to be at home, in slippers when my feet ache, warm when Londoners are out in the cold, the wind and the rain, travelling in dirty trains or stranded in dismal stations. I will be much happier when the machine allows me to make sufficient money to have more free time to go out and enjoy myself ... in the cold, the wind and the rain.

AUTHOR

Nélida E. Depiante, Freelance translator, 3 Coombe Lodge, London SE7 7PE, UK.

The translator as information user

Pamela Mayorcas-Cohen

Commission of the European Communities, Luxembourg

INTRODUCTION

As we know to our cost, non-translators have little understanding of the translation process, even labouring under the delusion that translation is a matter of looking up words in a dictionary and writing them down in the right order. Translators are not automatons; in a discussion on machine translation, Andreyewsky[1] noted the error of 'categorising translators as "wordsorters"'.

Assuming that the basic requisite linguistic skills have been developed, information is the key to high-quality technical translation: information in the form of subject and background knowledge and documentation, terminological information, reference materials and precedent.

The translator needs *information* in order to:

> do the translation at all
> understand the translation
> find terms in the translation
> find references to dictionaries/sources which will help with terms and information
> know where to look for and obtain sources of information on terminology and subject
> know more about changes and developments in techniques
> know more about the evolution and benefits of IT
> know more about professional status
> know more about their own profession

Figure 1. The translator's information needs

THE LESSONS OF TRANSLATION THEORY

If we consider briefly some of the research into translation theory, we find plenty of evidence that the translation task is one where information is at least as significant as language knowledge.

The early theories, whereby language was seen as a series of codes which could be uniquely identified and transcoded into other languages, ideas which influenced the very earliest theories on machine translation (MT), have given way to the view that meaning is bound into the grammatical, syntactical and lexical structures of a language, and that this meaning has to be extracted through a process of understanding and familiarity with the *subject* of the text.

Perhaps one of the greatest benefits brought about by the research into automatic language handling systems and natural language (which according to many translation experts has had little bearing on practical translation problems),[2] is that it has highlighted just what it is that the translator does. Thus modern translation teaching and training concentrates on sense and content, rather than translation drills.

The transfer phase which occurs between the reading and understanding stages, and composition in the final target language (TL) results from the bringing together of knowledge and information about the source (SL) and target languages. The translator adds or makes use of information on the nature and subject matter of the text.

Thus theorists tell us that concentration on translation theory has been to the detriment of a closer study and resolution of the problems which arise in translation in practice, and reassure us that the failure of translation theory to understand fully the complexities of the translation process has produced the paradoxical conclusion that translation is, at least in theory, impossible. One is reminded of Dr Johnson's view of women preachers.

Hence Margaret Masterman's appeal to translators, also at one of these conferences in 1981, that they should come forward and explain to the computational linguistics experts just what it is that they do, and how they go about the translation task.

Nor is it surprising to learn that at American Translators' Association (ATA) conventions which offer a wide range of theoretical and practical seminars and workshops, working translators regularly eschew the sessions on translation and linguistic theory for the practical hard subject information workshops, generally led by subject experts in such topics as civil engineering or chemistry. While not one word in a foreign language may be discussed, translators can gain valuable insight into the subject and useful guidance on the best reference books.[3]

The translation process is one which relies on the totality of the human experience of the translator. The whole problem of translation resides in the lack of experience, the difference between internal and external information. There is a lack of correlation between words and thought. Translators use their experience to look between the two. If they lack the experience or information they cannot do the looking.

A further theoretical definition states that translation is the 'replacement of textual material in one language (SL) by equivalent textual material in another language, with a view to transferring information from the scientific writer in the SL to the expert in the TL'.

The model in Figure 2 is adapted from the literature on translation theory.[2] Theorists point out that since the author writes for the reader, and not for the translator, and since the translator does not have the culture of either author or reader, it is extremely difficult for the translator to have a full understanding of signifier A. But, provided the information on which signifier A is based is valid, the translator can use internal and external resources to transpose it into signifier B. (The failure of machine translation (MT) is due to the fact that the computer can only look at the signifiers, and that it has no conception of the significant.) Where information is missing the translator cannot adequately perform the analysis of the SL and synthesis of the TL but has to paraphrase in a way which offers the 'best match'.

If we apply the model to technical translation, substituting content for culture, and if we say that content derives from information, then if the translator lacks the information available to both author and reader, translation will be impossible.

It has also been pointed out that the translator has to act as a substitute for the author and write as if he or she knew everything the author knew. The problem can be further complicated by the fact that the audience which the original author had in mind may not be the same audience for whom the translation is intended. For example, a report describing a complex piece of research on the health hazards of certain chemicals may be distributed to a working party of government representatives, trade

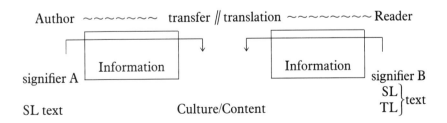

Figure 2. A theoretical model of the translation process

union officials, and manufacturers, in order to determine changes in industrial safety regulations.

THE RELEVANCE OF INFORMATION WORK AND INFORMATION TECHNOLOGY

In the information science literature we find that knowledge or information work involves activities in which the *acquisition, processing, storing, representing* and *communication* of information (knowledge) play a major role.[4] I think it can be argued that translation encompasses all these activities, which would mean that translators should also be classed as information workers.

The translation process itself necessitates the *acquisition* and *processing* of language information, in addition to preliminary research in order to *acquire* and *process* subject information. Subject and language information is subsequently *stored*, either in one's head, or preferably in some hard and recoverable form.

Representation corresponds to the linguistic conversion process itself, while *communication* is achieved with the end product, the target text. While I may be stretching this parallel somewhat, I think you will allow that these activities are all present in translation.

Knowledge work also involves the use of electronic mail, text processing, teleconferencing, telefacsimile, videotex, teletext and cable TV. The information profession has for some years been debating the merits and demerits of these jewels in the information technology crown. It would be interesting to know how many of these will, in the next ten years, become standard tools for the translator.

Another leading writer and consultant on information problems, Alan Gilchrist, has warned against being prematurely seduced by the new technology.[5] He provided some useful benchmark tests to help the user to decide whether and in what manner information technology provided real benefits. He suggested that the introduction of new technology occurs in three stages, each of which can only be regarded as a *good thing* if certain conditions can be identified:

> – in the *first* stage, it enables you to do the same thing more cheaply, faster and better;
> – in the *second* stage, it enables you to do things you could not do before;
> – in the *third* stage, use of technology changes your behaviour and ways of doing things to match the new capabilities bestowed by that technology.

I think you will agree that the use of word processing corresponds to the first condition, i.e., it enables you to do the same thing faster and better. Whether or not it is cheaper depends a lot on what system you buy, at the moment.

Coming to the second stage – doing things which could not have been done before. One example is use of the public information networks. It is possible to access information services worldwide: databases for bibliographic references, abstracts and, in some cases, full text; online terminology databanks; library services for finding and ordering reference books; photocopy services and document delivery; and Prestel, used privately or through a library service.

In theory, the fact that such services are remote from the workplace, and no longer only accessible to those living in the major metropolises where such information has always been available in traditional hard copy form, should not matter. In practice, telecommunications costs and the lack of suitable hardware still constitute significant obstacles.

Information technology facilitates the reception and transmission of texts, tables and graphics betweeen translator and client, between in-house department and out-house workers, between translator and reviser, or between the translation department and the graphics department in the same organisation, at a speed which was unattainable using conventional post and delivery services. Unfortunately both file transfer and facsimile transmission still leave a lot to be desired. Nélida Depiante's paper details some of the hazards that can arise in trying to transmit text between word processors, while telefax is only currently viable for relatively short and urgent documents. At a declared transmission rate of 20 seconds per page for Group 3 machines, but which is closer to 30–40 seconds in practice, it can take nearly an hour to transmit a sixty-page document, while the basic equipment costs in the region of £3,000.

In the European Commission we use telefax to transmit urgent documents and translations between requestors and translators, or between translation departments and the European Parliament when in session, and between Community institutions. Since a network of telefax machines has been installed to cope with the urgent transmission of documents between geographically-dispersed offices, especially in Brussels, it makes sense to optimise the investment by using it for translations as well. But the relatively high costs of installation and use may be a handicap for smaller organisations or individuals.

I am also concerned that the use of technology can mask certain inadequacies in the quality of the product. Word processing, a judicious choice of print style and layout, and high-class reproduction can produce work which looks marvellous in form, but which is rather poor in substance.

As regards the third stage (technology changing the user's behaviour), clearly post-editing of machine translation does require a change in approach by the translator, who has first to acknowledge the level of quality to be provided and then to develop specific techniques for correcting the typical errors generated by the particular MT system.

Electronic publishing systems can be used to produce off line prints from online terminology databanks or from the archives of dictionary publishers, to produce cheap and timely updates to printed dictionaries, or to dispense with hard copy altogether.

Conferencing software could be used between a group of translators in-house or working for an agency to update and consult an editing or technical manual. This would mean that the most up-to-date version would be available at all times and would eliminate the distribution and filing of loose-leaf sheets.

Leaving the machine translation issue out of the discussion, I think that the most significant way in which technology will change our behaviour and way of doing things is that we will cease to regard each translation as a new task to be tackled on an *ad hoc* basis. There are now new things we can do which were not possible before: word processing as an adjunct to the intellectual task of translation for enhancing the appearance of the text; transmission and remote access; information storage and retrieval. The whole approach to translation will change: it will be possible to organise translation on a more systematic basis, and to make far better use of all the know-how that the community of translators has acquired over the years.

It should also create a climate where the client has a better understanding of the work of the translator. In the past, translators were shadowy figures scribbling away in dark corners, with dusty books. They can now be recognised as part of the information and communication challenge to business and industry, using the same kind of tools as are familiarly seen in the general office. This should lead towards a more meaningful dialogue between translator and client, as regards both the function of translation and the support required for it to be done properly.

In 1981 Alan Negus[1] predicted that all translators would be using word processors or workstations as a clever typewriter, and online systems for obtaining information, and that the falling cost of disk storage would enable them to have their own private or local terminology banks. It is in fact taking quite a lot longer than had at first been thought. And I venture to suggest that the problems of price, choice of equipment, compatibility and communications, the rapid developments in techniques and systems, and the unsuitability of many systems for a specialist task are only part of the reason. No one has looked sufficiently closely at the types of information that translators need, or how they want to access it, organise it, store and retrieve it. So no one is really certain how the hardware and technology can be used. Being able to store large chunks of information is not the point; you need to know how to structure it in a way which matches your particular requirements.

We must be cautious about the advantages of information technology and the likely timescale. At the moment there is no real evidence that the paperless office or remote access is around the corner. While a terminal is now standard equipment for the airline or bank clerk, I would be particularly interested to know how many translators working for the large financial institutions, or indeed for the major telecommunications authorities, have access to the latest text-processing, data-processing reproduction and transmission equipment.

It is nevertheless a curious irony that so much interest in translation has been generated since technology came into it; machine translation has given translation a mystique, aura and status it has not known before. While interpreting and translating is considered to be the second oldest profession, and in terms of reward for effort, we may feel it has much in common with the oldest profession, the modern-day translator has little of the prestige or status awarded to the court interpreter or official translator in ancient or pre-Renaissance periods. It is only in countries which have a bilingual regime, such as Belgium or Canada, or in the 'minority' language countries, such as the Netherlands, that the profession of translator is officially recognised. (See Eveline Sleebos' paper on translators in Holland.) The predominance of English as a world language has certainly been to the detriment of the translation profession in this country and in the United States. Only now do I feel there is a glimmer of improvement; a quick glance at the delegates' list shows the range and variety of firms and organisations which now employ translators.

Unless we can educate first our direct clients, and then other professionals especially in the information field, to realise that we do have a specific need for information, we are not likely to get the necessary help and support in obtaining it. How we pay for it is another matter which I will also touch on later.

INFORMATION AIDS FOR TRANSLATORS – CASE STUDIES

I should like to provide some practical illustration of the aids used by translators, in the form of three case studies. The first is typical of problems encountered in organising technical translation work in the United States, described in a series of articles published in a special issue of *Technical Communication* devoted to technical translation.[5] I have picked out some of the key points regarded as typifying the ways in which high-quality technical translation can be assured and reflecting some of the problems we have been discussing so far. The other two are based on my own personal experience working with the European Commission.

Case 1: Ralph McElroy Company

The company, which is one of the largest translation agencies in the US, employing over 100 translators and editors, owes its success to a deliberate limitation of subject area and the building-up of customer information. The company concentrates on work for large corporations and in specific areas of chemistry, medicine, engineering, biology, geology, and physics. The translators get to know the appropriate house style and the political background of the clients, and are able to collect suitable background material.

The best translator is [one] ... who has worked for a particular customer on a particular subject.

It is also considered essential that translators devote time to building up stores of knowledge acquired in the course of their translation work; this includes banal but 'straight, objective information' such as the correct form of trade names, or uncommon abbreviations. Translators must also be equipped with the necessary background material, and standard technical references.

Satisfactory translation can only be assured if translators are able to acquire context and subject information. They may need help with passages which appear to be technically incorrect, which require confirmation from a subject expert, or perhaps the source used by the author for drafting his foreign language document. Where a document cites new technology, it is essential to check with the customer to ensure correct understanding; it may also be necessary to explain linguistic ambiguities to the customer.

The possibility of such consultation is a translator's ideal but is not always possible.

In the opinion of a senior member of the agency:

In addition to his skills as a technical translator, the person should have all the necessary resources for professional translation, and it is essential that he or she should have a technical background in the field in question.

These two qualities are regarded as interdependent and essential to fully professional performance.

The following quote struck a real chord with me, and I am sure you will appreciate it too:

Translation is a skill forever influenced by the winds of change; unlike learning to ride a bicycle, a translator of technical information must continually relearn his or her field based on technological advances and terminological changes. Areas such as plastics, textiles and wood chemistry challenge the translator to be informed, to judiciously and creatively discover the redefined present tense.

That seems to be it in a nutshell! The syllabus of the Ecole Supérieure de Traducteurs et d'Interprètes[6] in Brussels points out that:

le traducteur travaille un matériau en perpétuelle mutation en constante expansion, si l'on considère le nombre incroyable de termes qui naissent, associés à de nouvelles découvertes.

Both these quotations accurately and succinctly describe a situation and environment which we all recognise to be true, though we often have difficulty in getting customers, or people outside the world of translation, to understand this.

I should now like to come closer to home, both geographically and personally, and refer to my own working experience.

Case 2: European Integration Department (Special Translation Unit), Foreign Office
From 1970 to 1973, I was involved in the translation into English of EC secondary legislation prior to UK accession. I was particularly concerned with the translation of texts on non-tariff barriers to trade, but the team employed at the Foreign Office covered the full range of Community legislation from agriculture to external relations, through social legislation, the iron and steel industries, nuclear technology, transport, industrial and commercial policy, and consumer protection.

It would have been quite impossible to translate those secondary instruments without knowing the full corpus to be translated, or without having sight of all major documents, primary instruments, treaties, and other related Community texts which filled the gaps in our ignorance about the Community political and institutional framework and which helped to explain the Community decision-making procedures. There were special problems to do with Community terminology, particularly as regards the system of law which is quite different from the English one.

Liaison with Whitehall departments, manufacturers and research associations ensured that the technical language used would enable UK industry to implement the new laws properly.

On the whole the people we approached for information were extremely helpful, and appreciated that without their help and information the resulting English regulations would be unsatisfactory, and potentially difficult to implement.

Case 3: EC Commission Language Service

Turning now to my more recent experience in the Commission's Language Service and looking at the range of subjects which require information, I can single out as examples: harmonisation of technical legislation, nuclear engineering, new energy sources, environment, pollution, food science, measurement and testing, science policy, customs duty evaluations, and educational reforms.

Terminology (for source language and target language)

1. Dictionaries
   (a) bilingual
   (b) monolingual
   (c) multilingual
   (d) of abbreviations

2. Glossaries
   (a) internal (in-house; translators' own; group effort)
   (b) external
       (i) privately produced (professional and trade associations; specific industries; public utilities)
       (ii) commercially published
   (c) part works (published as appendices to monographs, in official documents or publicity material)
   (d) glossary sections of translating journals (e.g., *Babel*; *Lebende Sprachen*; *Technical Translation Bulletin*; *Banque des Mots*)

3. Online terminology databanks (public and private)
   (a) bilingual records (e.g., TEAM, Siemens AG, FR Germany)
   (b) multilingual records (e.g., Eurodicautom – available on ECHO host service)

4. Terminology information services
   (a) internal/in-house
   (b) external (e.g., other companies or organisations with translation/information departments)

5. Standard vocabularies and nomenclatures (e.g., ISO; CCITT; IEC; ISTC), customs nomenclatures (e.g., BN; CCT)

6. Card indexes
   (a) internal (in-house; translators' own)
   (b) external (commercially available, e.g., Institut Marie-Haps, Belgium)

Figure 3. Support documentation (English Translation Division)

The types of text for which background information is essential are: policy documents and statements, proposals for major multi-annual programmes, tender documents, commissioned studies, minutes, speeches, and official publications.

We are backed up by a substantial Terminology and Documentation Service, which maintains card indexes for all source and target languages, and stocks copies of translations, official publications, and glossaries; the Service provides a phone-in Help Desk and supplies copies of reference documents and subject literature.

Each target language division is divided into special subject groups in

---

Subject information and terminology

1. General reference works
   (a) encyclopaedias
       (i) monolingual
       (ii) multilingual
   (b) yearbooks
   (c) directories (company and trade; international)
   (d) literature guides

2. (a) EC legal texts: Official Journal; Budget; secondary legislation
   (b) EC official texts: Bulletin; Annual Report

3. Official and legal texts of other institutions: ISO; EFTA; UN; UNCTAD; FAO; CCC; ECC; CCITT

4. Subject-specific reference works (generally monolingual, and especially for TL)
   (a) handbooks and manuals
   (b) monographs and textbooks
   (c) manufacturers' product and equipment guides
   (d) technical guides and specifications
   (e) national and international standards
   (f) trade literature
   (g) scientific, technical and commercial journals and periodicals
   (h) daily and weekly 'quality' press

5. Consultation of authors, experts or subject specialists

6. Visits; lectures; films; exhibitions and conferences

7. Professional bodies and official bodies, especially in TL country

---

order to generate stores of knowledge and build up expertise in a particular area. Over the years the English Translation Division in Brussels has built up a large collection of original English reference material: dictionaries, handbooks, guides, catalogues, government publications, standards, treaties and agreements, specialist periodicals, newspaper cuttings, special supplements from newspapers and the 'better' weeklies, and some highly-specialised subject literature. Figure 3 shows some of the support documentation used in the Division.

Part of the art of drafting Community or indeed any other institutional or policy documents is careful wording and phrasing to highlight or allude to or camouflage a particular issue. Therefore the translator needs to be fully aware of the political significance and context of the text.

Another common dilemma which Commission translators frequently encounter is the request for quick translations, amendments to texts out of context or over the phone, all of which highlight the need for subject knowledge and background information.

Translators working abroad have a particular need to keep in touch with their mother-tongue country; unless one has access to the daily and specialised press, radio and TV, or can make regular visits, it is all too easy to lose touch. Apart from preventing the pollution of one's syntax, it is essential to keep track of changes in usage, in grammar and spelling, the shifts from proscribed to accepted use of jargon or slang, the birth of neologisms. It is also essential to keep up to date with new techniques and technologies, institutional and economic developments, political and legal changes.

Precisely to overcome this kind of difficulty, it was recommended by staff representatives at the Commission that translators should be given the opportunity to spend time in their home country to re-immerse themselves in the language, and also to attend conferences, symposia, special lectures, exhibitions and shows. Thus, for example, members of the English Translation Division's agriculture group have attended agricultural shows in order to see equipment, talk to experts, and collect technical and trade literature.

We also have the advantage of French, Italian, and Dutch colleagues close at hand who can help to solve problems of interpreting the source text.

To complete this look at the aids used in support of translation, it might be useful to look at the kind of environments in which translation is done (Figure 4) and a random list of the kinds of texts which translators handle (Figure 5). Information and support requirements will vary, depending on the nature of the organisation, the type of client, and the type of text. The material shown in Figure 3 is typical of that used by all Commission translators, but readers can probably identify material which is of relevance to them, and supplement the list with other material specific to their area of operation.

---

1. General (no order of size)
   (a) government departments, institutions and NGOs
   (b) manufacturing industry
   (c) trading and advertising sectors
   (d) scientific and research establishments; research and trade associations
   (e) data-processing firms, primarily translating software, sales and user literature
   (f) financial, legal and insurance bodies
   (g) translation bureaux services

2. Specific organisations
   (a) the European Commission, together with the other EC institutions, represents the largest multilingual and institutional translation service in Europe, very probably worldwide
   – in 1984, the Commission of the European Communities' Language Service translated some 570,000 pages, equivalent to 171 million million words per year!
   (b) Siemens AG, probably the largest private language service in Europe (electrical and electronics engineering and manufacturing)
   – over one million pages of documentation per year
   (c) Bundessprachenamt, the Federal Office of Languages, Bonn, probably the largest government service in Western Europe
   (d) The Translation Bureau of the Secretary of State, Ottawa, Canada
   (e) Teleglobe Canada, the Canadian telecommunications authority
   – translates some one million words per year
   (f) see also this year's list of delegates (see p.183) for the large number of smaller manufacturing and commercial firms which now have a translation department

Figure 4. Where translation is done

Advertising and sales literature
Product information
Instruction and operating manuals
Training course materials
Patents
Standards
Nomenclatures
Contracts
Cost estimates
Legal documents
Invitations to tender
Specifications
R&D results
Laboratory reports
Learned articles
Reports
Minutes
Site and inspection reports
Product documentation
Instructions for use
Books and monographs
Commercial and marketing information
Financial information
Handbooks
Internal and working documents
   e.g. discussion papers
      minutes and agendas
      opinions
      administrative and staff matters
Public information literature
Studies and reports

Figure 5. Types of translation

COST

We have to consider the cost of providing information for translators. We can also raise the perennial chestnut: what is the cost of not having information?

It is almost impossible to put a price on information deprivation. The same is true of information for managers and researchers. It is quite hard to justify to management what the cost would be if the work were not done, what the cost would be if the translation were not perfectly attuned to the latest idioms and terms of art, if references and quotations were not perfectly cited. However, it should be possible to evaluate the time spent by translators on researching reference material. Surveys have found that translators may spend 25–60 per cent of their time on such research.

After all, a translation badly done, or not done at all could cost a company or organisation hundreds of thousands of pounds in lost revenue or poor customer relations.

Since it is a well-recognised principle of business that time is money, time taken by a translator over weary research in order to track down a vital piece of information which might have been more readily available with the right kind of support is time lost, time wasted, time not spent on producing more translations, getting through the workload, and meeting vital deadlines. While in the case of the freelance translator, such lost time and money is his or her own in the first instance, the client will suffer in the long run, if the work has to be skimped because the translator cannot afford to spend too much time on checking material which should have been supplied by that client in the first place.

If we accept that information and background material *is* an essential requirement, what is the cost of providing it? Well, I haven't produced any figures, but I would like to itemise the main cost issues pertaining to various aspects of support for translation, and offer some considerations on which cost–benefit decisions might be based.

The cost of traditional information sources
Standard reference works, specialised dictionaries, manuals and guides are very expensive, and the problem is further exacerbated by the need to update them with the most recent editions.

Freelancers have to spend this money out of their own income, staff translators have to persuade or educate the powers that be into acknowledging the need and providing funds for such material.

The cost of introducing information technology
It is repeatedly being said that the cost of machines and mass storage is decreasing, while that of software and programs is increasing, as is the cost of setting up a system. Thus the objections raised to storing large quantities of data, for example previous translations or extracts from reference manuals, are no longer valid, provided that someone is prepared to pay for systems analysis, design and installation and user support.

But the larger the collection, the greater the problem of how to organise it, and further time, money and resources will need to be allocated in order to maintain it.

Then again, for translators who do not have access to some form of central storage at their own workplace, the low cost of mass storage is less relevant than the high cost of installation, of communications equipment, and of telecommunications and connection time.

An average online enquiry can cost between £20 and £30 for a fifteen-minute search which may produce only a bibliographic reference or at most an abstract. The full text still has to be ordered, obtained and paid for.

The cost of equipment

For the individual translator or translation department or agency it is not cheap to install word processors or telecommunications equipment, leaving aside the problems of compatibility with clients or other translation agents, character sets and keyboards, maintenance contracts, special stationery etc.

Are you likely to generate over £7,000-worth of additional income, or save the equivalent in salary costs by investing in a word processor?

It largely depends on how the equipment is used, and it is unfortunately true that a lot of time can be wasted in the beginning getting to grips with the machine. The cost of the annual maintenance contract must be added to the calculation of the initial outlay. But the work will look better, and therefore the client should be more satisfied; this should generate more work and enhance the image of the translation service.

For an organisation, the cost of equipping tranlators' offices can be absorbed into general office automation costs and overheads. While there is probably strong resistance to money being spent on sophisticated and expensive equipment for translators, company accountants should be asked to look at the cost of translators' time spent photocopying, or on long-distance calls to the author or subject expert, all of which represent lost translation time.

As an added bonus, the microcomputer or word processor can be used to improve the organisation of work, and to keep track of valuable information which would otherwise have to be searched for afresh with each new job.

The cost of terminology databanks and MT or CAT systems

The cost of researching, coding and checking terminology in a computerised dictionary or CAT system has been estimated at some $32 per word pair, and the major recurring expenditure in an MT system is the preparation of online glossaries and dictionaries. This is glossed over very quickly by the promoters of CAT systems. While it is true that systems will list missing terms, the cost of researching in the first place, inputting, coding and verifying the terms (and each and every word, even if it appears only once in the system, must be dealt with) is very high. It is impossible to amortise this unless it can be guaranteed that subsequent translations of sufficient size and using very similar terms will occur.

You might perhaps be interested to know that in the second evaluation of Systran, it was found that not even the EC (perhaps the largest translation client in the world) generates enough text in one language pair in one specialised subject for MT to be cost-effective.

The 'time is money' aphorism is a two-edged sword, depending largely on your standpoint, as translator or user of translation, and needs some careful thought.

Time wasted on unsuccessful research into essential information for the translation task is time that could be spent doing more translation. It's a vicious circle. Equally time and money misspent on the wrong kind of research is also time and money wasted. However, time spent on setting up information systems, on preparing and coding term and reference cards, on indexing and filing background documents, and on maintaining the collection, is time saved in the long run.

The cost of redoing translations

As far as the large company or institution is concerned it would seem quite ridiculous to waste money on producing a translation if one already exists.

However, if tracking down the translation and then obtaining it proves to be a lengthy process, if an in-house translator or editor has then to check it and perhaps extensively modify it, it may prove cheaper and quicker to redo the job. This is all a matter of experience, knowing the reliability of the sources available and the likelihood of finding an existing translation in a particular domain and target language.

A company or organisation with its own library or documentation service should be able to carry out the necessary research using the known sources of existing translations, and obtain the translation quite quickly. This can save unnecessary expenditure on the commissioning of translations in a difficult subject area and difficult language combinations for which the results might in any case be unsatisfactory.

For freelancers the issue is slightly different. If they suspect that the translation may have been done before, should they let on or do it again or perhaps crib from the original version – *shock, horror* – and take the credit, and money, for the *new* version? You could say that it serves the clients right if they haven't bothered to make enquiries; or alternatively call it part of the service if they do not have the resources to establish that a translation already exists. If they need the translation, they do not care how it is supplied.

But the freelance translator may decide to be virtuous and tell the client, especially if the existing translation can be obtained quickly and at reasonable cost; he or she could edit it, if necessary, and charge an appropriate fee, plus commission for obtaining the translation.

The result could well be a happy and impressed client who will entrust the translator with further such enquiries. My feeling is that the freelancer would benefit, since this would produce good client relations and more time for further work and further income.

Some time ago, members of the Translators' Guild launched an initiative to pool translations of legal documents since it was felt that there was nothing to be gained by duplicating the translation of highly complex texts. I believe the intention was to establish some system of payment and referral commission for those who notified translations to the register, and those who drew on this pool on behalf of their client. I do not know if this initiative materialised, but there is clearly scope here for both freelance and staff translators, in conjunction with an information provider.

We have an example of such a pooling arrangement at the Commission. An index is kept of the titles of all national legal instruments translated by the Commission's different language divisions. Further titles are supplied by the Ministry of Justice in Denmark, which, for reasons which may be obvious, has to translate a great deal of legislation both into and out of Danish. Copies of the texts, in the original version and in translation, are filed by the Terminology Division. Any new request for translation of a national legal instrument is first checked against this index, to avoid duplication of effort, or to supply translation in the same area or of the same source text but into a different target language.

It is unfortunately inevitable that certain EC texts will be translated concurrently by the EC translation departments, by government agencies, and perhaps by a private body. Where political or industrial confidentiality is involved, different bodies will want to obtain a translation of a particular text without it being known by other parties that they are interested in the document. It is also inevitable that different organisations will need translations at different times, and cannot wait for one of the other interested parties to produce a text.

Some years ago the English Translation Division in Brussels set up an information exchange system with the Health and Safety Executive (HSE) in Derby in order to avoid unnecessary duplication of effort. The HSE translations now appear in *World Transindex* so there really is no excuse for anyone outside the EC institutions wanting an English version of a Community proposal (particularly in the areas of industrial and agricultural vehicles, health legislation, mines and steelworks) not checking this index.

The major sources of translations to my knowledge are: *ASELT*, published by the EC; *BISITS*, published by The Institute of Metals; the British Library's *British Reports, Translations and Theses*, and *World Transindex*, both available in hard copy and online; SIGLE, sponsored by the EC; and the National Translations Centre, Chicago. Both the CNRS in Paris and the CNDST in Brussels hold translations registers. Copies of the translations notified to these registers can generally be obtained from the source body at reasonable cost. There is a good deal of overlapping between the indexes, and increasingly so as more and more data is put onto the various online systems, so it is worth double-checking. You can find further detailed information in *The Translator's Handbook*[7] and in 'The role of translations in sci-tech libraries', published as a special issue of *Science and Technology Libraries.* [8]

ACQUISITION OF SPECIAL SUBJECT KNOWLEDGE AND INFORMATION SKILLS

There are two issues which seem to require some attention, once it has been established that the translator is an information user, and a user of specialist information at that. First, how is subject-specific information acquired, and secondly, how is the information handled? There is a great deal in the translation literature about the importance of subject specialisation. Can I simply say that I feel it is inevitable that the majority of the new generation of technical translators will have an arts background? It is essential, therefore, that translator training syllabi should incorporate modules on technical subjects and on the best routes for acquiring special subject knowledge, and that this should be followed up by in-house training courses, as well as personal initiative. There is evidence to suggest that a number of training courses in the UK are starting to put a heavy accent on technical learning.

As regards the second issue (how the information is handled), some earlier research carried out when I was preparing an MSc thesis[2] suggested that only the Canadian, French and Belgian translation schools included information and documentation techniques in their courses. I thought it might be useful to see if this situation had changed since 1981, and sent a questionnaire to a number of CIUTI members (Conférence des Institutions Universitaires de Traduction et d'Interprétation) as well as to some non-CIUTI universities and polytechnics in this country. Unfortunately I do not have space to give you more than the most summary conclusions of this survey.

The responses indicated that while most courses stress the importance of special subject literature, and while some courses afford students the opportunity to become familiar with classification systems and the evaluation and use of reference works, none offered a comprehensive information retrieval module. This is largely due to lack of time, rather than lack of perceived relevance. The nearest thing approaching an IR project on the syllabus is the terminology project which requires students to research a highly technical topic, and to write a 3,000-word explanatory text in the foreign source language, accompanied by a detailed 300-word glossary and definition list, together with details of the specialist works and sources used, suitably identified and evaluated.

Full details of the results of the survey are being sent to Mrs Margareta Bowen, President of CIUTI, who has kindly offered to circulate the report to all members. A fuller report on the questionnaire and survey is being published in the *Technical Translators' Bulletin*, published on behalf of the Technical Translation Group by Aslib.[9] May I simply record here my sincere thanks to all the course directors who took the trouble to reply, and in some detail, to the questionnaire.

AN INFORMATION SYSTEM FOR TRANSLATORS

Generally, translators are badly informed about the wealth of information sources available for solving many of their queries, and poorly versed in efficient methods for handling the information that does come their way. Even where a translation department is part of a library or information service, translators are often left to devise their own Heath Robinson methods.

A great deal has been written on the creation of personal information systems, using integrated software. While the manufacturers' claims for such systems tend to fall short of reality, it is also true that end users need to have a very clear idea of what they require of the system.

A translator-dedicated information system would necessitate extensive analysis of the ways in which translators search for, select and use information.

Personal information systems

Do you realise that you have already developed your own personal information system? The dictionaries, notebooks, diskettes, files, card indexes, manuals, handbooks, modified glossaries and margin jottings, names of experts, cuttings, photocopies of earlier translations and background documents, collections of journals and specialist publications, all constitute your own personal information system.

Surveys of working methods have shown that translators can spend 25–60 per cent of their time looking for information in order to be able to produce high-quality, accurate, and reliable translations which conform to in-house, legal and political norms.

By 'looking for information', I would like to suggest that whenever translators have to interrupt their work and either leave their desk or pick up the telephone, it is because they experience an information need which must be met before the translation work can continue. So I would include new information, i.e., on terms or subject content which the translator has not encountered before; information which needs to be verified: formulae or nomenclatures which can be checked in manuals and handbooks, and terms or content for which the translator needs to go back to original sources in order to jog his memory, or confirm that the translation proposed is in fact correct; and finally, hard subject knowledge or information.

Some of this information will, therefore, already exist in dictionaries, in published or in-house glossaries, reference manuals, handbooks, encyclopaedias; further information can be elicited by consulting an expert, a subject specialist, or perhaps a fellow translator, a professional or trade organisation, specialist library or in-house documentation service. Much of the information required for translating a specialised text will require serious and sometimes difficult and time-consuming research as well as reading of the appropriate subject and background literature. The results of this research can be stored in notebooks or on index cards, on the word-processor glossary file or a small database program on a microcomputer. But pressure of work may preclude more than 5 per cent of it being noted down. Very often notes are scribbled on the backs of envelopes or the last telephone bill! So translators end up carrying a lot of this information in their heads.

Both individual translators and their colleagues (if they work in a team or unit) would benefit enormously if all the mentally-stored information, information which is to be found in the reference tools in the translator's own office or some other library, and the sources of other kinds of specialist information known to be available, were to be systematically stored, and organised and made accessible from one central source. Such information would then be accessible to the translator who had originally unearthed it. It could also be made available to other translators requiring information for the same text, or for other texts for which the same information was pertinent, and it would be very important as source material for new, inexperienced translators.

In the next twenty years, much of the information which is currently available in hard copy, and much of the in-house documentation which staff translators require for their work will be available in electronically-stored form. Worldwide telecommunications facilities also mean that translators working in any one place, or country, for any one firm or organisation, are no longer, in theory, limited to the information which is locally available. Since translators are working between pairs of languages, this obviously has enormous advantages: it will be possible to check original language sources for terminological and subject information in both the source and target languages.

But these electronic mammoths will inevitably suffer from disadvantages of size, and the fact that they may well have been designed for a different type of user, with different requirements.

Our information problems are very similar to those of other users of information systems, namely the authors of the scientific, technical or legal texts which we translate. I suggest, therefore, that what translators need is access to a suitably designed set of software tools which will enable them to set up their own personal information systems.

A few years ago in a paper published in *Journal of Information Science* S. Cooney[10] suggested that the resources spent on producing very large information systems and big databases might rather more profitably have been spent on improving personal retrieval systems for scientists who require the means to store and retrieve their personal notes, reports, reprints (photocopies) and document references.

This seems to be analogous to the world of translation, and probably reflects the views held by many translators, namely that the money and resources spent on automatic translation systems, which in any case are only as good as the information fed into them, could have been better spent on a completely different type of translation aid.

In the case of the individual translators, such a system would comprise their own personal and individually generated information and sources. In the case of a translation company or staff department, the information store would represent a pooling of the resources generated by each individual; this would then be available to other individuals in the group, including new, inexperienced translators.

Considerable effort would be involved in collecting, selecting, verifying and inputting the information, but it would produce a system of real and growing value. Let us not forget that this effort has to be expended in any case by the individual translators, and that their energies would then effectively be recycled since the results of such efforts would be available to them and other translators in a generally available information system. This would result in the effective and efficient recycling of translation energy.

Characteristics of a personal information system
In his paper, Cooney defined a personal collection as being one which comprises approximately 500 to 5,000 documents or references. A recent survey amongst EC Commission translators indicated that each individual might produce between 300 and 600 terminology or reference cards for their own private use. If we multiply this by the total number of translators, and add hypothetical quotas of 20,000 additional documents, files or references held at divisional level, we soon exceed this total. However, the Commission's translation service is broken down into target language units and further subdivided into subject groups. The total number of references held by a group would probably be close to the figure suggested

by Cooney. Thus the conditions for a personal collection exist. Provided the indexing and retrieval characteristics are identical for each of the 'personal' information systems developed for each group of translators or individual translators, it would be quite feasible to provide links to permit the retrieval and interchange of information between systems.

Cooney noted some significant differences between personal collections and general collections which I feel are significant to our environment:

1. The user whose queries are put to the system and who requires the system to perform the retrieval function is also the one who selects the input.
2. The range of documents and the user's range of subject interests for retrieval are generally biassed and selective, towards the specific needs and interests of that user or group of users.
3. Personal collections are generally physically and psychologically more accessible: physically in that they may consist of a card file on the desk or set of Leitz files on a shelf in the office; psychologically in that the translator personally has been instrumental in collecting, and indexing the documents.
4. Since personal collections are smaller than large general-purpose data-bases, the design and method of indexing can be simpler and more accessible to a non-professional information user.
5. Personal collections and indexes are generally kept by people who are amateurs in information techniques.

Does this begin to sound appealing, a system which can readily handle 500 to 5,000 documents, is simple and inexpensive to install, maintain and use, and can accommodate changes of interest and new fields of work?

While this list of requirements may seem straightforward at first glance, they do represent some fairly tall orders. But, by applying some of the basic rules of information storage and retrieval, good results can be achieved.

Decisions as to selection of the documents or records to be put into the system should be left to the individual or group of individuals. Only when the total of the collection starts to exceed the limit which has been defined for a personal collection, would it be necessary to have recourse to external sources for setting up an information retrieval system.

Alternatively, if the total collection is broken down into categories, none of which exceed the 5,000 ceiling, and provided a common indexing language is used for the different categories (terminology, bibliographic references, reprints and original documents, external sources of information), the system will remain personal and accessible.

Personal information software

A number of suppliers of large-scale information retrieval systems have designed micro versions of their information storage and retrieval software, for use on a range of personal microcomputers. The dBase II type of program generally permits only fairly simple record structure, limits the size and structure of fields within a record, and relies on lengthy and slow character-string match and serial searching of the entire set of records.

The new micro versions of the larger database systems are generally faster and more sophisticated, offering classic searching of inverted files, which contain data taken from individual fields and records. They will allow you to specify whether fields are to be of limited length (fixed length fields) or unlimited, and to specify different data structures in different fields. They allow for control or checking tables to ensure that formatted data such as dates, names and subject codes and controlled vocabulary terms have been entered correctly, and in accordance with rules defined by the user. You can use standard vocabulary for certain fields, i.e., in order to specify the type of information (book, photocopy, term card). So, if you know that the information you want on company takeovers is probably in a photocopy of a journal article, made during the last six months, you can specify 'Photocopy', select the appropriate subject code, and limit the search to 'new items entered since 85.06'.

This allows you to preselect certain types of record before pursuing a more detailed search. You can also use logical and value operators (AND, OR, AND NOT, GREATER THAN) or their symbolic equivalents, to combine search terms in a single field or in separate fields; alternatively queries can be put to the system via a suite of customised menus.

You can request screen displays of parts of records, and a variety of printouts, for example, a list of keywords in context as a handy manual reference to the information available, special subject lists or chronological lists.

These systems generally come with purpose-built menus which are used to set up the database, define the structure of the information and the way in which you wish to access it, and with further menus for updating old records. This is a simple and user-friendly approach which replaces the arduous programming required for setting up large-scale databases.

Such systems are not yet cheap enough for the individual, but are certainly within the means of a translation company or commercial or government organisation, especially if they are looking for an information retrieval system for other parts of the organisation. The cheapest are available for between £250 and £500; the top end of the market ranges from £2–4,000 to over £20,000 – the price of a small suburban flat! Further useful information on information retrieval systems and software can be obtained from the Library Technology Centre, 309 Regent Street, London W1R 8AZ.

Construction of a personal classification scheme

Cooney suggested a detailed but, even for a non-specialist, workable method for resolving the vexed problem of all retrieval systems – the method of describing a document in such a way as to ensure (one hopes) that it will always be retrieved when required and never retrieved when not relevant.

Keywords selected for indexing a small sample of documents are listed alphabetically. The frequency occurrence of each keyword is noted. Future users of the system provide a short text, briefly analysing the type of work in which they are engaged, or in the case of translators, the subjects covered by their translation work. Keywords are retained on the basis of the number of documents corresponding to any particular keyword: where the document number is too high or low, the keyword is either further divided, or grouped with others. The keywords are then assigned to between six and ten major topics or facets identified from the work description provided.

Each document or piece of information to be identified in the system is assigned a unique number. Keywords, taken from the personal classification scheme, are attributed to each document. Since the retrieval software described above allows you to have controlled vocabulary fields and free text fields, you can supplement terms taken from the classification with free indexing terms. Used in combination with controlled term searching, this will enhance the performance of the retrieval system. You start by selecting the main topic or facet or combinations thereof, corresponding to the enquiry. The system tells you which keywords correspond to that main heading, and how many documents correspond to each of those keywords. Depending on the data-handling capacity of your system, you can either continue to refine your search in order to limit the final number of documents which match your enquiry, or examine samples of documents from the initial set and rephrase the query.

If this type of exercise is beyond your means, you can use an existing classification scheme, for example UDC or Dewey for general texts, or something like the COSATI list of subject headings for general, scitech subjects. Those working in a very specialised subject area could investigate the thesaurus classifications which have beeen devised for particular industries or particular sectors of the economy. Aslib, which acts as the UK Thesaurus Centre, can give more information on the types of thesauri available.

It might also be a good idea to enquire into the indexing and classification scheme used by your company or organisation, and to see whether you could use this or a suitably simplified or modified form to classify the documents and material which you have collected. Since this should be related to the nature of your translation work, it is logical to suppose that the classification scheme used by the organisation's reference and library collections could be applied to your material.

CONCLUSION

This brings me, I suppose, to the burden of my message, which is to urge you all to go and identify and talk to the company librarian or information officer. If you are working freelance, you should make friends with this person in the companies or organisations for whom you work; if you are in a translation company you should establish good contacts with your custo-mers' information departments. By talking to them about the translation work that you are handling for them, I hope that you will discover that you are both working for the same client: the manager or the research worker.

This person needs material which has to be translated from foreign languages, as well as original material which will have been collected and organised by the library or information department. All this material can be of inestimable value to the translator.

By the very nature of their work, translators are inevitably thrown back on their own resources. Time is at a premium. But time spent on organis-ing and setting up an information retrieval system is time saved in the long run as well as contributing to the production of a higher quality product, and improving job satisfaction.

May I end with something that many of you will recognise as my pet hobby horse. I sincerely believe that we should not be using valuable funds to research MT systems.

I do not believe that we shall be able to build a system (fifth-generation computers, inference systems and knowledge representation notwithstan-ding) which will be able to cope with the subtlety, complexity, ambiguity and constantly changing nature of language. I am strengthened in this view by something which Margaret King, a senior participant in the EC Eurotra project said at one of these conferences in 1981: that in order to compete with human translators' extraordinary capacity for storing com-plex language conversion codes, their universal knowledge of the world which they apply in order to resolve ambiguity, and the constantly chang-ing nature of language, it would be necessary to feed in (to the Eurotra machine translation system) whole phrases and even whole sentences in order to ensure complete, satisfactory and fast translation by the machine. If you are going to do that, you might as well train more and better translators and develop general-purpose aids to translation and translators.

The expert systems of the future will need to be fed terminological, subject and context-specific information before they can make the right choices of lexis, register, syntax. So the MT system is itself an information user!

And we must ask, 'Where will all this information come from? By whom, and how will it be collected and verified?' Alan Readett, until his retirement a group head in the English Division in Brussels, pointed out that it is the translator who encounters the unknown word or concept first, not the machine, and it is the translator and terminologist who have to solve the puzzle, before the machine can apply the newly found SL–TL conversion to a text.

The translator's ideal information system will be constructed by translators, information scientists and computer and systems experts working closely together to understand the phenomenon of translation, and will provide hardware, software and telecommunications equipment which will provide translators with all the facilities they need for handling the material they use in the translation process and which matches the way in which they perform the translation task.

REFERENCES

1. MAYORCAS-COHEN, Pamela. Evaluative report: a state-of-the-art review of computer-aided human translation. London: City University, September 1982 (unpublished).

2. MAYORCAS-COHEN, Pamela. MSc thesis: The translator as information user. London: City University, October 1982 (unpublished).

3. *Technical Communication*. Special issue on 'Technical Translation Today', 29 (4) fourth quarter, 1982.

4. JÄRVELIN, Kalervo. Knowledge work augmentation and human information seeking, *Journal of Information Science*, (5), 1982, pp. 79–86.

5. GILCHRIST, Alan. Patterns of information transfer, storage and retrieval in various types of organisation revealed by recent research, Part 2. *In*: Taylor, H., *ed. Information management and organisational change: proceedings of an Aslib conference held at the London Tara Hotel on 6–8 April 1981.* London: Aslib, 1982.

6. École Supérieure de Traducteurs et d'Interprètes, Bruxelles, Belgium, Prospectus 1985.

7. PICKEN, C., *ed. The translator's handbook*. London: Aslib, 1983.

8. FEDUNOK, Suzanne. Printed and online sources for technical translations. *In*: The role of translations in sci-tech libraries, *Science and Technology Libraries*, 3 (2), Winter 1982.

9. MAYORCAS-COHEN, Pamela. Survey of information-gathering techniques taught to translation students, *Technical Translation Bulletin*, 32 (2), 1986.

10. COONEY, S. A standard procedure for generating personal classifications and indexes, *Journal of Information Science*, (2), 1980, pp. 81–90.

AUTHOR
Pamela Mayorcas-Cohen, Commission of the European Communities, PO
  Box 1907, Bâtiment Jean Monnet, Luxembourg – 2920.

The opinions expressed in this paper are those of the author, and do not
necessarily represent those of the Commission of the European Communities.

Session I:
Summary of discussion 2

In the chair: Barbara Wilson

(1) Anne Napthine asked where training was available on word-processing systems other than WordStar; Nélida Depiante replied that courses were organised by the University of Manchester, among others. Commodore Croft suggested that learning to use a dedicated word processor was easier and more straightforward than using a personal computer running WordStar.

(2) Professor Stanforth pointed out that software was now available to convert the BBC Microcomputer into a multilingual word processor, possibly obviating many of the difficulties Commodore Croft had mentioned in his paper, and Patrick Corness, from Lanchester Polytechnic where this software had been developed, offered to provide additional information for anyone interested.

(3) A gentleman from Finland, commenting on the difficulties of coping with Norwegian characters which Commodore Croft had described, pointed out that Finnish had an even larger character set than Norwegian but that perfectly adequate systems were available in Finland. Commodore Croft would, he felt, have been able to avoid makeshift solutions and gained better results if he had purchased a system in Norway.

(4) This raised the whole problem of translators working into languages foreign to the country where they purchased their equipment. Commodore Croft replied that translators working in the UK were usually obliged to buy their equipment there for, as Nélida Depiante pointed

out, it would be difficult if not impossible to obtain technical support in the UK for equipment or software purchased on the Continent.

(5)   Tom Evenson asked if there were any examples of co-operation between translators pooling information on computer and word-processing systems, and/or sharing the cost of equipment. Professor Benoît Thouin, from Ottawa, said that cost-sharing (bulk-buying) schemes existed in Canada. As for information pooling, he suggested that translators' associations could play an important part here: members should contribute information to their associations and expect their association to provide an information service and to act as a pressure group influencing manufacturers to respond to translators' needs. Pamela Mayorcas-Cohen pointed out that before trying to exert pressure on manufacturers, translators would have to agree on a set of specifications. The Chair, Barbara Wilson, and speakers agreed that these could perhaps be hammered out at Association seminars. It was pointed out, by Nélida Depiante, that this might be difficult because translators had very different requirements.

(6)   Dr Alan Melby, commenting on Commodore Croft's paper, stated that WordStar was outdated. Better word-processing packages for micro-computers were now available; for example, IBM had recently converted its dedicated word-processing software to run on the IBM Personal Computer. Other companies were producing similar products, with the result that microcomputers were now rivalling dedicated word processors. Commodore Croft and Nélida Depiante commented on the possible difficulty of using any microcomputer keyboard which did not have the labelled function keys normally available on a good word processor.

It was pointed out that WordStar had been designed for CP/M machines of 64K or less, and that if it were old-fashioned that was because it had been designed for machines that were old-fashioned. In any case an improved version was now available. The better word-processing packages which had been mentioned required a much larger memory.

(7)   Returning to Alan Melby's comment on the new IBM Displaywrite software, several speakers pointed out that although this had been announced, it was not readily obtainable. One translator working in Paris (Sarah Kaulback) had purchased English Displaywrite and Displaycom software in England because it was not available in France, but was then refused assistance by IBM in France when she experienced difficulties with the latter. Manufacturers should be made aware of the problems of people working in or into another country's language, and offer more co-ordinated international support. Another translator (Julie Slade) had been told by IBM that Displaywrite was not available to run on the PC in

England and had been assured by IBM that their dedicated word processor was a better buy.

(8) Julie Slade added that she was collecting information on translators' experiences with word processors for the Translators' Guild, and would be grateful for any contributions.

(9) Andrew Evans warned that the dividing line between dedicated word processors and microcomputers was becoming very hazy and might soon disappear. Having tested several systems at the Commission of the European Communities in Luxembourg, he reported that translators found the Wang word processors excellent; another word processor tested, the Olivetti ETS, had been found less satisfactory, but was acceptable because it could be linked up to the more powerful Wang system.

(10) Tom Evenson suggested that since research was the most time-consuming part of the translator's work, word processing was in fact less important than personal information systems and information retrieval, and more attention should be paid to these aspects.

RAPPORTEURS
Emma Wagner, Reviser, Commission of the European Communities, PO Box 1907, Bâtiment Jean Monnet, Luxembourg.
Andrew Evans, Translator, Linguiste de Liaison Informatique, Commission of the European Communities, Bâtiment Jean Monnet, A1/062A, L-2920 Luxembourg.

Session II: The impact of machine translation and high technology

Chaired by Brian McCluskey
and Barbara Snell

Translation and information processing: a Canadian viewpoint

Benoît Thouin

Programme Co-ordinator and President, CLC Ltd, Quebec, Canada

Translation – at least to some extent – and computer science come under the field of information processing. They both have played and are playing a major role in the information revolution which is dominating this second half of the twentieth century. They both help us realise that information is just as much a resource for an organisation as are people, equipment and capital.

It took quite some time for computers to become really useful to the language fields. Computer science (considered here to include electronic data processing) had to undergo a whole evolutionary process and its place today still gives rise to questions and debates, perhaps not for specialists, but at least for its potential users. This evolution in computer science has resulted in a number of tools for translators; it still is and will be a determining factor in the changes we observe or foresee in the translation environment. The major aspects of this evolution will be described below, together with some of their effects on the language profession. Some attention will also be given to translation and adaptation of software as a new field of activity for language specialists. This will lead to some thoughts on the future of machine translation (MT) and computer-assisted translation (CAT) systems.

THE EVOLUTION OF COMPUTER SCIENCE

Hardware
The concept of generations of computers is well known. The fifth generation, in any case, is the topic of much discussion, and not only in

specialised circles. These generations correspond to the successive technological advances made in the production of the main computer units:
first generation – vacuum tubes and germanium diodes, triodes and pento-
des; second – transistors; third – integrated circuits; and fourth – large-
scale integrated circuits, as used in present microcomputers. The fifth
generation has more of a software connotation. On the hardware side,
which is still at the research and prototype stage, it integrates circuits on
an even larger scale and might integrate newer technologies such as laser
memory, superconductivity at very low temperatures, and parallel processing.

The successive jumps from one generation to another have until now
resulted in a significant increase in processing capacity, the miniaturis-
ation of circuits and a decrease in production costs. These improvements
have led to the most extraordinary machine that the human race has ever
created. While machines can multiply our physical speed and strength by
factors of the order of thousands, the computer is capable of increasing a
million times over our capacities for calculation, data storage and information processing, which are much more fundamental human skills, all at
relatively low cost and with almost no energy consumption.

The consequences of this on the language profession are numerous. The
most obvious one is that computers are small, ordinary and cheap enough
so that small groups and even individual translators can afford them and
enter the electronic information age. The electronic medium is slowly but
surely taking over paper to the point that in some instances the translator
uses only magnetic and electronic media. But one should not forget that
these media have a lower level of compatibility, readability and security
than hard copy.

All this brings new problems and new opportunities to the language
profession. Translators now have to worry about investing thousands of
dollars in a single piece of equipment, something they never faced before.
They do such things as product comparisons, cost–benefit analysis, selection, purchase, installation, training. They see new products every week,
do not know what to choose, would like to avoid obsolescence, fast
depreciation, and incompatibility with their clients' equipment.

Larger translator offices are created to share the initial investment, but
translation permits few economies of scale and new problems arise with
overheads, quality control, co-ordination of large projects etc.

New formulas emerge: group purchase of equipment and supplies,
networks and co-operatives of translators, translation brokerage and dis-
patching.

These complex and sometimes dramatic changes in the translation
picture are welcome since they force translators to think seriously about
work organisation, to select appropriate tools, and not necessarily

computerised ones, according to the type and size of text, to get more information and training. But they must also be careful not to put too much emphasis on hardware and equipment, which is the most visible but least important aspect of the information processing revolution.

Software

Application software, those instructions to perform some function for the user, also has its generations, more or less five years behind those of the computer. The first programs were directly encoded in binary numbers or written in a language very close to the internal structure of the computer. Therefore, only specialists could use computers since there was no distinction between using a compter and programming it, and it was necessary to understand thoroughly the structure of a computer in order to write programs. Moreover, a program could never be transferred from one computer to another.

Then appeared the so-called 'high-level' programming languages that could give the equivalent of a number of machine instructions in a relatively understandable statement. Some of these languages, for example FORTRAN, were sufficiently standardised to enable the transfer of programs from one type of computer to another. This second software generation, however, did not give users direct access to the computer; instead, users had constantly to enlist the aid of computer specialists.

The third generation was that of software packages: general programs equipped with a specialised command language through which users can operate the computer without having to program it. A software package can be designed for a single purpose, such as word processing, bookkeeping or inventory control, or it can combine several applications. A good package has menus, pictograms, or other action-selection features, error-detection routines, easy-to-understand messages, a help facility and appropriate documentation, that make it easy to use. Trends in third-generation packages include improvements in human–machine communication: increased use of graphics and pictograms, touch-sensitive screens, some voice input etc., and the integration of several applications in one package through split screens and interconnection of parallel processes.

Fourth-generation languages began to appear several years after the fourth-generation computers. These languages, built around a database management system, allow the user not only to operate the computer but also to define and implement applications by him or herself much more rapidly than before and with a minimum of help from computer specialists. The emphasis is no longer on procedures to access and process data, which are relatively standardised, but on data definition and organisation. There is also a new emphasis on functional definition of systems rather than their technical structure, the *whats* rather than the *hows*.

The data administrator has emerged as the main user representative as far as computer applications are concerned, and his/her role has become much more important than that of the computer systems analyst.

Fourth-generation languages and software are still undergoing development, but the real phrase à la mode is 'fifth generation', defined by the key words 'artificial intelligence' (AI), with expert systems thought of as a sort of an intermediate step. It is expected that this generation will set itself apart by, among other things, the logical inference capabilities of its systems, human–machine communication in natural language, and knowledge representation systems, at least in some limited fields. Let us not delude ourselves, however; as long as we do not understand the working of our own minds and as long as we have not established that it is possible to simulate it through the limited operations of the computer, artificial intelligence will remain much more artificial than intelligent.

The scope of software applications has also evolved: from military to scientific to business applications before entering the domain of the humanities (including language) and new technologies. The first effect of that evolution on the language profession is that third-generation packages were made available to writers and translators. Nowadays, several user-friendly packages are used daily without too many problems.

The world of software covers many application areas that ignore each other, which results in duplication of effort and lack of utilisation of new developments in other areas. For instance, terminology banks and information retrieval systems have resulted in large and powerful database systems not encountered at all in management information systems. On the other hand, fourth-generation languages and techniques are underused in linguistic applications. In MT and CAT, integration of general database management systems with specialised linguistic and logic metalanguages is achieved only in a few instances, as is a recognition of various software tools as complementary instead of opposed to each other. The building of more bridges between subdomains of software is certainly a desirable step for the coming years.

Access to the computer
The methods of operating computers have also developed in a spectacular way over the short history of computer science. In the beginning, the user had to be by the computer in order to enter data through switches, but later he or she could prepare data independently by means of unit record devices, particularly punched cards. Batch processing would then most often be done: the user would group the records into batches, bring them to the processing centre, and later obtain printed results.

Developments in the theoretical study of processes, in parallel processing and in communication between processes led to improvements in operating systems, from monoprogramming to batch processing of input/ outputs, multitasking and time-sharing. Time-sharing enabled the introduction of online processing through terminals connected to a mainframe by relatively short cables, and later remotely connected by telephone.

Telephone links were used at a later stage to connect computers to each other, in increasingly larger networks. Computer specialists also learned to operate a number of CPUs together in the same location, thus increasing the reliability of computer installations and leading to various concentrations of similar functions within computing centres. A now typical application is the use of a separate computer, called a front-end processor, to handle communications with the terminals.

More recently, the replacement of standard terminals by so-called 'intelligent' terminals, which have their own processing capability, and then by true computers (generally microcomputers) has added a great deal of flexibility to all kinds of computer systems. While the user is back to a by-the-computer situation, he/she has immediate access not only to more powerful means at divisional or organisational levels, but also to national and international networks. The result is multilayered systems whose throughput can be maximised by optimising the distribution of data and workload among levels and among computers at the same level. Such distributed processing systems are now so sophisticated they no longer require that all databases be centralised, as was thought to be inevitable. We have not yet explored nor implemented all the new possibilities created by these developments.

Language specialists now have access not only to various system configurations, but to numerous makes and models of hardware and software of all kinds. It is very nice to have several alternatives, but too much is too much. Over 300 makes of microcomputers, a few times as many models, thousands of pieces of software ...

Moreover, any single user can have his/her computer custom-modified through chip programming and/or software: new character generators, multiple keyboards, printer drivers, special instruction sets, anything you can think of. Such customisation is more like 'modifications not authorised by the manufacturer' (did you read your warranty card?) than just selecting the colour or a few options on a new car. For one standard that is painfully set up, five are violated, if they ever existed. Multilingual character set definition, for one, is near chaos. Even standard pieces of software will modify such things as the BIOS (Basic Input/Output Supervisor) and make the most innocent and plain microcomputer behave like a non-standard one.

For sure, standards deserve what happens to them. How can one comply with a standard for French characters where ë and ï do not exist, and where ten accented letters are present only because ten standard characters (square brackets for instance) have disappeared? Indeed, stupid standards are in essence self-destructive.

Shall we give up compatibility between systems? Or create new standards that deserve this name? Sometimes the latter might be a difficult decision. One should admit, for example, that the old 8-bit byte is obsolete in a truly multilingual environment. The 16-bit and 32-bit architectures, plus lower memory and storage costs should help us make the step up to more powerful character representation systems.

Methodologies
Our ability to develop and implement systems that satisfy the user's requirements has always lagged far behind our technical skills. Until the Seventies, there was no defined systems development methodology. Phased approach and systems theory, for example, did not exist, although some successful project leaders had used similar methods more or less intuitively.

An important concept that emerged was that of the *system* – a set of inputs, procedures and outputs, and of human, material and financial resources, which perform a well-defined function. Only recently has information been considered as another type of resource involved in the development and operation of a system. The recognition that a systems development project is in itself a system with its own resources, inputs, procedures and outputs led to the phased approach of systems development, or the 'systems development life cycle'.

This approach was the first clear methodology available for recognising the need for a new system, and then developing and implementing that system. With a few variations, the approach consists of seven phases, which are as follows:

1. **Project initiation**   Analysis of the situation and identification of problems, user requirements and new opportunities, ending in the decision to develop or not to develop a new system.
2. **Feasibility study**   Examination of various possible system solutions and comparison of these in terms of their technical and economical feasibility. Recommendation of one solution, based on cost–benefit analysis, including estimates of the development and operating costs.
3. **Systems analysis**   Definition of *what* the system will do: description of the various functions and their interactions within the system, definition of inputs and outputs, all from a user's non-technical point of view.
4. **Systems design**   Technical description of *how* the system will work: screen and report layout for inputs and outputs, physical

organisation of data and files, programs, modules and interfaces.

5. **Programming and testing** Writing of programs and testing of individual modules, followed by more general testing of the interfaces between modules.

6. **Implementation** Physical installation of the system, data conversion, user training, and acceptance testing by the user under normal operating conditions. Final acceptance of the system.

7. **Post-implementation evaluation** An on-going review, detection of problem areas and maintenance of the system, in whole or in part, when any major problems are detected or improvements projected.

Since 1980, 'structured' techniques have been more and more widely used to develop and to maintain computerised systems.

Data flow diagrams represent the circulation of data and the processes that use and produce information. Each process can be further broken down at lower levels, to give not only a general overview of the system but also an accurate representation of details.

The data dictionary contains a definition of all data at the elementary and higher levels. It ensures that each piece of information used or produced by the system, or created temporarily within a process, is clearly and consistently described. Where necessary, it also contains a statement of the validation conditions for data elements.

Structured language is a means of describing processes. It is a subset of a natural language that imposes a strict use of designators as they appear in the dictionary, together with the primitives and connectors of structured programming languages like Pascal. Structured language also prohibits the use of vague verbs to describe the action performed over input data flows. It can very well be thought of as a system description Language for Special Purpose (LSP).

The structured-module representation of the processes describes how each process is divided into programs, modules and routines. It shows the arguments received and the results produced by each program component of the system.

All these structured techniques include a mathematical means of checking for consistency and balance between the various components of the system, both at the same level and between two consecutive levels. Data flow diagrams, the data dictionary and structured language are used mainly at the systems analysis stage, while structured-module representation is a systems design technique. Data flow diagrams can also be used to describe the existing systems, and the various drafts of the proposed ones, in the early stages of the development cycle.

Structured techniques do not in fact represent a new methodology. They only provide a more handy means of describing the existing system and of representing it under development during the two critical and complex phases of systems analysis and design.

It is only lately that there has appeared what can be considered as a real second-generation methodology, known as prototyping. Unlike the phased approach, which can be described as the vertical development of a whole system in five to seven phases, prototyping consists in the complete and relatively fast development and implementation of a prototype, followed by a horizontal expansion to the full system.

The prototype can be one of the many functions of the full system, selected because of its priority to the user, its self-contained character or its strategic position in the overall flow of information; or it can be a very simplified version of the whole system, without the special or difficult cases, just to see whether the general principle of the system is sound or not.

The availability of a fourth-generation package is important to prototyping, because it accelerates the development and implementation of the prototype, and provides a highly flexible tool to rework the data structure as needed in the course of expansion to the full system.

An advantage of prototyping often encountered is that the user is provided with 'something that works' very early in the development process. But more important is that the prototype allows one to see exactly what kind of a system one has defined and permits early adjustments that can't simply be thought of over a pile of abstract diagrams and definitions.

Methodologies appear to be far behind the development of computer hardware and software. Other emerging techniques, like automatic production and proof of programs, are almost always absent from linguistic systems. The reason given is that linguistic applications are too specialised to be developed in a general framework adapted to more classical environments. The evolution of systems development methodologies has little affected the language profession. Let us hope it will, be it only as will be seen below to help language specialists better participate in the adaptation of software.

User involvement

The client's participation in the development and utilisation of computer systems has also dramatically evolved since the beginnings of computer science.

At first, the computer specialists were the only designers/clients/users of computer systems. Then appeared other people: clients of computer specialists and consumers of computer services. They would be more or less afraid of those complicated and extraordinary devices and would have to rely totally on specialists, like someone who feels ill and can only believe the medical science that says there is a cancer there and that some precious but defective part of his/her body has to undergo some strange, painful but certainly successful treatment using the latest and extraordinary 'omega ray' generator.

With the almost simultaneous advent of the third generation of software and of the phased approach to system development, there appeared two different types of involvement of the user and/or client. Buyer and user of custom-developed software would be consulted at the project initiation and systems analysis stages, and would approve the deliverables of all phases. (A deliverable is any program, document or other concrete result that must be delivered during or at the end of one phase of the development process.) On the other hand, the user of third-generation software gets a user-friendly and well-documented package, but only a few people supposed to be representative of the target clientele are involved in its development, on a consulting basis, as members of test groups etc.

With fourth-generation software, the end-user becomes the main agent of the design and implementation process. The role of the computer specialist remains important in the general framework – building the fourth-generation environment – but becomes limited to special support upon request as far as applications are concerned.

Through their greater involvement in the development of systems, users have learned the golden rules of good computerisation: (1) define your requirements (qualitative and quantitative); (2) then look for or define the software that will satisfy these requirements and (3) last (and least), choose one set of hardware compatible with the above software.

The composition of research and development teams in linguistic systems has followed that evolution, from rather closed teams of mathematicians, computer scientists and theoretical linguists, to include eventually translators, writers, lexicographers and terminologists. The very nature of machine translation systems has changed, from fully automatic to human-aided machine translation, to computer-assisted human translation. Language specialists have become more and more interested in the development of their own working tools with the result that they get much more satisfactory products to work with, and offer less resistance to change.

Technology integration in the work environment
The evolution of computer science has led to the integration of systems along two different lines. One is the mix of several applications in one package. For example, accounting packages will include book-keeping, journals, general ledger and financial statements but also extensions and links to other applications such as purchase orders, billing, inventory control, production scheduling and material requirements planning etc. in an all-in-one type of superpackage.

The second line of integration is much more important in its scope and effects. Computer science has not only evolved dramatically as a field in itself, but also has imposed its tools (computers) and its methods (especially programming and top-down analysis) on other fields of activity. Here are a few examples of this remarkable and apparently unique phenomenon.

From the chisel to the pen, to printing, to the manual then electric typewriter, the evolution of writing instruments has now reached the computer stage. A word-processing system is nothing more than a computer specially programmed to that effect. It is thus not always necessary to buy a specialised piece of equipment; in fact, a word-processing program is part of the free package that comes with the purchase of most microcomputers.

Oral communications are also handled by computers: telephone exchanges and Programmable Branch Exchanges (PBXs) are simply computers with telephone receivers as terminals. Computer-controlled dictating machines have functions similar to word processing that allow for moving around paragraphs, deletion of portions of text etc., the operation being symbolically displayed on-screen while its equivalent is performed on tape. Drawing boards have become computerised as well, offering features such as automatic calculation of various sections and movement simulation on the screen, all in full colour and with more precision than conventional drafting and reproduction methods. In manufacturing, assembly lines have become gigantic robots, that is, computers which have sensors, articulated arms and various devices as peripherals, instead of the usual keyboards, screen and printers.

The adoption of computers and their methods in fields other than computer science leads to an easier integration of various functions and opens the door to a new synergy. Consider, for example, the development of workstations which group together the functions of a computer terminal, word processor and telephone receiver, and computer-aided design and manufacturing (CAD/CAM) applications by which plans designed through computer graphics are directly used in manufacturing to operate robots. Computer science has given birth to office automation, tele-processing or 'telematics', computer graphics and robotics – the integration of these new technologies in our working environments depends only on our imagination.

Besides the implementation of integrated workstations for language specialists, the integration of several advanced technologies has opened new opportunities to translators and given much research work to terminologists. Information, as the raw material necessary to disciplines of communication, appears to be not only a renewable, but a self-multiplying resource.

TRANSLATION AND ADAPTATION OF SOFTWARE

Our interest in computer aids for translators should not make us forget that with the advent of computers and computer science, data processing, word processing, office automation, teleprocessing and robotics, more work has come to the 'in-tray' of technical translators and a new specialisation has emerged. Moreover, since information systems have invaded more and more domains of activity, it has become a must for any specialised translator, if not for every translator, to be familiar with at least the fundamentals and the basic terminology of information systems. This demonstrates the effect of computer science on the language profession.

Added to the ever increasing use of computer means as an aid to translation, this has resulted in a closer symbiosis between the fields of translation and information technology. Besides that, the multiplication of computer systems and their use by ordinary people in a variety of locations and situations has resulted in a quite new and specialised activity: the translation and adaptation of the computer systems themselves.

Given the wider definition of a system (set of inputs, procedures, outputs, and various resources), it is clear that the translation of a computerised information system includes, but is not necessarily bound to, the translation of user documentation. Indeed, translation of the documentation is only the first of three levels of translation one can distinguish in information systems.

The first level consists in translating only the documentation of the system without modifying anything in the programs. More often than not, only the user documentation (and the operations manuals in the case of larger systems) is translated, while the system and program documentation is left aside. This implies that only individuals fluent in the language of origin of the system can understand it in all its aspects and modify it (which, by the way, implies rewriting the documentation of the modified parts).

This level of translation of a computer system is still quite frequent. Nevertheless it is very primitive and leads to problems of various kinds. As an example of these problems, let us mention the necessity of keeping the commands and messages of the system both in the source and target languages in the translated documentation, to quote exactly what the system displays and expects and to make it understandable for the target language reader, leading to either hybrid or heavy text.

Such a phrase as *la commande SUPPRIMER* will become in English 'the SUPPRIMER command', or 'the SUPPRIMER (delete) command', to be more explicit for a reader who has little knowledge of the source language. It is the same for sentences like *Le système affiche: 'Voulez-vous vraiment supprimer cette page (O/N)?'*, that would be translated, 'The system displays: "Voulez-vous vraiment supprimer cette page (O/N)?" (Do you really want to delete this page (O for yes – OUI, N for no)?)'.

There are several ways to translate in this type of situation, but all of them are either tedious or incomplete. Moreover, one cannot limit oneself to translating more explicitly at the first occurrence and less explicitly afterwards, since computer systems documentation is often used for reference purposes and very seldom read from cover to cover.

The second level of translation includes partial reprogramming of the system in such a way that at least the messages and reports, and sometimes the commands of the system, are in the target language and that the system seems to understand and speak the user's language.

Usually, this reprogramming affects only data areas in the system and not the algorithm itself. Field lengths must be redefined according to the target language wording. A little bit more delicate is the problem of commands abbreviated in short mnemonics, since two different commands in the source language may have the same abbreviation in the target language. Synonyms must be found, not always a satisfactory solution. In some cases, a report that takes up a certain number of lines in the source language will require more or less in the target language, resulting in slight modification of the algorithm (new statements to add or delete lines, more or fewer items per page etc.).

But this is little compared to the third level of translation, the only complete one, which tends to make the translated system as a whole look like a genuine system in the target language. In addition to what has been discussed before, this implies including the alphabet (and diacritics) of the target language in the keyboard, screen, printer, communications protocols and internal character representation of the system. This can be very complex since, for example, the traditional one-byte representation of characters is often insufficient, some letters change shape when followed or preceded by some others, left-to-right writing is not universal etc.

Some physical indications on the equipment may have to be translated. Moveover, the very principle of the system may have to be adapted to the new linguistic and cultural environment. For instance, the operations performed by an accounting system will be different from country to country (even those that use the same language). This latter case resembles the change of technical specification of any device so as to adapt it to another environment, which also reflects in the documentation.

It should be noted that the third and to some extent the second level of translation imply that translating and adapting a computer system is in fact an activity of system development, which requires more than linguistic knowledge and renders necessary the use of system-engineering methodology. Since few translators (in fact few individuals) master both fields, multidisciplinary teams become necessary, and must be properly organised and managed.

Several system development teams include one or more technical writers to prepare the user and technical documentation while the system is being designed and implemented. The concurrent development of versions in several languages or the design of truly multilingual systems brings new opportunities not only for writers, but for translators and terminologists, to do their communication work under new and exciting conditions.

The fact that so many software packages have been adapted to other languages has contributed to the development of foreign-language facilities on several computers and operating systems. It has also helped several translators to participate in the information systems revolution.

FUTURE DIRECTIONS FOR MT AND CAT

Looking at the general evolution of computer science, let me suggest some directions for research in MT and CAT. Certainly not all of them will prove fruitful, but they deserve to be honestly investigated.

Clearly, the integration of sophisticated database management systems, of fourth-generation languages and of parallel processing in MT and CAT systems should be examined.

Research on LSP and expert systems will at some time have common features inasmuch as experts use special-purpose languages in their domain. AI programming languages like Prolog and LISP might be interfaced with linguistic tools such as Q-systems and ATN.

Serious theories of translation, as well as psycholinguistic theories, should find an echo in actual MT systems. Research on knowledge-based systems could be made more effective by putting together the contributions of information representation and storage activities such as thesaurus building, lexicography and terminology.

As a final example of possible co-ordination of efforts, I can refer to the very many computer or high-tech firms that use or plan to use machine translation to translate their documentation. I am sure that in some cases, the documents to be translated describe a computer system whose formal description (data flow diagrams, data dictionary, description of procedures) is available somewhere in machine-readable form. I suggest that this description could be somehow used as a knowledge base, helping the MT system better to translate such things as the operator's and user's guide, overall system documentation etc.

These are only a few of the many possible directions for research in MT and CAT. In the meantime, we should not forget that translators and other language specialists require right now better tools to do a better job, to be more productive and to be happier. Such things as the translator's workstation can very well be developed and made ready to include MT as another module.

AUTHOR
Benoît Thouin, President, CLC Ltd, PO Box 420, Station A, Hull,
  Quebec, Canada J8Y 6P2.

Developments in OCR for automatic data entry

Julie Harnett

Editorial Consultancy and Services, Twickenham, UK

A team of researchers at International Resource Development predicts that optical character recognition (OCR), linked to online signature verification, will revolutionise the use of credit cards in the future. The US report predicts rapid movement of OCR and other image-processing technologies into a variety of specialised markets, including credit card verification, cheque processing, legal searches and so on. The team foresees a dramatic decline in credit card fraud and theft as a result of the new technology.

But if such research is going on into the development of new products we read very little about them in the press, even less about optical character recognition for full-page document input for word-processing applications.

Yet one might expect companies to be crying out for such technology, thereby encouraging manufacturers to progress such developments with greater urgency. Speed and efficiency are the selling points of word processors and computers – once the data is entered into the system. Keying it in, however, takes a long time. Re-keying it when it has already been created once on a typewriter is a tremendous waste of skilled resources.

For example, when companies install computers, they very often need to create their database from existing documents. It is estimated that the labour costs of keying that information are about 50 pence per record. Assuming an average database of 25,000 to 50,000 records, that overall cost will probably be far more than the computer system; and while staff are tied up re-keying existing documents, they are obviously not devoting any time to generating new business. That is equally true whether it be in the accounts office, which handles numerical data, or the translator's office, which handles words.

Document reading by machines using optical character recognition techniques would also appear to have a significant part to play in the day-to-day support of word processing. In their simplest form, present systems read text produced on a standard typewriter, in a stylised, but generally acceptable font (such as OCR-B) and record it on storage devices (such as floppy disks) to be edited by a word processor, if need be, prior to printing. This permits every typewriter to serve as an entry point to word processing, and reserves the word processor for editing, at which it is most cost-effective.

Just let me explain a moment the technique for those of you who are new to OCR. It is a technique for scanning a page of text with a light source to form a series of images. These are interpreted by software which tries to match the patterns it reads against a series of patterns from a pre-defined font of characters stored in its memory. If a good match is obtained, the appropriate computer code is generated and stored. If not, there are various techniques used, from outright rejection to recommended best matches. A main need for OCR is to handle external documents whose format, quality and type form cannot always be predicted.

Translators, of course, have to contend not only with different typefaces but with different languages, and machines which can recognise more than one language are few and far between. Not many machines, either, can recognise bold characters or underlining.

But 'All such problems can be overcome with proper planning,' as Michael Mason, Managing Director of Interlingua/TTI Group says. Interlingua bought a Compuscan Alphaword OCR machine back in 1979 and it was supplied capable of understanding English, French and German. Naturally, three languages were not enough for such a large translation company, so they asked the suppliers to adapt the machine to recognise twelve languages – which they did. The system has proved to be a good workhorse ever since.

Interlingua employs around 500–600 freelance translators every month who may not be the same people each time, but Interlingua needed the work each person produced to be input to the CPT word processor for editing and correcting. They could have equipped all of the freelancers with an IBM PC, but that would have been tremendously expensive. The alternative was to supply them with an OCR-B golfball element which the Alphaword OCR could recognise and input to the word processor, thus avoiding the necessity to re-key all the text produced.

Mr Mason did have some good advice to pass on – if a machine cannot understand underlining, for example, then translators should manually underline words in red, which the system cannot see. If there are corrections to be made, again, mark in red so only the word processing operator can see where to make the necessary changes. In other words, most problems can be overcome with imagination and patience.

The American company Compuscan has, since then, developed a more capable OCR machine, the Alphaword 3 + , which is available for around £22,000 in the UK from Formscan or from Kendata. It automatically identifies and reads up to eight resident fonts, including the most popular – Courier 10, Prestige Elite, Letter Gothic and so on – at the pitch for which they were designed. It automatically adjusts to read 10 and 12 pitch and varying line spacing, and automatically inserts appropriate information-processing codes, such as decimal tabs, centring codes, paragraph codes, etc. It is claimed that it makes less than one error in over 300,000 characters. It can be connected to most word processors and computers, typesetters and modems for communications.

The latest member of the Compuscan family, the Alphaword Series 80, is said to be able to capture text and data faster than forty typists. Margins are adjustable to permit reading of non-standard text and to avoid having to edit corrections to garbage that should not be scanned in the first place. Fonts are as powerful and encompass as many typesources as the Alphaword 3+ , including all commonly used characters on the IBM Golfball such as the degree sign and fractions.

Important indices, such as underlining, tabs, accents in foreign language texts and special symbols, are read as well and converted to the desired code or commands. It can also read right-justified text and outputs with full word-processing formats.

More intelligence is also claimed for the American Typereader TR3, the most sophisticated in the Hendrix OCR family which is available in the UK from General Audio & Data Communications. It features automatic recognition of up to four common typestyles and their font variations in both 10 and 12 pitch, with underscores and in any standard line spacing. The types of text it will read include correspondence, legal, fractions, accounting and foreign fonts of all available typestyles (for example, Courier 12, Courier 72, Letter Gothic, Prestige Elite, Prestige Pica, OCR-A, OCR-B and Hendrix Gothic).

With auto font and auto pitch recognition, the TR3 automatically detects different typestyles from page to page which means you don't have to pre-sort pages when using the automatic sheet feeder. Its error rate is one error in every 150,000 characters. Average reading rate is between 120 and 150 characters per second (cps) although the maximum rate is 264 cps. In addition, it offers dual output to multiple word processors or message communications devices.

For those organisations preferring a desk-top machine, the Japanese Totec TO-5000B from Mitsui, costing from about £12,500, may be more appropriate. Again, available in the UK from GADC, it not only looks like a desktop copier, it acts like one. It can read, without manual switching, the intermixed fonts of unmodified golfball or daisy-wheel typewriters, with the power to handle up to 300 pages an hour.

Currently it can read 16 fonts, with others under development. Special typefaces are available to order. But up to six fonts can be fitted at any one time. Its multilingual capability does not include French, Spanish and Italian, says Kendata, because the accents are too microscopic. However, as with most OCR devices, it is possible to build in codes for accented characters which show up on the word processor screen, enabling the operator to key in the correct character manually.

A notable feature of this machine is its straight paper-path which eliminates paper jamming, a common fault with OCR machines. Although there are formatters for most word processors, GADC say they can usually develop interfaces for non-standard systems at short notice.

A competitor of that OCR machine is the American DEST Workless Workstation from Lexisystems, a wholly owned subsidiary of Formscan. It inputs a page in 25 seconds, which is about twenty times faster than the average typist. It reads two up to eight multilingual typestyles, greatly expanding the translator's ability to read both in-house documents and those from outside sources. It will automatically format text to be compatible with the host system; it reads multiple typestyles on the same page – which means no dials or switches to set – and a 75-page paper tray feeds in face up and ejects face down, maintaining proper page sequence.

Prices for DEST Workless systems start at just over £6,000, but a multifont multilingual system would start at just over £8,000, with multilingual Courier 10 as standard and optional typefaces available in pack form from just over £1,500 for two extra fonts, £3,500 for a seven-font pack. Multilingual word-processing format processors cost just over £1,500, but it should be noted that these multilingual machines do not read proportional spacing.

However, it is the Kurzweil 4000 Intelligent Scanner, launched in the USA in 1984, which has created more interest than most in the field of character recognition. Indeed, since it was introduced, 200 systems have been installed worldwide, twelve of which are in the UK. It is not cheap at £41,000 from UK distributor Penta Systems, but then intelligence doesn't come cheap. It combines the high technology of artificial intelligence with optical scanning, whereby it learns new styles as it scans.

As you may realise from my previous comments, OCR is limited in the number and variety of type fonts and formats it can handle. Intelligent character-recognition technology, on the other hand, accepts the entire range of type styles and formats in everyday use, including proportionally spaced type as well as conventional typewritten copy.

Enhanced artificial intelligence capabilities enable the system to train itself to recognise a full array of bold and italic characters, engineering and mathematical symbols, foreign alphabets, and multiple fonts within a single document. It will also recognise word-processing and typesetting formats and font codes. When broken characters, smudged type or other problems make recognition uncertain, the system flags the operator for assistance, diplaying an enlarged version of the character and asking for an identification decision.

With reasonably clean copy, the system's training process is completed in minutes, at which point production scanning begins. Other special features include the ability to identify and code font changes, scan from left or right, and distinguish such characters as left and right quotation marks, hyphens and em rules, and horizontal and vertical spacing.

Currently, its multilingual capability includes German, Dutch, Danish and Swedish, with French and Spanish due shortly. The system can also make use of an electronic tablet costing around £5,000 which enables portions of text to be separated from surrounding graphics or allows selective automatic data entry. This system could, therefore, be used for reading and inputting text from books or newspapers.

Three years ago, industry observers predicted the development of an OCR for the home computer market and, indeed, less than a year ago a British invention, the Omni-Reader, was launched at the incredible price of £399, answering the need for a low-cost method of entering hard copy into a microcomputer or word processor. It is somewhat pedantic in the typefaces it will read, but a number of people have voiced their satisfaction with its performance providing they keep to Courier 10 or 12, although Letter Gothic 12 and Prestige Elite 12 are also incorporated. Other typefaces, I understand, can be downloaded from a computer.

In fact, a prominent laser print bureau which has no less than five large laser printers costing around a quarter of a million pounds each was very happy using the Omni-Reader for typewritten texts received from clients, which has saved the company many hours of unnecessary re-keying.

It consists of two moving parts, the precision read head and the tracking guide or ruler. It is connected to the workstation in the same way as a modem, through an RS-232C serial interface. The hard copy is placed under the ruler and aligned and the information is scanned by the read head running backwards and forwards.

The drawback is that alignment of the guide over the text line has to be accurate to avoid triggering the misread 'beep', but on the other hand you could use the ruler edge to 'hide' underlining and avoid the misreads that other OCR devices are sometimes prone to. Being manual, it is not speedy but the manufacturers, Oberon, had planned further developments, among which was supposed to be a semi-automated version. Whether that will come about now is debatable. Sadly the company is currently in financial difficulties. But perhaps someone will step in and rescue them. There are still a number of units apparently available through dealers.

I hope this unfortunate circumstance will not damage the prospects of another British invention shown to prospective backers recently. It is called the Typereader, invented by Frank O'Gorman (a computer scientist who was recently a research fellow at Sussex University working on artificial intelligence vision projects) in collaboration with Southdata Ltd, a database management software company.

As the MD Peter Laurie has said, the objective is to make an OCR machine which will read misaligned, dirty letters in almost any typeface in any size, in roman, bold and italic variants; and read lines of text at random angles (within reasonable limits). This is not as easy as it might sound, but they believe they have solved the problems which have baffled many people by bringing advanced computer vision techniques to bear.

It will be an accessory which can be connected to any computer – from mainframe to home micro – and will look rather like a photocopier. The simplest version will probably only accept separate A4 sheets fed into a slot, but larger versions would be able to accept text in sheet or book form, laid on a glass plate.

The backing that Southdata is hoping for will produce a production machine combining facsimile input hardware and computer boards to run the analysis software in a single box. It is thought that there is a mass market available for a machine costing about £4,000 which could read A4 sheets of text in more or less any typeface, perhaps with manual feed, just like a normal fax or copying machine, and with automatic feeder options.

It is also thought that there is a market available for a more sophisticated system at round £25,000 which would comprise a stand-alone facsimile transmitter (the prototype uses the Muirhead Mufax 7600) or similar hardware and a separate 68000 microcomputer running the copyrighted software. Laurie says that there is no reason why the production machine should not be able to recognise foreign language typefaces and the software could be readily adapted for that purpose. The prototype shows that such a machine would read about fifty words a minute.

Facsimile and other image-scanning techniques are thought by many to be the way that OCR will go in future. Image scanning is often confused with OCR but does not, in itself, have any ability to recognise characters. Image and graphics scanners physically record the sequence of light and dark images on a page with no provision for editing or converting those images into computer code. To be capable of recognition so that the information can be processed, not just viewed, the image-scanning process needs to be complemented by artificial intelligence, as indicated above with the Typereader invention and the Kurzweil system.

Many people believed that optical disk technology would provide the answer but, again, such systems do not 'understand' the images they read, they only capture and store images. Also, the optical disks currently available are non-erasable. Therefore, captured images cannot be edited or amended except for deletion and optical manipulation such as enlargement and reduction of the captured image. What is more, such systems currently cost around a quarter of a million pounds.

Some people may be interested to know if there are OCR machines which can read handwritten documents and, indeed, there are. One of the leaders in this field is Scan Optics with their Easy Reader 1750: but such systems are intended for applications such as sales order entry, subscription fulfilment, motor vehicle registration, money order records and other primarily form-filling applications. They are not intended for intensive word- or text-processing applications.

However, just to keep you up to date on the subject, a brand new OCR system was launched in November 1985 at the COMPEC computer show, which is claimed to be the only system on the market able to read a mixture of alphanumeric handprint, typewriter output and computer print, including dot matrix, without the need to predefine which fonts will be used. From Computer Gesellschaft Konstanz, a Siemens subsidiary, and available in the UK from DRS Data & Research Services, the CSL 2610 will read handprinting, in block capitals, completed in pencil, ballpoint or felt tip pen, and in blue or black inks. Again, uniquely, or so they claim, it will automatically adjust to cope with handprint slopes of up to forty-five degrees.

Potential users include banks, travel companies, bureaux; any organisation, in fact, which handles a high volume of data entry tasks involving multiline documents completed by the public. The maximum sheet size it can handle, however, is A5.

While it may not have immediate application in the translator's office it does illustrate that OCR research is just beginning to be taken more seriously by a larger number of manufacturers, even if it is only recently. Since DRS accepts systems commissioning projects, then maybe we can see adaptations for other fields.

It is somewhat surprising that the Japanese have not been faster off the mark in producing character-recognition equipment since they are the leaders in facsimile transmission and image-processing technologies. I do hear that NEC in Japan has been fairly active recently, although it doesn't expect to be considering export to other countries until at least mid-1986.

NEC has produced, for example, an optical character reader that can read handwritten alphanumeric data input, graphics images and characters printed from terminals, either separately or directly from the printer, with no special conversion of control programs. Its price in Japan is around the £10,000 mark.

New high-performance hybrid equipment is expected to be introduced by Japanese manufacturers, that incorporates the capabilities and functions of several products. For example, a combination of a facsimile machine, which has input and output, image transmission and communications capabilities, and a personal computer which incorporates information processing and storage capabilities – quite an exciting prospect.

But there is a word of warning which comes from the IRD report mentioned at the beginning. Apparently lawyers are potentially prime users of OCR equipment, but the space age, high-tech designs do not complement the decor of their staid offices and libraries, apparently. So, says IRD, the solution is simple: suppliers should design the OCR equipment with leather or velvet upholstery (slightly worn, of course) and/or mahogany panelling.

Could it be a case of only accepting new technology providing it doesn't look like new technology? Is it really the outward designs which are holding up progress? Let us hope such attitudes do not dampen the enthusiasm of the developers and designers of the equipment which we all need if we are to realise the full benefits of word processing and computerisation.

USEFUL ADDRESSES

DRS Data & Research Services plc
 Sunrise Parkway, Linford Wood, Milton Keynes MK14 6LR. Tel: (0908) 666088
General Audio and Data Communications Ltd
 70/82 Akeman Street, Tring, Herts HP23 6AJ. Tel: (044282) 4011
Kendata Peripherals Ltd
 Nutsey Lane, Totton, Southampton SO4 3NB. Tel: (0703) 869922
Lexisystems Ltd
 Apex House, West End, Frome, Somerset BA11 3AS. Tel: (0373) 61446
Oberon International Ltd
 2 Hall Road, Maylands Wood Estate, Hemel Hempstead, Herts HP2 7BH. Tel: (0442) 3803
Penta Systems (UK) Ltd
 719 Banbury Avenue, Slough, Berks SL1 4LH. Tel: (0753) 29064
Scan-Optics Ltd
 36 Sunbury Cross Centre, Sunbury, Middx TW16 7AZ. Tel: (09327) 88881

Siemens Ltd
  Siemens House, Windmill Road, Sunbury-on-Thames, Middx TW16
  7HS. Tel: (09327) 85691
Southdata Ltd
  166 Portobello Road, London W11 2EB. Tel: (01) 727 7564

AUTHOR

Julie Harnett, Editorial Consultancy & Services, 10 Post Lane, Meadway,
  Twickenham, Middx TW2 6NZ, UK.

The ALPS computer-assisted translation system in an academic environment

Patrick Corness

Department of Language Studies, Coventry Lanchester Polytechnic, Coventry, Warwickshire, UK

INTRODUCTION

May I begin with a few words about the background to the polytechnic's association with ALP Systems, or ALPS, as it is known to us in Coventry? This began in May 1984, when, searching for software which would help me to compile an electronic dictionary, I contacted, amongst other firms, ALP Systems of Provo, Utah. My colleagues and I in the Department of Language Studies became very interested in the advanced computer-assisted language translation facilities being offered by a number of commercial companies. We believed we saw in the ALPS interactive approach considerable potential for educational applications beyond the electronic dictionary look-up capability which was originally looked for, and beyond the automated translation capability seen purely as an aid to productivity for the busy professional translator. Subsequently, in the spring of 1985, Lanchester Polytechnic in Coventry became the first institution of higher education outside America to install an ALPS computer-assisted translation system.

At Coventry we only began to introduce ALPS to students in October 1985 and the Polytechnic is, for the time being, I understand, the only educational ALPS user in Britain, indeed so far the only one outside America.

I am therefore going to be talking rather more about plans and aspirations than about hard experience. My remarks are predicated on a certain degree of optimism and a good deal of confidence that the ALPS system, while it may in practice turn out to be less than everything one could wish for, is something which represents a significant advance in the application of technology to language translation, and something which has considerable potential for language learning purposes.

If this confidence in the system as a useful aid for translators is justified, then it follows that advanced language students should be acquainted with its principles at least, and hopefully they will have the opportunity to gain hands-on experience with ALPS.

I should emphasise at the outset that we see the system not only as an advanced tool for the translator, which students of translation can therefore with advantage learn to use, but as an aid to language learning in a much more general sense. It forms, in fact, a new element of the computer-assisted language learning (CALL) facilities which have been developed and introduced over the last three years or so in our language courses. In this development of CALL the principle has been adopted that the use of microcomputers, like the use of the language laboratory, should be fully integrated into the teaching at all levels, from beginners to final honours. The Department is continuing to develop this integrated approach, and intends that ALPS shall play its everyday part in an overall teaching scheme. The ALPS installation will not be a curiosity item, nor something exploited by a limited number of machine translation buffs, but a tool which all students will gradually learn to use for appropriate routine tasks.

This paper is not intended to be an advertisement for ALPS. The fact of the acquisition of this system by the Polytechnic obviously reflects confidence in its potential for academic purposes, but a full and objective assessment of the system will have to wait until there is extensive experience of its use in practice. Of course, users' needs vary, and ALPS offers different levels of assistance, designed to match these. As far as the applications of ALPS in the academic environment are concerned, it will be vital to demonstrate that they represent a real educational advantage and that ALPS, unlike Everest, is not simply being used 'because it is there'.

COMPUTER-ASSISTED LANGUAGE LEARNING (CALL)

Now a few words about computer-assisted language learning (CALL) and the prospects for its development, in order to consider the introduction of ALPS at Coventry Polytechnic in this particular educational context. Then follows a brief outline of the facilities ALPS offers, before some talk about the ways in which these computer-assisted facilities are being used at the moment for language teaching, and about the prospects for the fairly near future.

Today, students in some polytechnics and universities are beginning to use computers as an aid to language learning as naturally as they would a tape recorder. Indeed the tape recorder and the microcomputer are now being linked in a new development called audio-enhanced computer-assisted language learning, or AECALL.

I am not able to cover the latest research work in CALL in other polytechnics and universities. The CALL packages which have so far been developed in my own Department[1] – and which are, if I may mention it, also being widely used in other institutions – enable many kinds of self-correcting language-learning exercises to be produced. Such exercises are now extensively used on our languages degree courses; indeed this development has stimulated a different approach to the teaching of languages at Coventry Polytechnic. It would not be appropriate for me to go into the detail of the teaching method here: can I just re-emphasise the point that it is fundamental to our approach to CALL that work on the computers is fully integrated into the teaching scheme, rather than being an optional extra, or a peripheral activity.

In CALL, the programming of language-learning exercises can allow for a variety of acceptable responses to questions posed to students by the computer: it does not have to demand, completely unthinkingly, one response only, to the exclusion of other responses which may be reasonable alternatives. However, in self-testing CALL exercises, the number of acceptable alternative answers has to be finite. In other words, the fundamental problem of the language–computer interface is that while human language is infinitely creative, the computer can only accept what it has been told to accept, to the letter.

In practice, of course, the number of acceptable alternative responses in many language-learning exercises can reasonably be fairly limited. Other exercises, such as translation as a case in point, are, by contrast, very open-ended and creative. An obvious misgiving felt by sceptics who view CALL and computer-assisted translation with suspicion, and hesitate to jump, as they see it, onto the microprocessor bandwagon, is that because language is so fundamentally human a phenomenon, so rich, so unpredictable, it can only suffer if forced into a straitjacket by a machine which is very powerful but fundamentally brainless. The short answer to these misgivings is, I believe, that the machine is not supposed to be the brains: it is supposed to help the human translator to concentrate on the intellectual and creative aspects of the task.

The old conception of what machine translation means, that is to say fully automatic translation by computer, entails the false assumption that the computer can, indeed, become the brains of the operation. But the ALPS approach is based on a more realistic view of the relationship between language and the computer. The fact that the human translator retains control makes ALPS viable as an open-ended and creative CALL facility as well as a translation aid as such.

However, not everyone is convinced that computers of any kind are potentially an effective aid to language learning, and not simply a gimmick. The teacher's job is to assist students to increase their factual knowledge, to develop their intellectual understanding, to enhance their practical skills and to stimulate their enthusiasm and interest. The question is whether technological aids help the teacher to achieve these aims more rapidly or more effectively. In faculties of science and engineering it is taken for granted that technical facilities, including of course computers, are essential, but in the teaching of languages and the teaching of translation the relevance of the computer is still considered unproven by some.

The development of AECALL was mentioned earlier. This is an attempt to progress beyond the limitations of the first generation of computer-assisted language-learning exercises, in which the written language predominates. The purpose of AECALL is to incorporate the spoken language in computer-assisted learning exercises. It is of course axiomatic that spoken language is primary, and written language secondary. Audio-enhanced CALL is, therefore, one important direction in which CALL research must move. The use of speech recognition and speech synthesis techniques is not relevant here, by the way, or not yet. What is being developed in AECALL is computerised control of human voice recordings for language-learning purposes.

A second, no less important, aspect of CALL research is the exploitation of information retrieval techniques as interactive computer-assisted learning resources. These include dictionary look-up, concordance look-up and other online help files. It is in this vital area of the application of computerised information retrieval to language learning that we are looking at the ALPS system to see what it can offer.

OUTLINE OF THE ALPS SYSTEM
There are three levels of ALPS translator assistance, called respectively:

- SDL (selective dictionary look-up)
- ADL (automatic dictionary look-up)
- CTS (computer translation system).

These terms represent a range of facilities, adaptable to different needs. The different levels are appropriate, for example, for differing degrees of specialisation of subject matter, differing length of text etc.

The processing capabilities include the following:

- multilingual word processing
- dictionary building

- dictionary look-up
- keywords in context (KWIC) look-up
- vocabulary frequency analysis
- grammatical and syntactical analysis
- interactive translation.

Once a source text has been entered, using the word processor or an optical character reader, the next step is to provide a purpose-built dictionary, called a document dictionary, for that text. The document dictionary will contain all the vocabulary items found in the source text, and, depending on the level of automatic assistance required, may contain the grammatical and syntactic information codes which the translation program will need to examine.

The first step in building the document dictionary is a process called dixtraction, which scans the source text and scans the appropriate permanent dictionaries, as instructed by the user, and then creates a bilingual dictionary containing all the required vocabulary found in the dictionaries searched.

Dixtraction also lists, if required, all the source text vocabulary not found in any of the dictionaries searched. The user can then use this Words Not Found (WNF) list to complete the document dictionary. Further assistance to the translator in editing dictionaries is provided by the KeyWords In Context (KWIC) list facility and the word frequency count facility which are also available. When the dictionary is ready, the translator can call up whichever level of assistance is required.

Using SDL, a translation may be typed on the screen using the word processor, to be subsequently saved, printed out etc. During this process the dictionary may be accessed as necessary, to find suggested translation equivalents for particular items.

In ADL, the translation is built up on the VDU screen, sentence by sentence, in the Work Area window. The translation equivalents for all the words or phrases are automatically displayed in the Target Area window, and are numbered so that they can be entered into the target text in the appropriate order, and subsequently rearranged if necessary, by one or two keystrokes. Typing is thus reduced to a minimum, but a translation equivalent offered can always be rejected in favour of a different word or phrase actually typed in by the translator, and the target text can be edited subsequently if necessary.

In CTS, grammatical and syntactical processing is also done by the computer. A draft translation of the text is offered automatically, sentence by sentence, but first of all the computer interrogates the user in order to clarify structural or semantic ambiguities, and to supply missing vocabulary. Editing of the translation offered by the computer can be carried out rapidly if necessary.

The ALPS computer-assisted translation system at the CTS level is not intended to replace the human translator and it cannot translate entirely automatically a text fed into it. However it can accelerate the translation process.

It is important to realise that the analysis is limited to one sentence at a time. This means that the computer has no knowledge of the world beyond the purely grammatical structures it is programmed to recognise and beyond the meanings of words and phrases it is programmed to recognise. In other words, it cannot resolve for itself the ambiguities contained in a sentence such as, 'Coventry Polytechnic is a big computer user'. The intervention of the human translator is needed here: knowledge of Coventry Polytechnic's actual use of computers is needed to resolve the ambiguity as to whether the Polytechnic is being described as a 'big user of computers' or as a 'user of big computers'. Even such background knowledge may not resolve the ambiguity, since both interpretations may be valid. The human translator may be able to tell which meaning is intended from the context, since the rest of the text may refer consistently to users of big computers or consistently to big users of computers. However, the computer programs which are analysing a sentence have no knowledge of the context beyond that sentence. The system can be programmed so that 'big computer user' is always translated as 'big user of computers' or always translated as 'user of big computers', but in principle this is unsatisfactory, since it limits the usefulness of the program to one particular text. The translation might as well have been done by hand in the first place.

What is needed is an automatic system which is independent of particular texts and particular vocabulary items, a system which enables all such ambiguities to be resolved as they occur. What the ALPS computer-assisted translation system does is to ask the human translator to resolve the ambiguity, by displaying on the screen a question such as:

Is the text speaking of
(a) big computers
(b) big users?

The translator presses either *a* or *b* on the keyboard to tell the ALPS computer what the correct choice is in this case. If the computer's dictionary contains more than one possible translation for a given expression, the translator will again be asked to make a choice by pressing *a*, *b*, *c* etc.

The translation which is offered by the computer after the ambiguities have been resolved may not be satisfactory. Some editing will usually be needed to produce an acceptable final version. Much depends on the dictionary which has been built up in advance by the translator.

At Coventry there is presently a two-workstation installation, incorporating all three levels of ALPS translation assistance (SDL, ADL and

CTS) from English into French, into German, into Spanish and into Italian, running on a Data General minicomputer, the Model 20 Desktop. We are awaiting the software for translation into English, and also we hope soon to have ADL facilities for Russian.

ALPS AS A DEVELOPMENT OF CALL: PRINCIPLES

One of the problems of language learning, including translation training, is that of heightening awareness of contrasts in structure between the native language and the foreign language, awareness of the variety of stylistic expression available in a given language, and awareness of the many factors influencing the choice of particular forms and structures in a given case.

One can see in ALPS new opportunities to demonstrate these contrasts, giving students – literally at their fingertips – a display of a variety of possible translation equivalents for a given word or phrase, showing examples of their occurrences in a variety of contexts and meanings. As they proceed with their translation, students either make choices from a number of suggested translation equivalents shown on the screen, or else decide on equivalents of their own. In the latter case they then update the dictionary by adding the new equivalents as additional entries for future reference. Naturally this work has to take place under the supervision of the tutor, but it results in a translation which is the product of a series of conscious decisions which the computer obliges the user to take in a systematic way.

There might be a suspicion that working with pen and paper is really more creative than doing what the computer apparently tells you to do, but pen and paper translation would normally involve reference to dictionaries too: one difference between the traditional method and working with assistance from ALPS is in the speed and convenience of access to helpful information. ALPS users are not banned from looking at traditional reference works, by the way! And the translator is not obliged to accept the suggestions on the screen any more than the suggestions in a traditional dictionary.

As I see it, one principal advantage of ALPS as a language-learning aid consists in the power of the computer to make rapidly available a wide range of online look-up facilities during the translation process, as required. We are planning in Coventry to build up further, specifically education-oriented, look-up facilities in addition to the dictionaries and KWIC lists. These will include a set of help files for convenient reference to information, for assistance on problems of grammar, for example. The extent of the available help can also be controlled by the tutor, depending on the nature of the exercise involved. Access to certain files can be temporarily restricted for testing purposes, for example.

The fact that students can be made aware that a dictionary does not represent tablets of stone, but is rather the object of creative development work, to which they themselves can contribute, learning by doing, also seems to me to offer a distinct pedagogical advantage.

A further significant feature of ALPS as a learning aid is the labour-saving facility. Since words and phrases are selected from the screen menu of translation equivalents and entered into the target text by a very small number of keystrokes, the time and effort spent on sheer writing or typing is considerably reduced, and so the system should enable the student to concentrate on the actual intellectual activity of translating, of making intellectual decisions. Writing or typing everything out by hand does have its own pedagogical advantages, of course. It helps the learner to remember what was written. But the potential advantages of more intensive and extensive exposure to the languages and their points of similarity and contrast which the language student will eventually have as an ALPS user do seem to be considerable. Besides, students will not do all their work on an ALPS terminal. They will still do plenty of writing in longhand.

ALPS AS A DEVELOPMENT OF CALL:
THE EXPERIMENT SO FAR

We are experimenting at the moment with some fairly general texts for translation from English into German, using ADL, with first year students. The subject matter of the texts is modern German history and the ADL level is being used in this way to provide exercises in what we call 'guided translation' into the foreign language.

In this context I should mention that the Department's microcomputer network has been used during the last three years or so to give practice, amongst other things, in what is called 'text reconstruction'. In this exercise, an original German text, say, previously translated into English by the students, has to be faithfully reconstructed by them on the computer from memory using the English translation as a guide. This is, of course, not a translation exercise as such, but is used to reinforce knowledge of target language structures in context. The idea behind this is not too far removed from the hallowed principle of learning poetry by heart to reinforce knowledge of a language.

Now that the ALPS system is installed, we are introducing, experimentally, exercises in a more open-ended form of guided translation, using ADL. In these exercises, students are expected to produce their own translations with varying degrees of assistance from the computer, and a model translation is made available for purposes of comparison only. The student's version and the model version can be displayed and printed out in parallel columns for easy checking and comparision.

One such type of exercise using ADL is very closely guided translation practice, which is really more of a grammar test than a translation task. In this case the appropriate vocabulary is defined in advance by the lecturer, who builds the dictionary. The student is then automatically provided with the vocabulary to be used, and is required to compose the translation using the words offered, in their correct grammatical forms, building a correct sentence structure.

Certain grammatical information is available in the ALPS dictionaries, and can be looked up as needed. This grammar look-up facility is being extended (something not normally needed by a professional translator) for language-learning purposes. It is planned to make such help available on ALPS on a fairly comprehensive basis ultimately.

Other ADL assignments, designed to be more like translation exercises, involve more interaction. A relatively wide range of suggested translation equivalents is displayed, and the student is required to translate the text with the help of this display and the other online look-up facilities available. Working with a normal dictionary, learners might not bother to look a word up, but assume that they knew the best translation for it. ADL can ensure that students consider a range of possibilities, including some they may well not have thought of. We will be developing look-up facilities which will show the use of vocabulary in various contexts, to assist in finding the best translation, and enhance students' awareness of the problems involved.

Professional translators using ADL would design their dictionaries in such a way as to minimise interaction and save time, but for language-learning purposes it may be appropriate to deliberately maximise interaction.

CTS is being used to demonstrate some of the problems of translation arising out of contrasting structures. My colleague Gwyn Howells is experimenting in this area, systematically testing the capability of CTS to cope with the translation of specific structures from English into Spanish.

CONCLUSION: ALPS AS A LANGUAGE-TEACHING AID

For language students, the three different levels of ALPS systems (SDL, ADL and CTS) offer the benefit of hands-on experience with a range of information retrieval and information-processing techniques, from word processing and database handling to computer-assisted translation. This provides them with basic skills in these areas, which they are likely to need if they become professional linguists.

The ALPS computer can also be used as a broader CALL facility. The ALPS company[2] has provided some education-oriented software, so that the system can be more readily adapted at all levels for language-teaching purposes. This software helps teaching staff to prepare controlled translation assignments, which students can carry out without the need to learn complicated procedures and without the risk of crashing the system. This is a big advantage, enabling all students to be given some experience as ALPS users with only a small installation.

The information storage and retrieval facilities are equally useful for purposes of accelerating the translation process and for purposes of accessing information for the language learner. They offer an open-ended, creative CALL facility which complements the self-correcting testing programs.

The vocabulary analysis – both alphabetical and frequency lists, as well as KWIC lists – can be used to assist the teacher to design graded teaching materials.

Last but not least, the CTS system and how it works, with its limitations just as much as its positive capabilities, presents a rich field of enquiry for the theoretical linguist.

To conclude, we believe that experience with ALPS will help students become more aware of the nature of language in general and of the problems of translation in particular.

REFERENCES

1. UNITEXT (for roman-alphabet languages) and RUSTEXT (cyrillic) suites of authoring and testing programs, written by R.M. Benwell of the Department of Applied Physical Sciences, Coventry Lanchester Polytechnic, in co-operation with the Department of Language Studies.
2. European Office: Automated Language Processing Systems, Route de Boudry 14, CH2016 Cortaillod/NE, Switzerland.

AUTHOR

Patrick Corness, Department of Language Studies (CALL Consultancy Group), Coventry Lanchester Polytechnic, Coventry CV1 5FB, UK.

A user's experience of the LOGOS machine translation system: a manager's viewpoint

Wolfgang Heitmann

Nixdorf Computer AG, Paderborn, West Germany

I work in the Field Engineering Division of Nixdorf Computer AG, as Manager of the Technical Documentation Group.

Nixdorf is a company with worldwide activities; it has no fewer than 400 marketing and service centres in forty countries of Europe, America, Asia, Australia and Africa. The company obtains 55 per cent of its income from sales, the remaining 45 per cent deriving from services and rentals. As far as the geographical distribution of company turnover is concerned, almost half (49 per cent) comes from Germany, 40 per cent from the rest of Europe and 11 per cent from the overseas markets.

As at the end of 1984, Nixdorf field service personnel throughout the world numbered 4,540, with 3,280 staff members in Europe (half of them in Germany) and 660 overseas.

The tasks of the field service personnel are to provide:

1. Installation and technical start-up
2. Maintenance
   - preventative maintenance
   - general overhauls
   - diagnostic evaluation
   - installation of technical alterations
3. Repair
   - exchange of functional components and printed circuit boards
   - repair through adjustment and component compensation
4. Software maintenance
5. Remote diagnosis and remote maintenance
6. Network management

7.   Technical customer support

In providing these services, the priorities for the Field Service main office are as follows:

1.   Measures for quality control
     – products
     – testing devices
     – methods
2.   Execution/development of:
     – technical customer service processes
     – technical organisation facilities
3.   Creation of:
     – field service documentation
     – field service information
4.   Service
     – technical training/media
     – support of modification services
     – control/planning of field service material
     – support in the case of difficult technical problems
5.   Measures for introducing products
     – create field service specification manual/specifications for product development
     – acceptance tests of 'prototype products'
6.   Special tasks
     – revision ⎫
     – support ⎬ of the field service performance
     – analyses ⎭
7.   Marketing
     – observing market/competition prices and conditions
     – services, field service methods

The pattern of operations can be illustrated by Figure 1.

The services provided by the Technical Documentation Group include drafting, writing, drawing, translation, typesetting, distribution and management.

The documentation chiefly consists of reference manuals of various kinds – general descriptions, system descriptions, model descriptions, equipment descriptions, component descriptions and data sheets. The group also provides customer service information of the 'quick information on paper' type, internal information, and hand-outs.

Up till 1984, the group had produced some 1,000 reference manuals

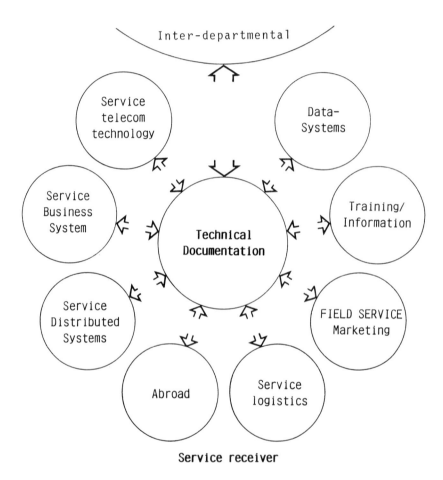

Figure 1. Pattern of operations, Nixdorf's Field Services

varying in length between 60 and 800 pages. Of these, 60 per cent were in German and 40 per cent in English. During 1984, it was planned that the group should produce about 720 customer information brochures averaging 6 pages long, 55 per cent being in German and 45 per cent in English.

The Technical Documentation Group at Nixdorf numbers eleven staff members, seven of whom deal with planning, writing, setting, distribution and management, three (two in-house plus one freelance) with translation, and one with drawing. There is a measure of overlap between the functions.

The Technical Documentation Group was recently confronted with a major problem, which had its origins in the two following facts: as from 1985, the corporate language was to be English as well as German, and Nixdorf was becoming the No. 1 firm in Europe in its field.

The structure of the Technical Documentation Group presented a problem in itself; within the group, the translation service would have to provide all the reference manuals, customer service information, hand-outs and internal information. However, the translation requirement is rising steeply; in 1981 the volume translated was 4,580 pages (114,500 lines). By 1983 this figure had risen to 6,560 pages (164,000 lines), and after that there was a sharp increase – 9,000 pages (225,000 lines) in 1984, and no fewer than 13,000 pages (325,000 lines) in 1985, 284 per cent of the 1981 figure.

At the same time, the life cycle of EDP equipment is diminishing. From over six years prior to 1984, the life cycle is now down to about three years in 1986, and by the year 2000 it will be less than two years.

Table 1 sets out the possible ways of solving the translation problem.

Solution principles	Translation performance by:			
	Human translator		Machine-based system	
Variations	extent of his/her capacities		service	
Variations divided into	*internal* – fixed employment contract – paid-up contract	*external* medium – paper – floppy disk – TC[1]	*external* medium – paper – floppy disk – TC[1]	*local* medium – paper – floppy disk – TC[2]

1. Telecommunication: Nixdorf 8860 to host
2. Telecommunication: Nixdorf 8860 to Wang

Table 1. Simplified representation of problem solution principles

The target volume for translation is estimated to be a minimum of 2,300 pages, or 56,000 lines, a year; by 1986 the volume should be 4,400 pages (110,000 lines) and from 1987, the volume anticipated is well over that figure. In order to achieve this target, the processing time for translation has to be reduced by 20 per cent as between 1984 and 1985, and by 60 per cent from 1987 onwards.

At the same time, however, standards must be maintained. In other words, 'the translation must be professionally/objectively understandable', and the user must not suffer in any way.

In fact, the desired objectives could be summarised as follows:

- enhanced translation quality
- improved, more uniform, company style and more uniform presentation of documentation
- a dictionary should be created and kept up to date
- there should be less diversity of terminology

Let's have a look at the basic data we were working on: we assume that a page of translation amounts to 25 lines, and that a translator can produce 15 pages, or 375 lines, in a day. Over a year, assuming 204 working days, this represents a total of 76,500 lines. The costs are 1.12 DM per line, or 85,000.00 DM per year. The Technical Documentation Group as a whole can produce 10 pages a day of text input (i.e. ready for publication). Looked at in another way, if in 1984 we had to produce 225,000 lines of translation and the annual output per translator was 76,000, this meant that to achieve this output we needed 2.94 translators.

Table 2 compares the cost of expanding the translation service by increasing staff numbers (and assuming a translator actually achieves 75 per cent of target performance), with the adoption of a translation system (i.e. machine translation), provided either by a bureau service or by making use of a rented LOGOS system locally.

As far as as the potential quality of translation is concerned, it was estimated that Nixdorf could bring influence to bear if extra in-house translators were to be recruited, but not if the additional capacity took the form of freelances. The same applied to the processing of the texts. When machine translation systems were studied, it was found that translation provided by a service bureau could not be influenced in any way by Nixdorf, nor could anything be done about the text processing stage. If a LOGOS system were adopted, however, Nixdorf would be able to bring influence to bear both on the translation and the text processing stages.

Figure 2 shows the configuration adopted for the machine translation process.

Overhead estimate for 75% translator performance 57,375 lines				
	Capacity extension		translation system	
	Internal	External	Service	LOGOS (local)
Translation	85,000	103,275 (1.80 DM/line)	87,576 (Computer costs, Revision, Dictionary maintenance)	21,630.29 100,279.20 (RENT)
Editing		19,125 50 pages/day	19,125 50 pages/day	31,874.99 30 pages/day
Text processing	63,311	45,900 0.80 DM/line	45,900	15,861.11 (40 pages/day)
Total	148,311	168,300	152,601	169,645.59
Percentage	100%	113.47%	102%	114.38%

Table 2.

The plan was to apply the translation system to all types of document: simple, moderately difficult, and difficult, of ten pages or more.

There would be no so-called 'good deeds', e.g. translating 'Mein lieber Herr Gesangsverein' as 'My nice gentleman Gesangsverein' without a New Word Search (NWS). As regards the number of lines translated, there should be a very marked increase, with the number rising from 1,445 in February to 57,375 by the beginning of the following year. A

Table 3.

Creation time estimate for 75% translator performance 57,375 lines				
	Capacity extension		translation system	
	Internal	External	Service	LOGOS
Translation	153	153	No data 1)	76.5
Editing	0	45.9 2)	45.9	76.5 3)
Text processing	229.5	229.5	229.5	57.38
Total	382.5	428.4	313.65	210.38
Percentage	100%	112%	82%	55%

1. In benchmark (comparison) test: 32 days including postage. Assumed value for bureau service machine translation: LOGOS time × 0.5.
2. Editing service 50 pages/day.
3. Editing service 30 pages/day.

comparable increase was to be expected in the number of words entered in the dictionary, from 107 in February to 4,100 by the beginning of the following year.

Various considerations were taken into account when evaluating the quality of completed translations. In the first place the old adage 'garbage in – garbage out' (GIGO) holds good for translation just as much as for any other field. There is no getting away from the fact that a highly sophisticated text requires a much greater editing effort, whereas a clear, plain style makes it possible for a machine system to provide an almost perfect translation. Where a text is worded with a certain amount of nuance, the meaning which lies behind the words, and which would be readily apparent to a human translator, is completely missed by the machine, which can only translate literally.

In view of the foregoing, therefore, measures had to be taken to

Configuration:

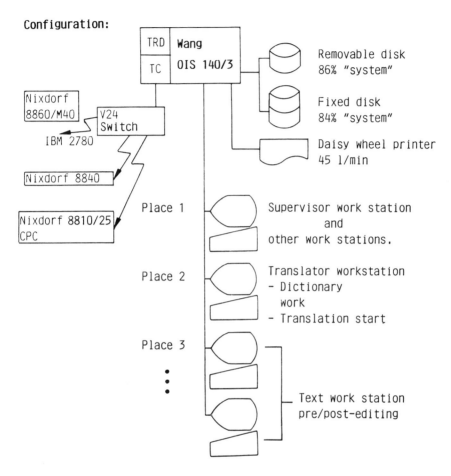

Figure 2. TRD: Translation Device (co-processor beside CPU O/S 140)

minimise the editing effort. There were two principal approaches, the first being to pre-edit the source texts, and the second to adopt standard paragraphs. As a result of this different approach to translation, there were a number of side effects: one was that texts were examined carefully for correctness of style in both German and English. As a result the text processing capacity rose by a factor of 2 to 3.5.

From the point of view of the manager, the machine translation system could be diagrammatically represented as shown in Figure 3. There the process of translation by the LOGOS system is regarded as merely one part of the editing procedure as a whole.

Use of the LOGOS translation system has resulted in optimum organisation of the Technical Documentation Group, a clear division of responsibilities, which had hitherto not been the case, and a high level of system availability. All these factors lead to enhanced efficiency and a high degree of economy.

Figure 4 indicates how the various stages in the text processing sequence are allocated. It can be seen that the human translator intervenes at only two stages.

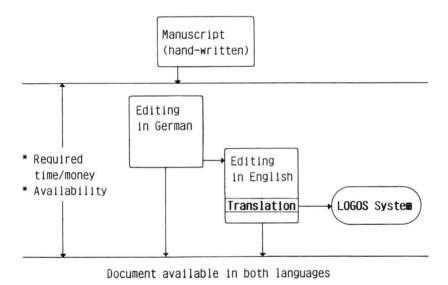

Figure 3. Diagrammatic representation of the machine translation system

('Editing in English' means in this case preparations for the translation, i.e. LOGOS-compatible format.)

Preparation and editing steps	Typist	Supervisor	Translator
		In charge Responsible	
1. Data communication from Nixdorf 8860⇔LOGOS		*	
2. Text preparation for conversion	*		
3. Conversion into LOGOS format	*		
4. NWS for orthography		*	
5. Preparations for translation	*	*	
6. NWS collection for translation		*	
7. Dictionary update for translation			*
8. Start of translation		*	
9. Formal check of the translation		*	
10. Post-editing			*
11. Preparing the printer's copy	*		
12. Data back-up		*	

Note

When a document has to be input manually, steps 1 to 3 are replaced by a LOGOS-compatible entry of the manuscript by the typist.

Figure 4. Allocation of the stages in the text processing sequence

Examples 1 and 2 set out in figures the time saved by the adoption of the new translation system.

Example 1:   May/June 1985

Editing of an application manual of about 400 pages in German and in English.

Preparation and editing steps	Required time in days	
	Previously	Today
Text entry (German)	40	20
Preparations for translation	1	2
Dictionary update	0	2
Translation	27	2 *1
Post-editing	0	14
Text entry (English)	40	0
Preparations for printing	2	5
	110	43
	100%	39,1%

Note
In both cases the manual costs DM 60.00 per copy.

*1   The translation was performed over a weekend.

Productivity has risen steadily – after the introduction of the LOGOS system, production in 1985 rose to 121 manuals, whereas in 1984 it had been 95 manuals.

In the opinion of Nixdorf Computer, the introduction of the LOGOS system was well supported by LOGOS, and their observance of deadlines was considered to be very good. Documentation was satisfactory, and training good. The support and co-operation provided by LOGOS were both felt to be very good.

As far as the LOGOS software was concerned, Nixdorf came to the following conclusions. The translation quality achieved, the operating

Example 2:   August 1985

For an important seminar, a manual of 85 pages had to be available in English for photocopying within 4 days. (The manual had been entered before in German.)

Preparation and editing steps	Required time in days		
	Previously		Today
	max.	min.*2	
Preparations for translation	0	0	1
Translation	6	3	(1)*1
Post-editing	0	0	1
Text entry	8,5	3,5	0
Preparations for printing	0,5	0,5	1
	15	7	3
	100%	46,7%	20%
		not possible	possible

Note
In both cases the manual costs DM 12,75 per copy.

*1 Editing steps were performed over night
*2 2 translators, 2 typists (parallel work)

---

environment, and user friendliness were all good. Training was felt to be very good, and throughput was also considered good.

Turning to the installed hardware and the stability of the equipment, the central processing unit was found by Nixdorf to be very good, and the magnetic disk good. The TRD, TC and screens were all very good, while the printer was no more than satisfactory.

The supervisor in the Technical Documentation Group, Mrs Emde, gave the following impressions. In the first place, her opinion of the system was good. The break-in period was short, and handling was simple. Text processing was particularly easy, with excellent menu support. She particularly liked the simultaneous operation in the case of TC sessions. Data backup and data set maintenance were very simple, and throughput was high. In fact, when asked if she had any criticisms, she said she would have to think hard, because none spontaneously occurred to her.

In the opinion of Nixdorf's staff translator Mr Plöger, the translation quality varied. Sometimes he felt it could be described as almost excellent, and yet in other parts considerable editing effort was required. He found it frustrating to have to edit a translation which was almost perfect apart from petty blemishes like incorrect plurals and 'of/by'. (For the German *von*, often 'of/by' is offered for selection, so that one always has to delete either 'of' or 'by', which is a bit tedious.) He would like to be able to have more time to spend on terminology, but overall his opinion of the LOGOS system was positive. He had some criticisms of it, of course, but found editing on screen extremely straightforward. He also thought that the text processing functions were excellent.

Comparing 1985 with 1986, in 1985 the hardware comprised an O/S 140/3, with four display workstations, and one daisy-wheel printer. In 1986, this was to be stepped up to a VS65, with eleven display workstations, a line printer and a daisy-wheel printer. The sole translator present in 1985 would in 1986 have one colleague working in-house, plus one external translator for post-editing on screen.

In 1986, *all* documents were to be entered in the LOGOS system and translated by it, with the aim of achieving higher production rates, earlier availability of documents, higher efficiency, and increased terminology standardisation.

AUTHOR
Wolfgang Heitmann, Nixdorf Computer AG, Furstenallee 7,
    D-4970 Paderborn, West Germany.

Session II:
Summary of discussion 1

In the chair: Brian McCluskey

The discussion session focused on four main areas.

(1)   Frederick Mostert (Merck Sharp & Dohme, Holland) was interested to learn whether existing optical character readers (OCRs) are able to read printed books (as opposed to typescripts). Julie Harnett (Editorial Consultancy & Services) replied that no system is absolutely 'spot-on' yet and that OCR performance with printed material is determined in large measure by the typefaces. However, the authorities looking into this problem are interested in the potential offered by the Kurzweil system. It was reported that one of the uses of the electronic tablet which comes with the Kurzweil system is for reading from books. The system has a selective auto-data entry and can recognise roman typefaces, among others.
   This claim was substantiated by a spokeswoman for a Stockholm dictionary company which has used the Kurzweil system to enter some 7 million characters in a variety of typefaces (including bold, italic and roman) with extremely good results.
   Veronica Lawson (Associate Editor *Computers & Translation*) added that the Kurzweil can actually read badly printed Russian books, but only with considerable help from editors and probably not for £40,000 (Julie Harnett's upper price limit for OCRs).

(2)   Replying to a question from Rebecca Ray (Automated Language Processing Systems) on the use of the Logos system, Mr Wolfgang Heitmann (Nixdorf Computer AG) reported that special Nixdorf software applications were employed in the technical documentation department to pre-edit the source text on the English and German sides.

Val Butterfield (Staefa Control System) wished to know whether Nixdorf gave preference to British or American English for computer terminology; how technical differences between countries were resolved; how Nixdorf trained their translators and whether these were of English mother tongue. Mr Heitmann replied that Nixdorf uses American English and that technical differences (e.g. voltage conversions) were simply dealt with at the editing stage. Nixdorf train their translators for one year.

Barbara Wilson (Foreign and Commonwealth Office) observed that it is the common experience of human translators that source text ambiguities only become apparent during the translation process. She therefore wondered whether Nixdorf might find it useful to have the translator present at the editing stage. Referring back to his presentation, Mr Heitmann emphasised that the Nixdorf procedure with the Logos system was for technical editors to revise the raw German version first. The translator then went to work and finally the edited English version was produced.

(3)   Dr Harold Somers (UMIST) asked whether the usefulness of the ALPS computer-assisted translation system at Lanchester Polytechnic in enhancing students' awareness of linguistic problems might not be adversely affected by subsequent improvements to the system. In other words, might it not be of greater instructional benefit if ALPS actually did not perform well?

Mr Patrick Corness (Lanchester Polytechnic) stressed the different uses to which the different levels of ALPS are put. In the Lanchester context, with its specific aims of enhancing students' awareness of translation problems, inter-language contrasts and choices available in the given context, the most useful level of ALPS was the automatic dictionary look-up (ADL) facility. The limitations of the system in actually translating a sentence suitably are probably of greater interest to the theoretical linguist.

Arguing that students would be better able to make judgements in their native language, Mr G. Pollhammer (Leeds Polytechnic) was surprised that the language direction chosen at Lanchester was *into* the foreign language. He felt that students would require considerable assistance from tutors in explaining linguistic differences and that speed of work would suffer as a result.

Patrick Corness explained that the into-English directions on ALPS were not yet available for use at Lanchester. While agreeing with the principle that translators should work into their mother tongue, he emphasised that ALPS was not being used at Lanchester with the prime purpose of training translators. The language-teaching potential of the into-German and into-French directions lies in asking students (under tutorial supervision) to construct a text in the foreign language using the help facilities available on ALPS. This represents an extension of established language-learning facilities on microcomputers. The procedure is not open-ended and ALPS will indicate if the student's solution is not in its repertory of acceptable answers. Patrick Corness concluded by reiterating that ALPS is used as a language-teaching tool rather than as a translating tool as such, and that a language-learning situation requires that students be able to work in both directions.

(4)   Rebecca Ray (ALPS) asked Professor Benoît Thouin to indicate briefly where he felt the greatest advances would take place in the areas of linguistic processing and of user interface for machine-aided translation systems.

Professor Thouin (University of Ottawa) spoke about the current situation in Canada in the hope that this might be representative of trends in other parts of the world. Organised and subsidised research into machine translation in Canada has been halted for a number of years now. The resultant rethinking process has led to a restructuring of the entire research industry. One of the key concepts to emerge has been 'integration' – integration of theories of translation and psycho-linguistics under the label of artificial intelligence and expert systems. The past year has witnessed the creation of totally new research centres (e.g. in computer science and in office automation), each of which has a division for natural language processing or machine translation. The trend is thus for linguistic processing to become integrated in other activities.

Moving on to the second part of the question, Professor Thouin indicated that researchers would dearly like to do away with trivial interfaces. The move instead is towards more general interaction between groups of experts in the fields of the texts for translation and the designers of the translating system. This will demand close co-operation between specialists in various information representation disciplines, e.g. lexicographers, terminologists and mathematicians.

RAPPORTEURS
David Beattie, Senior Translator, Medical Department, Hoechst UK Ltd, Hoechst House, Salisbury Road, Hounslow, Middlesex TW4 6JH, UK.
John Stowell, Medical Department, Boehringer Ingelheim Ltd, Southern Industrial Estate, Bracknell, Berkshire RG12 4YS, UK.

Machine translation as an integral part of the electronic office environment

Ian M. Pigott

Systran Project Leader, Commission of the European Communities, Luxembourg

INTRODUCTION

In 1981, Peter Walker of the EC Commission wrote a paper laying down the ground rules for an integrated machine translation operation, combining document preparation with telecommunications, translation, printing and distribution.

I am pleased to report that significant progress on all these aspects has been made, with the result that in 1985 machine translation is no longer looked upon as an isolated application but has, for the majority of users, become part and parcel of the general problem of multilingual document preparation and distribution.

PROGRESS AT THE COMMISSION

Perhaps more than any other organisation involved in multilingual communication, the Commission has come to recognise the vital role automation can play in speeding up the translation process.

In 1981, three Systran language pairs were available (English–French, French–English and English–Italian). Today, with the addition of English and French into German, there are five. Intensive development work is now being carried out on French and English into Dutch, which should reach production quality by the end of 1986. Finally, we have just started to develop systems from English into Spanish and Portuguese.

Over the next five years, with the expanded multilingual action plan, efforts will be made to cover all EC languages at one level or another. Work has yet to start on Danish and Greek at any level and we shall certainly see the integration of new source languages such as German.

What, you may ask, has happened in the past year to make us so confident about predictions for the future? On the one hand we have seen specific applications of the Systran system within the Commission which demonstrate very clearly its value in certain situations. In addition, we have seen increasing use made of our systems and others outside the Commission.

IN-HOUSE APPLICATIONS

One of the most successful trials conducted with Systran in recent years has been the provision of service to our energy department in Brussels.

Here, information documents such as reports and technical analyses of two to ten pages have been sent through telecommunications networks for Systran processing, post-editing and transmission back to the end-user. With these facilities it has been possible to reduce to a few hours what used to take up to a week using conventional methods.

I should make it quite clear at this point that machine translation has not been the only factor responsible for the significant time savings involved. The telecommunications links themselves have eliminated physical transmission of paper from one building to another which, at the Commission, can take a day or more in conventional document handling; in other words, the routing of even the shortest text from a requesting department to a translation department and back can often take three or four days. The incorporation of Systran into the production environment has clearly demonstrated that these delays can be reduced to minutes.

However, machine translation has also offered benefits of its own. At the Commission's energy department clear distinctions are made in the translation quality required for different types of document. Many written communications do not require a high standard of stylistic presentation but rather an accurate translation of the message of the author. Applying what we refer to as the 'rapid post-editing option' to machine translation, it has been possible for translators to turn out up to four or five pages per hour.

Not all translators like working under these conditions but for the end-user the service has proved to be a great asset. Indeed, with one exception, all the reactions received from end-users have been extremely positive, with the result that an official request has now been made for more extensive Systran services. Extensions are currently being made to the agriculture department (DG VI) and the Commission's Secretariat General.

Compatibility
Systran service at the Commission would indeed have progressed much

more rapidly if it had not been for the enormous problem of compatibility between different types of equipment. For the time being, only three types of word processor – Olivetti, Philips and Wang – have been officially accepted but many more types are actually used.

Data-processing experts will know only too well that the problem of compatibility is restricted to characters outside the English alphabet. The figures from 0 to 9 and basic punctuation pose no real problems but the accented letters for French, German and Italian do cause considerable trouble. The reason behind this is that while standards such as ASCII have been adhered to for years for the English alphabet, no similar standards have been implemented for multilingual communications.

Thus, while English language documents can be transmitted faultlessly from one type of equipment to another, an E acute on one machine may well produce a U umlaut on another owing to lack of standardisation in character representation.

It goes without saying that if machine translation (MT) is to be widely used in any organisation, then the text processing systems of any user should be able to serve as input and output devices for the MT system. We have therefore tried to solve the problem in two ways: the first, a rather pragmatic one, the second a more co-ordinated approach.

The pragmatic solution has been to create one-to-one character conversion tables between different devices. Here we have succeeded in copying Olivetti to Wang and Philips to Wang, with the result that any Olivetti or Philips user can submit his or her source document by telecommunications without any requirement for manual adaptation or retyping. In reverse, users are able to receive output which can be correctly copied onto their own device for any further processing which is required. While this approach has done much to extend availability of the system, it depends to some extent on hardwiring of workstations of the types in question, with the result that in many cases diskettes have to be transmitted to a central point where a hardwired communications configuration exists.

The more co-ordinated approach now under development depends more on the general networking of various kinds of equipment through one or more minicomputers which are able to act both as mailboxes and/or conversion tools. Initial results here have proved quite promising but full-scale tests have yet to be conducted.

In my opinion, problems with accented letters will however continue to cause problems in the MT environment until such time as widely acceptable telecommunications protocols such as teletex are universally implemented.

Finally, for dealing with the very worst situations – i.e. cases in which equipment cannot be or has not been rendered compatible or in which documents are submitted on paper rather than in machine readable form –

we have fallen back on optical character reading. Our experience here has been very positive. We have found that an experienced secretary can capture up to sixty pages of text per day using a combination of OCR and human editing. Before OCR, we could not expect more than twenty pages per day.

EXPERIENCE OUTSIDE THE COMMISSION

One of the most important developments in MT since around 1983 has been in the area of software development for personal computers. Now that there has been a proliferation of PC-compatibles, a software package designed for one PC will usually function faultlessly on a wide range of equipment.

The most successful MT supplier in this area has undoubtedly been Weidner, together with its Japanese parent organisation, Bravice International. Weidner packages for PCs using the MS-DOS operating system have been selling well both in the United States and Europe for European language combinations while up to 200 packages a month are being sold in Japan for the Japanese–English software.

While these systems have a number of shortcomings including dictionary size and sophisticated text format recognition, they are obviously well adapted to existing office equipment environments.

Other manufacturers such as ALPS and Smart have also moved forward in the microcomputer market, combining machine translation with increasingly sophisticated multilingual word processing. ALPS supplies hardware/software packages which not only provide a number of tools specifically developed as aids for the translator but serve as terminals for speeding up document preparation and communication in the multilingual office. Smart, by adapting its MS-DOS editing and machine-translation packages to run under Unix, hopes to increase marketing to Europe where it is as yet little used.

Finally, LOGOS, which for years was married to Wang, is now extending availability of its packages to other machines including IBM equipment and is hoping to strike into the microcomputer market in the near future.

These examples of combining software with office equipment clearly show the direction in which MT development is moving: packages are increasingly being adapted to run on desk-top equipment to serve translators and support staff at the office or even at home. Indeed, many translation agencies are now encouraging their staff to work at home on compatible equipment in order to speed up service for the client by making full use of communications and electronic document delivery.

BUREAU SERVICE

This brings us to another, all-important aspect of machine translation: bureau service. Until fairly recently, machine translation was available only to a limited number of large companies and organisations who were in a position to finance the on-going development of MT systems. Now, with drastic reductions in the cost of MT systems, a number of translation agencies have begun to offer MT facilities to their clients as a quicker, cheaper and more reliable way of handling the more routine types of translation processing.

1985 has seen yet another major step forward in this direction with the creation of Systran service bureaux in Europe. Systran's late arrival on the open market was due to problems of user rights coupled with the difficulty of running the package in the office environment. User rights have now been made available to bureaux serving the private sector and running problems have been overcome by combining telecommunications with local text processing facilities. In other words, while the package actually runs on a mainframe – which may be hundreds or even thousands of miles from the user – translators can receive a raw machine translation of documents up to fifty pages within fifteen to thirty minutes, most of this time being spent on electronic document transmission. They can then use sophisticated text processing equipment to automate much of the post-editing work.

As Systran translation quality is extremely high for the more mature language pairs, it is fair to assume that it will prove to be a serious competitor to microcomputer translation packages in the translation bureau environment.

Finally, Systran itself may well become available on office computers within the next two or three years if the proposed conversion of the package to Unix goes ahead. This option is being seriously considered by the Commission as a means to increase portability for distributed processing within its own translation services.

FRINGE BENEFITS

I have already discussed the benefits of machine translation in overcoming the general problem of document transmission. The very fact that input to and output from MT systems is in machine readable form means that texts can be communicated from office to office, from building to building and even from country to country.

Such transmission facilities would of course be available for handling requests for human translation too but, in our experience, machine translation has certainly acted as a catalyst in making translators aware of possibilities in this area.

Another advantage of having text in machine readable form is that with minor adaptations, post-edited texts can be transmitted directly to photo-composition equipment for high-quality printing. Indeed, with the sophisticated packages now on the market, it is extremely easy to merge graphics with text.

The Xerox Corporation and General Motors have implemented all these features to the full in connection with Systran and are now able to publish foreign language documentation on new products in parallel with the original English. Whereas it used to take them from six months to a year to produce foreign language versions of maintenance manuals, these companies are now able to increase turnover by introducing products on foreign markets immediately. This approach also makes for sizeable economies as far as clerical work is concerned.

Recently a number of other companies such as Nixdorf and Hewlett-Packard have begun to use the LOGOS system in the same way, while the Smart Corporation in New York runs an integrated bureau service for translating and printing technical maintenance manuals for a wide range of companies. More often than not, Smart's clients are quite unaware of how their documentation has been produced. All they are interested in is time and money, and as it appears to be both quicker and cheaper to use the automated approach, the business is expanding rapidly.

FUTURE DEVELOPMENTS

Development of MT systems is proceeding on two fronts. Some manufacturers are concentrating their efforts on providing ever more user-friendly features in their software packages while leaving much of the quality improvement work to the end-user. By combining simple dictionary-making features with small but fairly reliable basic systems, this strategy seems to be working well for many applications.

The alternative strategy, which has been adopted by developers of larger packages such as Spanam, Metals and Systran, has been to centralise development for the benefit of all users. In regard to Systran, the Commission has always insisted that development work undertaken by or for one user should become immediately available to all the other users. As a result, the rapidly expanding dictionaries now offer many well-documented subject sectors, from aerospace to nuclear physics or from agriculture to informatics, in one and the same system which can be used by all without the need for subject sector parameters.

Of these two strategies, the former might prove more successful from the sales point of view, simply because the potential for selling software packages on diskettes or cartridges is enormous and production costs are low. However, from the point of view of quality, which after all is what the translator wants to see, the second – the fully co-ordinated approach – will no doubt continue to produce the best results.

As for completely new developments, we are likely to see significant progress in the six or seven systems now being developed in Japan for translating into and out of Japanese. In my opinion, these could also be extended to cover combinations of the principal European languages in the next few years and may well become serious competitors for American and European developments.

For the time being, it is still difficult to predict whether any of the three major European developments will in fact produce quality levels significantly better than those of current systems. All have got off to a fairly slow start and all are proving quite difficult to manage.

On the wider front, the advent of automatic dictation and related voice analysis systems is likely to have a major effect on translators' working methods over the medium term. These systems are developing quickly and it may well be that within five or ten years, translators will be able to 'dictate' their post-editing corrections to the computer rather than having to work on a keyboard.

Looking even further ahead, automatic dictation techniques coupled with MT systems may produce computerised, simultaneous interpreting systems by the end of the century.

But to return to the Commission itself, now that machine translation has been recognised as a viable alternative to more traditional methods, I am sure that we will see considerable changes in the working methods of translators as problems of compatibility are overcome and suitable equipment is widely installed. The new five-year multilingual action plan provides for the development and implementation of new language pairs within the translation services, while parallel plans have been accepted for other computerised projects combining the use of machine translation with access to terminology banks, databases and document retrieval and transmission services.

CONCLUSION

Machine translation is now becoming an essential component of the multilingual electronic office as equipment is introduced to combine word processing with document transmission and sophisticated printing facilities.

More generalised access to machine translation will result from the increasing availability of bureau service facilities.

Availability of machine translation services will also encourage users to choose between various levels of translation quality depending on whether they require speed and basic accuracy or high standards of stylistic perfection.

Over the medium term, enhancements to existing systems and new developments from Japan are likely to represent the major impetus in the area of machine translation. The future of the various European projects still remains uncertain.

The Commission itself is now committed to the extension of the Systran system to additional language pairs over the next five years as part of its general modernisation of the translation services.

FURTHER READING

CAMPANELLA, D. Chi ha paura della traduzione automatica? *Bulletin Terminologie de la Commission des Communautés Européennes*, (45), 1984.

DETEMPLE, A. La T.A.O. au CDST. *Revue de presse et d'information CNRS/CDST*, (5), March–April 1983, reprinted *Multilingua*, 2–4, 1983.

HEARD, J. Machines are mastering the language of multinational business. *Business Week*, 9 September 1985.

LOFFLER-LAURIAN, A-M. Pour une typologie des erreurs dans la traduction automatique. *Multilingua*, 2–2, 1983.

NAGAO, M. La traduction automatique. *La Recherche*, no. 150, December 1983.

PIGOTT, I. Electronic translation grows cheaper and better. *Intermedia*, July/September 1984, 12, (4/5).

ROUVRAY, D., and WILKINSON, G. Machines break the language barrier. *New Scientist*, 22 March 1984.

STRAUSS, S. Teaching computers to translate languages. *Toronto Globe and Mail*, 18 March 1983.

VAN DER ELST, N. Traducteur et ordinateur. *Entreprise et formation permanente*, no. 102, Spring 1983.

WHEELER, P. Changes and improvements to the European Commission's Systran MT system 1976/84. Paper presented to the Cranfield conference on machine translation, February 1984.

WILKINSON, J. The language machine. *British Airways Highlife*, October 1985.

AUTHOR

Ian M. Pigott, Systran Project Leader, Commission of the European Communities, Bâtiment Jean Monnet B4/24, BP 1907 Luxembourg.

Machine translation: Japanese perspectives

Toyoaki Nishida and Shuji Doshita

Department of Information Science, Kyoto University, Kyoto, Japan

This paper overviews Japan's approach to machine translation (MT). It gives a survey of technical developments in machine translation, as well as a few case studies of experience with early products. It especially points out that most of the current MT systems are rather general purpose. This partly reflects the fact that Japan has few existing mass-production lines for technical translation into which computers may be incorporated. Instead, our approach is to design the entire environment in which humans and computers can co-operate using the state-of-the-art technologies.

(1) INTRODUCTION

It has been a common recognition among MT researchers in Japan that deep analysis is needed to achieve a realistic machine translation system between the Japanese and European languages, since these languages differ from each other both in linguistic and conceptual structures. As a result, Japanese researchers have long been working on basic problems.

Recently, however, as social demand for machine translation has increased and technology for natural language processing in general has made some progress, intensive efforts have been made to produce commercially available products for machine translation. Since 1984, major computer industries started to announce the release of their first commercial products.

This paper is intended to overview machine translation activities in Japan, both from the technical and practical viewpoints. It is organised as follows: Section 2 gives a brief introduction to the Japanese language. Those issues which are thought as relevant to machine translation are listed and difficult issues are distinguished. Section 3 attempts to present some common features of activities in research and development in Japan. Section 4 overviews the technical aspects behind state-of-the-art products. Various techniques for overcoming difficulties in language translation between completely different language families are summarised. Section 5 provides some case studies on the experiences with early products and Section 6 presents a number of new research programmes directed towards more advanced machine translation.

(2) BRIEF INTRODUCTION TO THE JAPANESE LANGUAGE

The Japanese language differs from Western languages both in linguistic and conceptual structure. Some prominent aspects of the Japanese language are listed below, from the easiest to the most difficult.

1. Large character set. The character set for Japanese can be divided into Kana, Kata-Kana and Kanji characters. JIS (Japanese Industrial Standards) specifies standard 16-bit code for these characters. The first level contains about 3,000 characters and the second level 3,400 more. This aspect is not a problem at all, as most Japanese computer products involving microcomputers support Japanese I/O (input/output) as well as fancy graphics. See [ICTP 83] for technical aspects.

2. No delimiters between adjacent words (but punctuation does occur between sentences and optionally between long phrases). Though we have breath-group notation, we are not generally familiar with it. Thus, word boundary is not a stable notion among ordinary Japanese people.

This aspect is problematic for machine translation as more than one segmentation is usually possible for a given sentence and this squares the complexity of analysis. However, Japanese computer industries succeeded in handling this problem by taking an engineering approach. Therefore, this delimiter-free problem is thought of as a relatively minor one to the current machine translation researchers.

3. Word order roughly corresponds to postfix notation or 'reverse Polish notation'. (Prefix notation is sometimes called 'Polish notation' because it was introduced by a Polish logician. Postfix notation is called 'reverse Polish notation' to emphasise the fact that it came from the same principle as prefix notation.) Thus, if the meaning of a sentence is represented as a case structure tree as in Figure 1(a), the word order in Japanese may be obtained by traversing it in postorder. Mood, tense, and aspects are indicated by left-embedding.

This is not a serious problem for the current technology, because we can use efficient algorithms for parsing sentences. It raises a problem only

(a) Case structure tree which means "I read the book which he gave (me)."

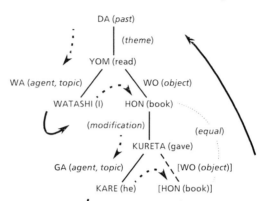

(b) Rules for traversing a case structure tree

    (a) start from the top node.
    (b) go along the tree until any terminal node is reached.
    (c) during going downward, neglect words.
    (d) when you arrive at a terminal node, read it, and go upward.
    (e) during going upward, read words.
    (f) when you come to any node with any branch you have not yet traversed, traverse them in turn, and then go back to the upper node.
    (g) finish traversing when you return to the top.

(c) Result: Japanese sentence for (a)

    WATASHI WA KARE GA KURETA HON WO YOM DA.

Figure 1. Case Structure Tree and Word Order in Japanese: Example.

when the concrete syntactic analysis fails for the input sentence, for we cannot use the word order of the input sentence as a default.

4. Surface case labels are explicitly attached to case elements as post positions (called *joshi*'s) to make word order flexible.

Freedom in word order makes typical phrase structure analysis awkward, but this specific aspect can be handled by semantic processing. The real difficulty arises when we try to obtain a deep case relation from a surface case structure. This is common to Western languages in that one surface label usually represents more than one deep case label.

5. Word ending inflects. This brings about no essential problem except that it slightly complicates the analysis and synthesis of Japanese sentences, for inflections are completely rule-based. All that is needed is inflection tables and dictionary entries which indicate inflection type.

6. Ellipsis is allowed as far as information is recoverable from the context. In general, short, concise, and insightful sentences are preferred in Japan

to rather long, detailed, logical sentences. This allows writers to eliminate as many words/phrases as possible.

This phenomenon is a real problem to computers. In order to recover eliminated words and phrases, a large chunk of common-sense knowledge is needed for the subject field. If this is not available, the machine translation program must be able to use a number of heuristic para-phrasing techniques to generate target language expressions without refer-ring to unrecoverable information.

7. Conceptual differences. It is often impossible to find a corresponding word or phrase when we translate sentences between Japanese and West-ern languages. Some features are given below with examples.

(a) Word level. It is sometimes hard to find a single word in the target language which can cover the entire meaning of a given source lan-guage word. For example, there seems no single adequate Japanese word for 'take', 'integrate' nor any two words distinguishing 'ambiguity' and 'vagueness'.

(b) Phrase level. For example, the Japanese language does not allow prenominal negation. Therefore a phrase like 'few researchers are working on this issue' should be paraphrased as: 'the number of researchers working on this issue is very small'.

There are a number of ways to translate an indefinite determiner in English into Japanese. However, the corresponding adjectives are not neutral; they may represent additional incorrect information:

" KARE WA INU TO SAMPO SHITEITA"
he <subj> (a) dog with walking was ; he was walking with a dog

⇒ indefinite determiner for "INU" is not indicated; neutral.

"... IPPIKI-NO INU TO..."
one dog with

⇒ the speaker seems to stress the number of dog is one; not two or more.

"... ARU INU TO..."
certain dog with

⇒ the dog seems to be extraordinary; the speaker may start a story about the dog.

(c) Sentence level. Japanese does not allow a non-animate subject. For example, 'the wind opened the door' should be paraphrased as, 'the door opened due to the wind'.

The way of capturing events also differs between Japanese and European languages. The meaning conveyed by the English sentence, 'he touched me on the shoulder' must be expressed in Japanese something like, 'he', 'touched', '*my*', 'shoulder' (direct, phrase-by-phrase translation from Japanese).

(d) Discourse level. Japanese generally like stories to proceed from the concrete to the abstract. Hence, strictly speaking, sentence-to-sentence translation is not a good translation.

(e) Social level. The Japanese language has honoratory expressions. To generate them, social relationships between the speaker, the hearer, or the referent should be taken into account. This issue, though hard, is important in the business field; if the honoratory expression is not generated adequately, the result would be completely unacceptable.

Nitta [85] discusses these issues from somewhat different viewpoints.

(3) CHARACTERISTICS OF JAPANESE RESEARCH AND DEVELOPMENT IN MACHINE TRANSLATION

It is now evident that the translation between Japanese and European languages cannot be achieved by any simple method. Before going into some details, we will attempt to extract some common features in research and development in Japan.

Historical notes [Nagao 82a,85a] {Tamati 85}

From the early days, the so-called first generation method [Hutchins 78], by direct, word-by-word replacement, was thought inadequate for translation between Japanese and European languages. From the beginning, researchers in Japan aimed at building systems by second or third generation methods [Tamati 63], {Yamada 64}, {Wada 65}, [Sakai 66,69], [Sugita 68], {Kurihara 73}, {Shudo 73,77}, [Uchida 80], [Nagao 80b], {Miyazaki 83}, {Ikeda 84}, [Yoshida 84], [Muraki 85].

The 1960s and 1970s were mostly spent on basic research. Hardware and software for Japanese input and output were investigated on the practical side. At the same time, adequate computational theory for MT was sought by building and scrapping small prototypes on the basic research side.

The years around 1980 were a turning point for the following reasons:

– the progress in basic research in natural language processing
– significant improvement of cost performance in computer facilities
– the success of Japanese language word processors.

From the practical point of view, the last issue is significant, because the success of the Japanese language word processors implies success in Kana-Kanji conversion, which indeed is an artificial intelligence (AI) problem in the sense that no complete solution is expected unless the machine can understand the input completely. (See the word processor section of [ICTP 83] for technical details.) The developers of the Japanese language word processors solved this problem by an engineering method.

In 1982, Japan's Agency of Science and Technology, a minor organisation of Japan's Ministry of International Trade and Industry (MITI), launched a three-year project (later extended to a four-year project) {Nagao 83d, 85c}[Tsujii 85], called the Mu project, to develop a practical system by integrating the state-of-the-art technologies. Around this time, some of the major computer industries had finished the initial developmental stage and started evaluation through internal use. Central Research Institute for Electrical Power Industries (CRIEPI) started to evaluate ATLAS-1, Fujitsu's early product for English–Japanese translation {Terano 85}. In the Fifth Generation project, machine translation was one of the early subjects and basic research focused on dictionaries and conceptual analysis of translators' knowledge and skills {Tanaka 84}. Major research projects and investigators are listed in the appendix.

Japanese perspectives
As a whole, the Japanese approach differs from that of Western countries in several respects:

1. The language pair demanded for translation is starwise: one to many. The investigation by the Japanese Electronic Industrial Development Association (JEIDA) revealed that Japanese language is almost always included at one end of desired language pairs. As to its partner, demand for English is most significant, followed by French, Chinese, and Spanish {JEIDA 82,83,84}. This is contrasted with the European Community, (EC) where all pairs between seven and nine languages are required.

2. Unlike the EC, we have had few industry-like mass-production lines for translation. This means that we do not have a mother system into which computers may be incorporated. This is the major reason why Japanese industries have not started building machine aids for human translators.

3. Therefore, the situation is quite product-driven. Potential requirements have not been explicit until the users have seen actual products. Since the demands for machine translation were rather widespread and vague, the computer industries had to develop a rather general-purpose, powerful translation engine for it to be usable in unexpected environments.

Thus, it is evident that we have to wait a few more years to adapt these systems to individual environments. But it is anticipated that a number of new environments which are suitable for state-of-the-art machine translation systems will be invented, quite like Japanese word processors, in the near future.

(4) TECHNOLOGIES FOR MACHINE TRANSLATION – SURVEY
The target of the current research and development in Japan can be characterised as a full implementation of so-called second generation machine translation systems featuring:

– the separation of linguistic data from the program
– the use of intermediate representation
– the use of semantic information.

No current machine translation product can be categorised as an interlingua system; no interlingua is defined which is completely independent of any specific language in its vocabulary, syntax, semantics and concepts. Therefore, all of these systems have somehow to transform a source-language-oriented representation into a target-language-oriented one. Thus, they are transfer systems. They differ in the level at which the transfer is performed. In the remainder of this section, we will review technical aspects from this viewpoint.

Morphological analysis
The morphological analysis of English is mainly devoted to the detection of word stems and the recognition of compound words consisting of relatively few words. It is fairly safe to separate the morphological analysis phase from the syntactic analysis phase. However, this is not so for the Japanese language, as the delimiter-free problem cannot be handled independently from syntactic and semantic analysis. No method developed so far can perfectly separate the unsegmented Japanese input into a word sequence. Hence, if the Japanese analyser is organised in tandem, from morphological analysis to syntactic analysis, then the accuracy of the whole system is bound by that of the morphological analyser. On the other hand, if the morphological analysis and syntactic analysis are done simultaneously in a uniform manner, then the complexity of the analysis will increase tremendously beyond manageable limits.

The approach taken by the Mu project was, like other methods, to incorporate local syntactic analysis into the morphological analyser to increase accuracy. They used a table-driven method to store word-continuation information. They also used some heuristics to cope with failures that may occur in the 'left-to-right dictionary-look-up and cut-a-word' method. If there still is ambiguity, parallel results are passed to the subsequent phase {Sakamoto 83}.

Syntactic and semantic analysis
The general problem here is how to resolve ambiguities that arise from a purely syntactic analysis. The usual method is to introduce selective restriction or preference. The most common approach to this problem is to use syntactic and semantic markers (or equivalently, features). Another approach is taken by the KDD group, who defined the notions of forbidden trees, recommended trees and exclusive trees to capture the semantic constraints rather as exceptional cases to pure syntactic analysis. They proposed a method of managing the (probably very large) set of these trees so that those trees are stored and retrieved efficiently {Sakaki 82,83,84}.

In ATLAS-II, a Fujitsu product, the notion of a world model is used to handle structural transformation at the conceptual level [Uchida 85]. Logically speaking, this approach seems to be essentially the same as the semantic marker method. However, from the engineering point of view, it is good for avoiding complexity, because the knowledge for structural transformation is separated from the main processing flow as an independent module and is managed by an ordinary database management system.

What should be realised in building a practical system, however, is that ambiguities may still remain unresolved or equally preferred, as it is almost impossible to incorporate into computers all semantic and common-sense knowledge for a full account of ambiguities. This aspect should be handled either by interactive or heuristic methods.

The Hitachi group uses shallow trees to allow certain ambiguities to remain unresolved [Nitta 82,84]. The shallow tree will be modified when further information is available from the semantic analysis. The English–Japanese version of their system, called ATHENE/E, does not use a chronological backtracking regime to recover from misdirected analysis; they do this instead by rewriting the structure when failure occurs {Okajima 85}. The Toshiba group similarly incorporates syntactic preference to cope with such cases [Amano 85].

The Mu project accumulates cues from multiple levels into a single structure called an Annotated Tree Structure (ATS) [Tsujii 84]. This makes it easy to give preference by considering the combination of cues at various levels. Nagao {83a} reported in detail their attempts at analysing conjunctive noun phrases.

Yiming Yang, a graduate student at the authors' group, takes a similar but more specific approach to give preferential interpretations to Chinese sentences [Yang 84,85a,b].

Transfer phase

It is generally believed that there are basically two types of approach to the transfer phase. One type is to use rather shallow structures, such as phrase structures augumented by features. The advantage of this approach is that many cues, such as information about surface subject or word order, are preserved which might not be able to be conveyed adequately by deeper representation. It is obvious, though, this approach suffers from a complication of the transfer phase. Accordingly, the other type is to use deeper, conceptual representation as an intermediate representation.

However, it seems that there is no substantial difference between the two. It is somewhat a matter of preference and trade-off. Almost any transformation that can be done by the deeper method can be simulated by the shallower method. This observation has led to a third approach in which physical structure does not play any essential role; a rather neutral structure is used as a physical structure and the structural information is virtually conveyed by annotations.

1. **Using shallow structure as an intermediate representation**   The IBM Japan group takes this approach to translate computer manuals {Tsutsumi 82}. The background of this approach is their observation that the use of syntactic structures does not seem to complicate the structural transformations required in this field as much as had been thought, because the sentence types in computer manuals are, and should be, rather restricted.

2. **Using deep structure as an intermediate representation**   The basic method is to determine the target language expression by examining the case structure and semantic markers [Ishihara 74a,b][Nishida(F) 80,82]. In spite of the use of deep, conceptual structures, this approach still requires an enormous amount of structural transformation due to conceptual differences between languages. Since translation at the conceptual level does not seem to be governed by a small number of universal rules, lots of word-specific rules should be prepared as lexical knowledge for conceptual transformation. Tanaka's active dictionary {Tanaka 85} and the NTT group's frame system {Nomura 82}[Iida 84]{Iida 85}{Shimazu 85} are attempts to allow sophisticated word-specific rules in each lexical entry that requires complex conceptual transformation. This approach needs to be supported by user-friendly, highly sophisticated software to develop and maintain dictionary entries. However, this has hardly been addressed.

3. **Using physically neutral structure**   The Mu project uses physically rather neutral structures in which syntactic, semantic and contextual

information are virtually embedded by means of annotation. This allows both surface and deep information to be accessed rather uniformly. Accordingly, it has advantages of both deep structure approach and shallow structure approach. Additionally, this ensures that translation at a deep level gracefully degrades to that at syntactic or default level, when analysis at a deep level fails.

To decrease the complexity in the structural transformation, the Mu project's system has two more subphases for the transfer phase: the pre- and post-transfer loops [Nagao 84a]. At the pre-transfer loop, source-language-oriented conceptual structures are paraphrased into more neutral ones. At the post-transfer loop, an attempt is made to paraphrase target-language theoretically independent structures into target-language-oriented expressions. These substages are expected to be useful when the system is extended to multilingual translation.

Generation phase

On the one hand, if shallow information of the source language is preserved in the transfer stage, then it is somewhat easy to generate target language expressions, in the sense that the discourse structure of the source language is preserved in the transfer phase and serves as a default discourse structure which may not completely fit in the target language, but which might be much better than nothing. On the other hand, if only a conceptual structure is passed to the target language, the discourse structure should be generated to make the translation understandable. This, however, has not been fully investigated yet and is left for the future. Therefore, current machine translation systems somehow preserve surface information and transfer it to the target language.

The Mu project divided the transfer phase into two: core syntax generation and style generation [Nagao 84a]. The core syntax generation subphase generates phrase structure from annotated tree structure. It in particular generates lexical or morphological entries for tense, mood or aspect from the underlying information in annotations. The style generation subphase adjusts styles. A long infinitive subject, for instance, will be replaced by an 'it-that' construct.

Morphological synthesis

There is no additional complexity in generating Japanese sentences for current computers.

Dictionary problems

The quality of a machine translation system depends heavily on the quality of dictionaries. The dictionary-related problems are divided into two issues: lexical acquisition and dictionary maintenance.

1. **Lexical acquisition** Work has been done on the construction of dictionary databases. Early work by Professor Nagao was related to the automatic construction of dictionary databases from ordinary dictionaries, Longman's for instance [Nagao 80a]. Now some terminology databases easily interfaceable to microcomputers have become available. Other researchers have been working on automatic collection of technical terms from existing document files. But there still remains much to be done before these can be used for machine translation.

Therefore, dictionaries have to be constructed by hand coding. Problems arise as to how to manage quality and coherence. The Mu project designed special forms for each part of speech and detailed manuals to fill them out [Sakamoto 84]. However, they were still faced with errors and incoherencies.

2. **Dictionary maintenance** It is a hard problem to maintain a large number of dictionary entries and to tune them up for a given situation. This issue has hardly been worked out.

Human–machine environment
Sophisticated interactive tools are needed to make the machine translation system effective in an integrated human–machine environment. There have been relatively few studies in this area, too. The Mitsubishi group has done some preliminary work on an interactive machine translation system {Fukushima 84, Arita 83}. Masaru Tomita at Carnegie-Mellon University developed an interactive front end for disambiguation which only requires the user to have knowledge of the source language [Tomota 85]. Tomita implemented a number of versions, including the one for the authors' system {Tomita 84}. Okajima *et al.* at Hitachi discussed a linguistically motivated editor for post-editing {Okajima 83}. The editor for pre-editing is discussed rather in the context of controlled languages than in a general context.

Software environment
Most computer companies in Japan preferred efficient implementation, sometimes using very low level programming languages such as C or a macro assembler. This would work when the goal is rather restricted and high performance is desired. However, it is hard to extend such systems. The NTT group, the Mu project, and the Hitachi group each take an approach using a high level grammar description language to achieve high quality translation. The NTT group uses a frame language to write semantically-oriented sophisticated rules for translation {Kogure 84}. The Mu project developed GRADE, a high level tree manipulation language [Nakamura 84]. Grammatical rules as well as lexical rules for analysis,

transfer and generation have beeen coded in GRADE. The Hitachi group has started to use a similar language {Kaji 85}.

Evaluation method

The Mu project designed a qualitative evaluation method to measure accuracy and understandability {Nagao 85a}. This method was also applied to evaluate ATLAS-1[Sawai 82] at CRIEPI. However, no quantitative method for evaluation has yet been proposed in Japan.

(5) MACHINE TRANSLATION SYSTEMS AT A PRACTICAL LEVEL

Titran

This system can be thought of as the first system that reached the practical level. This system, developed by Prof. Nagao's group, was designed to translate titles of scientific and technical literature. There were three versions. The earliest system was for English–Japanese[Nagao 82b]. Two other versions were developed for Japanese–English and Japanese–French. The English–Japanese version {Nagao 83c} was tested against some 3,000 titles and the accuracy rate was 80 per cent on average. This version was originally implemented at Kyoto University and later it was transported to RIPS (Tsukuba Research Information Processing System) of Japan's Agency of Industrial Science and Technology, where extensive evaluation was carried out. The Japanese–English version was tested against more than 6,000 titles and a 90 per cent accuracy rate was achieved. For the Japanese–French version, no extensive evaluation was carried out [Hubert 83]. Through these evaluations, it was experimentally proved that a relatively small set of patterns is sufficient for translating titles.

Commercial systems

Current systems, available from major computer companies in Japan, are not restricted to simple phrases like titles. They are summarised in Table 1.

Published experiences with early commercial products

Some published experiences with commercial systems are summarised below.

   1.   **Fujitsu–CRIEPI**   CRIEPI (Central Research Institute for Electrical Power Industries) introduced ATLAS-I in 1982 {Terano 85}. They wanted to use the system to provide a database service in which abstracts

Table 1. Commercial Machine Translation Systems in Japan

Industry	Name of the Product	Source Language	Target Language	Time Available
FUJITSU	ATLAS I	English	Japanese	9-1984
	ATLAS II	Japanese	English	7-1985
NEC	PIVOT	Japanese	English	(12-1985)
		English	Japanese	(9-1986)
TOSHIBA	TAURUS	English	Japanese	(12-1985)
SHARP	?	English	Japanese	(?-1985)
BRAVIS	MediumPack	Japanese	English	6-1984
	MicroPack	Japanese	English	8-1985

of English literature are made available in Japanese. Terano used the evaluation method of the Mu project to evaluate the results {Nagao 85b}. Though the results were only partially published, it seems that they think ATLAS-I usable for their service. Terano's plan for the future is to build an environment for a full, automatic translation facility for abstracts. The human beings are supposed to be involved only in offline dictionary updates.

2. **Fujitsu–Fellow Academy** Fellow Academy is a school which teaches students translation skills. They introduced ATLAS-I in 1984 and started an evaluation. Seminars for advanced students are held to let them have practical experience with state-of-the-art technology. Their short-term goal is to evaluate the limitation of current machine translation systems from the translator's point of view {Oka, personal communication}.

3. **Systran–Technical Service** Technical Service introduced Systran and formulated a computer network for translation services {Yamaguchi 85}. This was intended to cope with the overwhelming amount of raw translation coming out from a machine translation system. Through the computer network, drafts (raw outputs from the computer) are sent immediately to translators at workstations to be returned to the chief editor after post-editing. Some early results, if urgently required, will also be sent to customers through the computer network.

Many other joint projects between computer companies and translating companies have started recently. Some interesting results are anticipated as they can design the entire environment by taking advantage of the state-of-the-art technology.

(6) RESEARCH PROGRAMMES TOWARDS NEW GENERATION MACHINE TRANSLATION
At the research level, different groups are taking different approaches.

Machine translation by formal semantics
Viewed as a software system, a machine translation system should be among the most complex. The difficulty with designing a machine translation system is to achieve the following two rather contradicting demands at the same time:

– the system should be powerful enough to cope with various linguistic phenomena
– the system should be understandable enough to make it easy to maintain and improve.

The authors' group proposed to solve this by combining functional programming and object-oriented programming methodology [Nishida(T) 82, 83a, 83b, 84]. Each lexical entry is implemented as an object in an object-oriented language. Each object can interact with others by sending and receiving messages. Like Tanaka's active dictionary {Tanaka 85}, each lexical entry is active, in the sense that it is not simply a linguistic datum to interpret but it can embody procedures to manipulate linguistic structures with which it has semantic relations. This makes it possible to write arbitrarily detailed, word-specific rules for exceptional words or for those which have wide usage and which require complex judgement to assign adequate expression in the target language. Functional programming principles are used to prevent grammar writers from writing *ad hoc* rules. Formal semantics proposed by Montague serve as a theoretical basis of this research. The notion of semantic type introduced by Montague semantics gives a rigid protocol for interactions among word-specific rules. A prototype was implemented and was tested against scientific and technical literature.

Translation by analogy
This approach is motivated by the observation that (a) it is a painstaking task to construct a precise and detailed dictionary for machine translation, (b) success in detailed syntactic analysis does not ensure the quality of the translation, and (c) human beings are guided by examples. A method proposed by Prof. Nagao [Nagao 81] is based on breath group analysis, use of ordinary dictionaries, examples involved in them, and thesaurus look-up.

Use of a controlled language

Full automatic, high-quality translation – a dream – is strongly desired in some fields where rapid translation is desired in spite of an overwhelming amount of information flow. Use of controlled language seems to be a practical approach for the current development of technology. As it is hard for untrained humans to write a text in any controlled language, the development of dedicated word processors is necessary. Approach in this direction was taken by Prof. Yoshida at Kyushu University {Yoshida 83}, Prof. Nagao at Kyoto University, and Fujitsu. Prof. Nagao proposed MAL (Machine Acceptable Language) and special purpose word processor for MAL {Nagao 83b, 84b}. The design principles behind MAL involve the domain independence and readability for humans. What MAL controls is the use of punctuation. When the word processor detects syntactic ambiguity, it will ask the user which modification is intended. A number of Nagao's papers are actually written in MAL. However, it has not yet been proven how MAL is effective in machine translation. Fujitsu is attempting to design another controlled language for Japanese to achieve industrialised translation {Hayashi, paper presented at the International Symposium on Machine Translation, 14 October 1985, Tokyo, Japan}.

More basic issues related to machine translation are investigated in the natural language processing field by many groups. This field, natural language understanding in particular, has become very active in Japan. Most reports from these groups, though they are in Japanese, can be found in Transactions of the Information Processing Society Japan (IPSJ), WG Preprints from the Working Group on Natural Language Processing of IPSJ, and convention records of the IPSJ. Some can be found from proceedings of IJCAI or COLING (International Conference on Computational Linguistics). It is strongly anticipated that basic results in natural language understanding (story understanding and generation techniques; see for example Schank [77]) will contribute to third generation machine translation.

SUMMARY

Japan has recently begun to see the first products in machine translation. More products will appear soon. A number of contrasts can be found in these products. Some were developed by domestic companies and others are modified versions of commercial products which were already available for languages other than Japanese. Some use large time-sharing computers and others networked personal computers. Some take a general approach and others a rather domain-specific approach. Some aim at HAMT (human-assisted machine translation), in which computers take initiative, asking human beings for help when they come into difficulty; others aim at MAHT (machine-assisted human translation) which is a human-centred organisation. Thus, there are many perspectives currently competing with each other in Japan.

ACKNOWLEDGEMENTS

The authors would like to thank Prof. Jun'ichi Tsujii, Prof. Jun'ichi Nakamura, Dr John Bateman, Mr Oka, Mr Hiroshi Kushima, and Mr Takao Terano for useful and informative discussions.

REFERENCES
Note: [] refers to those written in English; {} to those in Japanese.

[Amano 85] Amano, S., Toshiba Machine Translation System, *Proc. International Symposium on Machine Translation*, 45-48, 1985.

{Arita 83} Arita, H. and Fukushima, M., Another Approach to a Machine Translation System from Japanese to English, *WG Preprints*, WGNL 48-7, IPSJ, 1983, (in Japanese).

{Fukushima 84} Fukushima, M. and Arita, E., WGNL 41-5, 1984, (in Japanese).

[Hubert 83] Hubert, J., Ibuki, J., Kume, M. and Nagao, M., A System of Japanese-French Automatic Translation for Paper Titles, *Records of Convention of IPSJ*, 1983.

[Hutchins 78] Hutchins, W. J., Progress in Documentation, *J. Documentation*, Vol. 34, No. 2, 1978.

[ICTP 83] *Proceedings of ICTP'83*, CLCS-IPSJ, Tokyo, Japan, 1983.

[Iida 84] Iida *et al.*, A Case Analysis Method Cooperating with ATNG and its Application to Machine Translation, *Proc. COLING-84*, 1984.

{Iida 85} Iida, H., Ogura, K. and Nomura, H., On Semantic Relations in English Complex Nominals and Handling These Relations by Computer, *WG Preprint*, IPSJ, 1985, (in Japanese).

{Ikeda 84} Ikeda, N., Machine Translation by Phrasal Rule Convertion Method, Proc. *Symposium on Natural Language Processing Technology*, IPSJ, 107-114, 1984, (in Japanese).

{Ishihara 74a} Ishihara, Y. and Tamati, T., On the D-Tree Model and Language Analysis for English-Japanese Machine Translation Based on the Model, *Trans. IECE Japan*, Vol. 57-D, No. 7, 435-442, 1974, (in Japanese).

{Ishihara 74b} Ishihara, Y. and Tamati, T., On an English-Japanese Machine Translation System Based on the D-Tree Model and its Experiment, *Trans. IECE Japan*, Vol. 57-D, No. 7, 443-450, 1974, (in Japanese).

{JEIDA 82, 83, 84} JEIDA, *Survey on Machine Translation Activities*, JEIDA (Japan Electronic Industry Development Association), 1982, 1983, 1984, (in Japanese).

{Kaji 85} Kaji, H., Grammar Design Language for Japanese-English Machine Translation System ATHENE/N, *Records of the 31th Convention of IPSJ*, 2H4, 1985, (in Japanese).

{Kogure 84} Kogure, K., Yokoo, A. *et al.*, The Frame Editor for Dictionary Editing, *WG Preprints*, WGNL 45-1, IPSJ, 1984, (in Japanese).

{Kurihara 73} Kurihara, T., Machine Processing of Natural Language, *Information Processing*, Vol. 14, No. 4, 267-281, IPSJ, 1973, (in Japanese).

{Miyazaki 83} Miyazaki, T. and Yasuhara, H., Generation of English Sentences from Semantic Representation Based on the Case Grammar for Japanese, *Proc. Symposium on Natural Language Processing Technology*, 67-71, 1983, (in Japanese).

[Muraki 85] Muraki, K., NEC Machine Translation System VENUS: Two-phase Machine Translation System, *Proc. International Symposium on Machine Translation*, 39-44, 1985.

[Nagao 80a] Nagao, M., Tsujii, J., Ueda, Y. and Takiyama, M., An Attempt to Computerized Data Bases, *Proc. COLING-80*, 1980.

[Nagao 80b] Nagao M. *et al.*, A Machine Translation System from Japanese into English, *Proc. COLING-80*, 414-423, 1980.

[Nagao 81] Nagao, M., The Framework of a System of Mechanical Translation between Japanese and English by Analogy Principle, presented at NATO Symposium: Artificial and Human Intelligence, Chateau de Chapeau Cornu, Oct. 26-30, 1981.

[Nagao 82a] Nagao, M., A Survey of Natural Language Processing and Machine Translation in Japan, 1980-1982, in Kitagawa (ed.), *Computer Science and Technologies*, North Holland, 64-70, 1982.

[Nagao 82b] Nagao *et al.*, An English-Japanese Machine Translation System of the Titles of Scientific and Engineering Papers, *Proc. COLING-82*, 245-252, 1982.

{Nagao 83a} Nagao, M. *et al.*, Conjunctive Constructions in Japanese Abstracts and Their Analysis Procedures, *WG Preprints*, WGNL 34-4, IPSJ, 1983, (in Japanese).

{Nagao 83b} Nagao, M., An Approach towards a Controlled Language, *Proc. Symposium on Natural Language Processing Technology*, IPSJ, 91-99, 1983, (in Japanese).

{Nagao 83c} Nagao, M., Tsujii, J., Ibuki, J. and Ueda, Y., A Japanese-English Translation System of Titles of Scientific Papers, *WG Preprint*, WGNL 36-4, IPSJ, 1983, (in Japanese).

{Nagao 83d} Nagao, M., Outline of a Machine Translation Project of the Japanese Government, WG Preprints WGNL 38-2, 1983, (in Japanese).

[Nagao 84a] Nagao, M., Nishida, T. and Jun'ichi Tsujii, Dealing with Incompleteness of Linguistic Knowledge on Language Translation, *Proc. COLING-84*, 1984.

{Nagao 84b} Nagao, M., *et al.*, Document Production Assistant System Based on Controlled Language, *WG Preprint*, WGNL 44-5, IPSJ, 1984, (in Japanese).

[Nagao 85a] Nagao, M. and Tsujii, J., Machine Translation, in H. Buhlered., *Proceedings of Xth World Congress of FIT*, Wilhelm Braumuller, Wien, 1985.

{Nagao 85b} Nagao, M., Evaluation of the Quality of Machine-Translated Sentences and the Control of Language, *J. Information Processing Japan*, IPSJ, Vol. 26, No. 10, 1197-1202, 1985, (in Japanese).

{Nagao 85c} Nagao, M., *et al.*, Outline of Machine Translation Project of the Science and Technology Agency, *J. Information Processing Japan*, IPSJ, Vol. 26, No. 10, 1203-1213, 1985, (in Japanese).

[Nakamura 84] Nakamura, J. *et al.*, Grammar Writing System (GRADE) of Mu-Machine Translation Project and its Characteristics, *Proc. COLING-84*, 1984.

[Nishida(F) 80] Nishida, F. *et al.*, English-Japanese Translation through Case-Structure Conversion, *Proc. COLING-80*, 447-454, 1980.

[Nishida(F) 82] Nishida, F. *et al.*, Japanese-English Translation Through Internal Expressions, *Proc. COLING-82*, 271-276, 1982.

[Nishida(T) 82] Nishida, T. and Doshita, S., An English-Japanese Machine Translation System Based on Formal Semantics of Natural Language, *Proc. COLING-82*, 277-282, 1982.

[Nishida(T) 83a] Nishida, T. and Doshita, S., An Application of Montague Grammar to Machine Translation, *Proc. ACL Conference on Applied Natural Language Processing*, Santa Monica, 156-165, 1983.

[Nishida(T) 83b] Nishida, T., *Studies on English-Japanese Machine Translation System based on Formal Semantics*, Doctoral Dissertation, Kyoto University, 1983.

[Nishida 84] Nishida, T. and Doshita, S., Combining Functionality and Object-orientedness for Natural Language Processing, *Proc. COLING-84*, 1984.

[Nitta 82] Nitta, Y., *et al.*, A Heuristic Approach to English-Japanese Machine Translation, *Proc. COLING-82*, 283-288, 1982.

[Nitta 84] Nitta, Y., *et al.*, A Proper Treatment of Syntax and Semantics in Machine Translation, *Proc. COLING-84*, 1984.

[Nitta 85] Nitta, Y., Problems of Machine Translation Systems -- Effect of Cultural Differences on Sentence Structure, *Proc. International Symposium on Machine Translation*, separate issue, 1985.

{Nomura 82} Nomura, H., Shimazu, A. and Iida, H., Artificial Intelligence Approach to Machine Intelligence, *WG Preprint*, WGNL 30-5, IPSJ, 1982, (in Japanese).

{Okajima 83} Okajima, A., Nitta, Y. and Yamana F., Editing Functions in Machine Translation, *WG Preprints*, WGNL 40-5, IPSJ, 1983, (in Japanese).

{Okajima 85} Okajima, A., Yamano, F. and Okamoto, E., On Recovery Processing in an English-Japanese Machine Translation System, *Records of the 31th Convention of IPSJ*, 1H2, 1985, (in Japanese).

{Sakai 66} Sakai, T., and Sugita, S., Mechanical Translation of English into Japanese, *J. of IECE Japan*, Vol. 49, No. 2, 46-53, 1966, (in Japanese).

{Sakai 69} Sakai, T., Sugita, S. and Watanabe, A., Mechanical Translation from Japanese into English, *J. of IPS Japan*, Vol. 10, No. 6, 418-427, 1969, (in Japanese).

{Sakaki 82} Sakaki, H. and Hashimoto, K., A Method for English-Japanese Machine Translation Using Pattern Matching, *WG Preprints*, WGNL, IPSJ, 1982, (in Japanese).

{Sakaki 83} Sakaki, H., Hashimoto, K. and Nogaito, I., A Parsing Method Utilizing Forbidden Tree Patterns, *WG Preprints*, WGNL 37-1, IPSJ, 1983, (in Japanese).

{Sakaki 84} Sakaki, H., Hashimoto, K., Suzuki, M. and Nogaito, I., A Parsing Method Having Filtering Procedure, *WG Preprint*, WGNL43-1, IPSJ, 1984, (in Japanese).

{Sakamoto 83} Sakamoto, Y., Design for Japanese Morphological Analysis in Machine Translation, *WG Preprint*, WGNL 38-3, 1983, (in Japanese).

[Sakamoto 84] Sakamoto, Y., *et al.*, Lexicon Features for Japanese Syntactic Analysis in Mu-Project-JE, *Proc. COLING-84*, 1984.

[Sawai 82] Sawai, S., Fukushima, M., Sugimoto, M., and Ukai, N., Knowledge Representation and Machine Translation, *Proc. COLING-82*, 351-356, 1982.

[Schank 77] Schank, R. C. and Abelson, R. P., *Scripts, Plans, Goals, and Understanding*, Lawrence Erlbaum, Hillsdale, New Jersey, 1977.

{Shimazu 85} Shimazu, A., Naito, S. and Nomura, H., Semantic Relations in Japanese Noun Phrases and Their Analysis, *WG Preprint*, 1985, (in Japanese).

{Shudo 73} Shudo, K., On Machine Translation from Japanese into English for a Technical Field, *J. of IPS Japan*, Vol. 14, No. 9, 661-668, 1973.

{Shudo 77} Shudo, K., Tsurumaru, H. and Yoshida, S., A Predicative Part Processing System for Japanese-English Machine Translation, *Trans. IECE Japan,* Vol. J60D, No. 10, 830-837, 1977, (in Japanese).

[Sugita 68] Sugita, S., *A Study on Mechanical Translation from English into Japanese,* Doctoral Thesis, Kyoto Univversity, 1968.

[Tamati 63] Tamati, T., Kurihara, T. and Yoshimura, A., The Translation Process and the Design of an Automatic Translator as an Information Processing Machine, *Information Storage and Retrieval,* Vol. 1, No. 1, 1963.

{Tamati 85} Tamati, T., A Historical Overview of Machine Translation, *J. Information Processing Japan,* Vol. 26, No. 10, 1140-1147, 1985, (in Japanese).

{Tanaka 84} Tanaka, H., *et al.,* Approach to More Natural Translation I, *Proc. Symposium on Natural Language Processing Technology,* IPSJ, 115-121, 1984, (in Japanese).

{Tanaka 85} Tanaka, H. and Mizoguchi, F., Semantic Based Machine Translation System, *J. Information Processing,* Vol. 26, No. 10, 1191-1196, 1985, (in Japanese).

{Terano 85} Terano, T., *An Experiment of a Machine Translation System and Some Remarks on its Practical Use,* Economic Research Center Report No. 584008, CRIEPI, 1985, (in Japanese).

{Tomita 84} Tomita, M., Nishida, T. and Doshita, S., A Front-End for Disambiguation in an Interactive English-Japanese Machine Translation System, *Proc. Symposium on Natural Language Processing,* IPSJ, 1984, (in Japanese).

[Tomita 85] Tomita, M., *An Efficient Context-free Parsing Algorithm for Natural Languages and Its Applications,* CMU-CS-85-134, Department of Computer Science, Carnegie-Mellon University, 1985.

[Tsujii 84] Tsujii, J., *et al.,* Analysis Grammar of Japanese in the Mu-Project, *Proc. COLING-84,* 1984.

[Tsujii 85] Tsujii, J., Science and Technology Agency's Machine Translation Project: Mu Machine Translation Project, *Proc. International Symposium on Machine Translation,* 49-68, 1985.

{Tsutsumi 82} Tsutsumi, T., On the English-Japanese Machine Translation of Computer Manuals, *WG Preprints,* WGNL 32-3, IPSJ, 1982, (in Japanese).

[Uchida 80] Uchida, H. and Sugiyama, A Machine Translaiton System from Japanese into English, Based on Conceptual Structure, *Proc. COLING-80,* 455-462, 1980.

[Uchida 85] Uchida, H., Fujitsu Machine Translation System: ATLAS, *Proc. International Symposium on Machine Translation,* 29-38, 1985.

{Wada 65} Wada, H., Mechanical Translation, Present Status and its Prospect, *Information Processing*, Vol. 6, No. 3, 1965, (in Japanese).

{Yamada 64} Yamada, S., Analysis of the Input Japanese Text in Mechanical Translation, *Information Processing*, IPSJ, Vol. 5, No. 3, 134-141, 1964, (in Japanese).

{Yamaguchi 85} Yamaguchi, S., An Example of Automatic Translation of Practical Level and Translation Distribution Service, May Issue of 事務と経営*(Office and Management)*, 14-17, 1985, (in Japanese).

[Yang 84] Yang, Y., Nishida, T. and Doshita, S., Use of Heuristic Knowledge in Chinese Language Analysis, *Proc. COLING-84*, 222-225, 1984.

[Yang 85a] Yang, Y., Doshita, S. and Nishida, T., Partial Constraints in Chinese Analysis, *Proc. IJCAI-85*, 1985.

[Yang 85b] Yang, Y., *Studies on Constructing Chinese Analysis System*, Doctoral Thesis, Kyoto University, Japan, (forthcoming).

{Yoshida 83} Yoshida, S., Tanaka, T., *et al.*, Controlled Japanese for Technical Writing, *WG Preprints*, WGNL 37-4, IPSJ, 1983, (in Japanese).

[Yoshida 84] Yoshida, S., A Consideration on the Concepts Structure and Language in Relation to Selections of Translation Equivalents of Verbs in Machine Translation Systems, *Proc. COLING-84*, 1984.

Appendix: Major Machine Translation Projects and Investigators in Japan

1. The Government

The Mu project
   Kyoto University:
      Prof. Makoto Nagao, Prof. Jun'ichi Tsujii, Prof. Jun'ichi Nakamura,
   Electro-Technical Laboratory (ETL):
      Dr. Yoshiyuki Sakamoto,
   Japan Information Center of Science and Technology (JICST):
      Mr. Tsuyoshi Toriumi, Mr. Masayuki Sato
   Tsukuba Research Information Processing Center (RIPS)

      {Nagao 83d, 85c}, [Nagao 84a], [Nakamura 84], [Tsujii 84, 85],
      {Sakamoto 83}, [Sakamoto 84]

2. Universities and Research Institutes

Kyoto University
   Prof. Makoto Nagao, Prof. Jun'ichi Tsujii, Prof. Jun'ichi Nakamura
      [Nagao 80a,b, 81, 82b, 85a]

   Prof. Shuji Doshita, Prof. Toyoaki Nishida, Ms. Yiming Yang
      [Nishida(T) 82, 83a,b, 84],[Yang 84, 85a,b]

Kyushu University
   Prof. Sho Yoshida, Prof. Toru Hitaka [Yoshida 84]

   Prof. Tuneo Tamati   {Ishihara 74a,b}

Fukuoka University
   Prof. Kimiaki Shudo   {Shudo 77}

Tokyo Institute of Technology
   Prof. Hozumi Tanaka   {Tanaka 85}

University of Osaka Prefecture
   Prof. Fujio Nishida, Prof. Shinobu Takamatsu   [Nishida(F) 80, 82]

Toyohashi University of Technology
   Prof. Tadahiro Kitahashi, Prof. Makoto Hirai

Electro-Technical Laboratory
   Dr. Shun Ishizaki, Dr. Hitoshi Isahara

   Dr. Naoshi Ikeda   {Ikeda 84}

ICOT (the Fifth Generation Project of Japan)
   focus is attentioned on basic issues; see {Tanaka 84}

3. Computer Industries

NTT
   Dr. Hirosato Nomura, Dr. Akira Shimazu, Dr. Hitoshi Iida, Dr. Katagiri, Dr.
   Ogura, Dr. Kogure, Dr. Naito
      {Nomura 82},{Shimazu 85},{Iida 85}

FUJITSU
   Dr. Hiroshi Uchida, Dr. S. Sawai   [Uchida 80, 85], [Sawai 82]

TOSHIBA
   Dr. Shin'ya Amano   [Amano 85]

NEC
   Dr. Kazunori Muraki, Dr. Ichiyama [Muraki 85]

HITACHI
   Dr. Yoshiyuki Nitta, Okajima, K. Kaji   [Nitta 82, 84, 85]

KDD
   Dr. Hiroshi Sakaki, Dr. Kazuo Hashimoto   {Sakaki 82, 83, 84}

MITSUBISHI
    Dr. Eiichi Arita, Dr. Masatoshi Fukushima   {Fukushima 83}, {Arita 84}
OKI
    Dr. Hiroshi Yasuhara, Dr. Toshihiko Miyazaki   {Yasuhara 83}
SHARP
    Dr. Suzuki
IBM Japan
    Dr. Taijiro Tsutsumi   {Tsutsumi 82}

AUTHORS
Toyoaki Nishida, Department of Information Science, Kyoto University, Sakyo-Ku, Kyoto 606, Japan.

Shuji Doshita, Department of Information Science, Kyoto University, Sakyo-Ku, Kyoto 606, Japan.

Session II:
Summary of discussion 2

In the chair: Barbara Snell

(1)   The session was opened by Dr M. Sieny from Saudi Arabia, who wanted to know from Ian Pigott why only 10 per cent of the EEC Commission's translations were made using Systran. The answer was that a number of factors were involved. The system ran US software, obtained in 1976, which needed three to four years' development work to make it suitable for use by translators; in addition, user-friendly equipment was needed, so that it was not until 1981, when a few word processors were introduced on a pilot basis in the three translation divisions in Luxembourg, that the system really began to be used. End-users had only recently become aware of the benefits of the new technology. There were still problems with equipment compatibility, and with the fact that not all translators were interested in using the system, which was in any case only being used experimentally at the Commission, and not in any other EEC bodies. Mrs Wagner, also from the EEC Commission, added that the amount of work done on Systran was more like 3 per cent, and that it was used for documents that would not otherwise have been translated.

(2)   The next question came from Mr Marques, of UNESCO, who asked Mr Pigott to describe the philosophy of the Eurotra system and give an account of the progress made on it since 1981. Dr Harold Somers of UMIST was asked to answer. Eurotra started in 1978 as a research project of the EEC Commission to develop an advanced machine translation system, ultimately intended to cope with all seventy-two language pairs. In 1982, funding was approved for an initial five and a half years, during which time a prototype would be developed. All member states were represented on the project, which had some 150 people working on it. It

was still only at the research stage. Prototype software was being run in a number of centres. In reply to a question from the floor, Dr Somers revealed that the system had not actually translated anything yet.

(3)   Dr Sieny asked Dr Nishida about work in Japan on translation into and from Chinese, and for details of progress made in developing electronic Chinese typewriters. It transpired that the Fujitsu company was developing a system for Japanese and Chinese, although no firm details were known about that or about Chinese typewriters.

(4)   The next questioner (Dr Fulton) asked whether there was a Systran bureau in the UK yet: there was not, although negotiations were in progress to set one up. To date, such bureaux existed only in Brussels (run by Orda-B, a computer bureau, and Mendez, a translation agency), in Paris (Gachot) and in Luxembourg (Ecat).

(5)   Peter Arthern then asked if there was any move by manufacturers towards establishing an industry standard that would make all hardware compatible. Ian Pigott replied that the only proposed standard was that of Teletex, but it was not widely implemented because it was only a telecommunications protocol; the need was for something much wider. Each new machine seemed to have its own character set, as often as not with restricted capability for handling foreign characters. The problem was that people were prepared to buy, which meant there were lots of quick sales to be made – even without compatibility – and that was all manufacturers were really interested in.

(6)   Benoît Thouin added that the character set was the main stumbling block, as it governed the way the screen, keyboard and printer operated. The only way to resolve this problem was from within the hardware's internal memory representation, i.e. on the basis of the machine codes used to form individual characters. He said that the International Standards Organisation (ISO) was currently working on a broadly multilingual character set based on 16-bit code.

By comparison, different disk sizes, disk sector sizes and so on (i.e. varying hardware formats) were a relatively minor problem; automatic devices could act as interfaces. Worse problems were encountered at software level, in that different control codes were used for text presentation features such as underlining and bold text. Similarly, there was no agreement at user level on how to represent groups of information in databases. It really was up to the users to decide among themselves precisely what it was that they wanted the manufacturers to provide.

(7)   The next question was directed at Ian Pigott and came from Mrs P. Thomas, at the University of Surrey, who was actively involved in running the British termbank project in conjunction with UMIST, and was about subject classification and whether it worked or not. Mr Pigott replied that at the EEC Commission coding by subject field did not work because all subjects were covered, and some texts were on several different topics. It had been decided to keep very general meanings for one-word equivalents, with sophisticated rules and semantic, syntactic or scanning checks to identify the subject field and actual meaning in a given context. This approach had been found to work well.

Mrs Thomas then added that Surrey University was now marketing the results of a terminology course held in March 1985, in the form of a terminology manual. She also mentioned another terminology manual from the Austrian Standards Institute, by Professor Helmut Felber.

Mr Keil from Saarbrücken said he did not agree with what Ian Pigott had said about subject fields, because his experience had been completely different. At his university, documents were scanned to find their terminological content. The computer decided on the basis of that scan what the text's subject was; any ambiguities were sorted out by human operators.

Towards the end of the session, Mr Le-Hong, of Daimler-Benz, Stuttgart, remarked that although compatibility problems were important, it was even more essential for translators to make a catalogue of minimum requirements for machine aids. They had to accept the challenge offered by high technology, but at present they were too afraid to say how they wanted the new technology to work for them. If nothing was done, we might end up with a phenomenon that could be called HAT – human-assisted translation.

At that point proceedings came to an end, and after a few closing remarks from Catriona Picken, delegates dispersed.

RAPPORTEUR
Patrick Sutton, Translator, Department of Health and Social Security, Room A311, Alexander Fleming House, Elephant and Castle, London SE1 6BY, UK

Biographical notes on speakers

Patrick Corness is Senior Lecturer in the Department of Language Studies at Coventry Lanchester Polytechnic. He teaches German and Russian on the BA Honours Degree course in Modern Languages. His research interests include computer-assisted language learning.

Commodore Christopher J.L. Croft was educated at Sherborne and Queens College, Cambridge and has served in the Royal Navy as a specialist in electrical and electronic engineering. A lifelong involvement with Norway is reflected in early qualifications as a Civil Service interpreter, an addiction to mountains, snow and skiing, and some thirty years' experience as a part-time technical translator, both official and freelance. He is now based in Winchester and continues to combine part-time translation with other interests on both sides of the North Sea.

Nélida E. Depiante was born and educated in the Argentine. She has degrees as a translator and teacher of English as a foreign language. After working in the Argentine as a teacher and freelance translator, she travelled to England on holiday and has been on a working holiday ever since. After seventeen years as a staff translator with Shell, she is now trying to make the best of an opportunity to start again as a freelancer.

Ian Frame was a linguist initially, starting as a translator with Shell in 1970 before moving on to the International Labour Organisation in Italy.

Disenchanted with translation he became a lawyer (1978) only to rediscover the delights of translation – so he then became a lawyer-linguist (the official title given to translators at the European Court of Justice).

Josette Guédès was educated in western France, and after some experience of teaching, turned to translating. She spent four years with Office and Technical Translations, dealing mostly with work for the motor industry, then three years as Technical Translator/Editor at the Central Office of Information, before going freelance in 1973. Present translation work includes film scripts, publicity work, legal work, electronics (telecommunications especially), feasibility studies in the fields of transport and the petroleum industry.

Julie Harnett is a freelance journalist and consultant specialising in office automation. For ten years, until the end of 1983, Julie was Editor of *Office Equipment News*, a leading monthly publication, and in her dual role as Editorial Director of AGB Business Publications, was responsible for publications in the fields of microelectronics, business management, finance, marketing, industrial relations and environmental planning. She was also responsible for the launch and development of the first magazine devoted to business information technology.

Wolfgang Heitmann is an information scientist by training and is Technical Documentation Group Manager at Nixdorf Computer AG. He has previously worked for CTM in Konstanz and the Gesellschaft für Kerfornschung, Karlsruhe (Society of Nuclear Research).

Geoffrey Kingscott has been a technical translator for the past twenty years. He is Editor of *Language Monthly* and Director of his own company, Praetorius Limited.

Pamela Mayorcas-Cohen is working on the CEC SYSLING Project in which she is developing an integrated resources system for the language service.

Dr Toyoaki Nishida is Assistant Professor at the Department of Information Science, Faculty of Engineering, Kyoto University, Japan.

Ian M. Pigott graduated in modern languages (French and Spanish) at Newcastle University in 1967. He gained considerable experience as a technical translator in Austria and Canada before joining the European Commission in Luxembourg in 1973. Since 1976, Mr Pigott has worked full-time in the field of machine translation at the Commission, in particular on the development and quality improvement of the Systran system. His interest has, however, extended to all other machine translation developments worldwide and he has spoken at a number of conferences and published several papers on the subject in recent years.

Eveline Sleebos joined Shell (London) as a staff translator in 1969 and became head of the Dutch section. She worked for Gist-Brocades in Delft as a staff translator 1974–82. Since 1982 she has been a freelance translator and official court interpreter at the District Court of The Hague.

Benoît Thouin works for Computational Linguistics Consultants Limited, CP 420, Succ.A, Hull (Quebec), Canada.

Jeremy M. Verrinder's varied work experience as a translator includes British Iron and Steel Federation, Ever Ready Company, Vickers Limited and Translations Manager for Able Translations Limited. He has worked for the Linguaphone Institute in a managerial capacity and since September 1981 has been the Course Leader for the Postgraduate Diploma Course in Technical Translation at the Polytechnic of Central London. He is currently Dean of the Faculty of Languages.

List of participants

ADAMS KVAM, Ms Gail, Self-employed Translator
N-6770 Nordfjordeid, Norway
AIREY, Mr Michael, Editor
Foreign Broadcast Information Service, Room P 13, American Embassy, Grosvenor Square, London W1A 1AE, UK
ALGHITA, Mr Musa, Managing Director
Technocrat Limited, 62 King Street, Maidenhead, Berkshire SL6 1EQ, UK
ALI, Mr Firas, Research Assistant
Technocrat Limited, 62 King Street, Maidenhead, Berkshire SL6 1EQ, UK
ALLISSAT, Mr Heinrich, Head of Department
Fried. Krupp GmbH, Krupp Gemeinschaftsbetriebe/Sprachendienst, Altendorfer Strasse 104, 4300 Essen 1, Federal Republic of Germany
ALLOTT, Mr Alan R., Head of Translation Department
Arthur Andersen y Cía., S.R.C., Raimundo Fdez. Villaverde, 65, Planta 14, 28003 Madrid, Spain
ALSTERBERG, Mr Stefan, Assistant to Technical Counsellor
Swedish Embassy, Office of Science and Technology, 11 Montagu Place, London W1H 2AL, UK
ANTTILA, Mr Paavo, Owner/Translator
Tek-Text Paavo Anttila, Lähderanta 6 Q, SF-02720 Espoo 72, Finland
ANXOLABEHERE, Ms Véronique, European Marketing Assistant
Automated Language Processing Systems, 3 avenue Beauregard, CH-2035 Corcelles, Switzerland
ARTHERN, Mr Peter, Head of English Translation Division
Council of the European Communities, rue de la Loi 170, B-1048 Brussels, Belgium
AUGER, Mr Michel, Ingénieur
Electricité de France, 1 avenue du Général de Gaulle, 92141 Clamart Cedex, France

BAILEY, Mr David, Translator
SOGREAH Consulting Engineers, 6 rue de Lorraine, F-38130 Echirolles, France

BARRAQ, Mr Ali, Translating Department
Moody Press International Limited, 56 Tabard Street, London SE1 4LG, UK
BARRETT, Mr Chris, Abstractor/Translator
De Beers Industrial Diamond Division (Pty) Limited, Charters, Sunninghill,
Ascot, Berkshire SL5 9PX, UK
BEATTIE, Mr David, Senior Translator
Hoechst UK Limited, Medical Department, Hoechst House, Salisbury Road,
Hounslow, Middlesex TW4 6JH, UK
BELL, Mr Colin, Head of English Language Section
EUTELSAT, Tour Montparnasse, 33 avenue du Maine, F-75755 Paris Cedex,
France
BERGER, Mr Hans
Sprachen- und Dolmetscher-Institut München, Amalienstr. 73, D-8000 Munich,
Federal Republic of Germany
BERTODANO, Alfonso, Freelance
Ferraz 73, 28008 Madrid, Spain
BIRDWOOD, Dr George, Medical Editor
Ciba-Geigy Scientific Publications, 100 Wigmore Street, London W1H 9DR,
UK
BLAHA, Mr Herbert
Siemens AG, Department KSDTD, Hofmannstrasse 51, D-8000 Munich 70,
Federal Republic of Germany
BOKX, Mr Hans, Head of Translations Department
Unilever Research Laboratory, PO Box 114, 3130 AC Vlaardingen, The
Netherlands
BOUDJEDID, Mr Meyer, Terminology Coordinator
Aerospatiale Company, 12 rue Pasteur BP76, 92152 Suresnes, France
BOURKE, Mr Desmond, Director
Commonwealth Bureau of Horticulture and Plantation Crops, East Malling
Research Station, Nr Maidstone, Kent ME19 6BJ, UK
BOURREC, Mr Tone, Translator
Elf Aquitaine Norge A/S, PO Box 168, N-4001 Stavanger, Norway
BOWDEN, Mrs Elizabeth, Head, Foreign Language Services
Shell UK Limited, Shell Centre, London SE1 7NA, UK
BRACE, Mr G., Technical Translator/Reviser/Rewriter
Institut Français du Pétrole, BP 311, 92000 Rueil-Malmaison, France
BRAZIER, Ms Mary, Translator
Departments of the Environment and Transport, Room P3/156, 2 Marsham
Street, London SW1P 3EB, UK
BREKKE, Dr Magnar, Senior Lecturer
University of Bergen, English Department, Sydnes plass 9, N-5000 Bergen,
Norway
BROOKES, Mr Robert, Freelance Translator
Sunnybank Cottage, Low Row, Richmond, North Yorkshire DL11 6NE, UK
BUCHMANN, Mr Beat, Researcher
Issco, University of Geneva, 54 Route des Acacias, CH-1227 Geneva, Swit-
zerland
BUGGE HOVERSTAD, Mr Torstein, Poet, Freelance Translator (Literary)
Norwegian Association of Translators, Karlsborgvn. 3, N-0193 Oslo 1, Norway
BURTON, Mr Thomas, Head of Translation Service
Customs Cooperation Council, 26–38 rue de l'Industrie, B-1040 Brussels,
Belgium

BUTTERFIELD, Ms Val, Sales Support and Marketing Manager
Staefa Control System, Staefa House, Moor Lane, Staines, Middlesex TW18 4XN, UK
BUUCK, Mr Günter, Head of Translation Office
Thyssen Stahl AG, Kaiser-Wilhelm-Str. 100, D-4100 Duisburg, Federal Republic of Germany
BYRNE, Mr T.P.
Techtrans Ireland, Project Management Bldg, Dasco Ind. Estate, S. Douglas Road, Cork, Ireland
BYRNE-SUTTON, Mr Geoffrey, Director, Division of Languages
International Atomic Energy Agency, Wagramerstr. 5, PO Box 100, A-1400 Wien, Austria

CARDNO, Ms Sheilah, Freelance Translator/Interpreter
Transtex, Rua. Presidente Arriaga, 34/1°, 1200 Lisbon, Portugal
CAREY, Mr John
Translation Bureau, Secretary of State, Ottawa, Ontario K1A OM5, Canada
CARISTAN Clement, Agency Manager
TAO International, 37 ter rue de Metz, F-31000 Toulouse, France
CASTELLANO, Dimity
The Translators' Guild, Mangold House, 24A Highbury Grove, London N5 2EA, UK
CASTELLANO, Lanna, Freelance Translator
39 Northumberland Place, London W2 5AS, UK
CAVE, Mrs Frances, Information Officer
Gras Savoye, SA, 115–123 avenue Charles de Gaulle, 92202 Neuilly-sur-Seine, France
CAZALS, Mr Jean-Paul, Translator
CERN (Conseil Européen pour la Recherche Nucléaire), CH-1211 Geneva 23, Switzerland
CHAFFEY, Mr Patrick, Lecturer in Translation Studies
ADNOM, University of Oslo, PO Box 1003, Blindern, N-0315 Oslo 3, Norway
CHALOUPKA, Mr Bedrich
TII, 1952 Kidwell Dr., McLean, Va., USA
COLE, Mr Philip, Translator
Shell UK Limited, Shell Centre, London SE1 7NA, UK
COLTOF, Dr Hans, Management Consultant
Van de Bunt Management Consultants, PO Box 7960, 1008AD Amsterdam, The Netherlands
CONVENTS, Mr Jan
Council of the European Communities, rue de la Loi 170, B-1048 Brussels, Belgium
COOK-RADMORE, Mr Derry, Reviser
European Space Agency, 8–10 rue Mario Nikis, F-75015 Paris, France
CORDON, Ms Anna, Translations Manager
British Telecom, BT Research Laboratories, Martlesham Heath, Ipswich IP5 7RE, UK
CORFIELD, Mr Peter, Director
Linguasoft, 15–19 Kingsway, London WC2B 6UU, UK
CORNELIUS, Mr Peter, ECHO Help Desk
ECHO (European Commission Host Organisation), 177 Route d'Esch, L-1471 Luxembourg, Luxembourg GD

CORNESS, Mr Patrick, Head of German
Coventry Lanchester Polytechnic, Coventry CV1 5FB, UK
CORNEY, Mr Fred, Translator
Hoechst AG, Pharma Forschung, PO Box 80 03 20, D-6230 Frankfurt (M) –
80, Federal Republic of Germany
COTTET, Mr Marcel, Head of the Translation Section
Nestlé Products Technical Assistance Co. Limited, CH-1800 Vevey, Switzerland
COX, Mrs Claire, Translator
British Nuclear Fuels plc, Risley, Nr Warrington, Cheshire WA3 6AS, UK
CROFT, Commodore Christopher, Director
SCANTECH, Downlands, Sleepers Hill, Winchester, Hampshire SO22 4NB,
UK
CYNKIN, Mr Christopher, Director
Interverbum AB, PO Box 12 258, S-102 26 Stockholm, Sweden

DAHL, Mr Emilio, Freelance Translator
Vibergsvägen 17, S-151 48 Södertälje, Sweden
DAVIES, Ms Suzanne
44 Woodland Rise, London N10 3UG, UK
DELAHAYE, Mrs Mary, Head Librarian
Institut Océanographique, 195 rue Saint-Jacques, 75005 Paris, France
DEMPSTER, Dr Andrew, Publisher
Elsevier Science Publishers, PO Box 330, 1000 AH Amsterdam, The
Netherlands
DEPIANTE, Miss Nélida, Freelance Translator
3 Coombe Lodge, London SE7 7PE, UK
DEPPE, Ms Jeannette, Management Assistant
Wolters Samson Group, PO Box 362, 2400 AJ Alphen a/d Rijn, The
Netherlands
DERAMAT, Mr J.M., Chief, Translation and Editorial Services
World Health Organisation, Regional Office for Europe, Scherfigsvej. 8, DK-
2100 Copenhagen Ø, Denmark
DIAZ-RECIO, Mr Fernando, Translator
ITT, Great Eastern House, Edinburgh Way, Harlow, Essex CM20 2BN, UK
DOWNS, Ms Linn, Vice-President
TE Corporation, PO Box 140, Campton, NH 03223, USA
DREIER, Mr H.
Siemens AG, Department K SD E, Hofmannstr. 51, D-8000 Munich 70,
Federal Republic of Germany
DREW, Mr Robert, Reviser
International Labour Office, CH-1211 Geneva 22, Switzerland
DUDZINSKI, Mr George, Office Manager
AD-EX (Translations) Limited, PO Box 428, 296 Kingston Road, London
SW20 8LZ, UK
DYSON, Dr Mary, Lecturer
University of Reading, Department of Typography and Graphic Communication, 2 Earley Gate, Whiteknights, Reading RG6 2AU, UK

EBEID, Mr Farouk, Chief, Conference Services Section
Economic & Social Commission for Western Asia (Baghdad), c/o Palais des
Nations, CH-1211 Geneva 10, Switzerland

EIE, Ms Eva, Translator
Ruglandveien 163A, N-1343 Eiksmarka, Nr Oslo, Norway
EISENGA, Reinder, Senior Translator
Akzo Nederland, Velperweg 76, 6800 LS Arnhem, The Netherlands
ELLESTAD, Mr Everett, Foreign Language Editor
Ehrenstråhle & Co., Box 5188, S-10244 Stockholm, Sweden
EVANS, Mr Andrew, Translator, Linguiste de liaison informatique
Commission of the European Communities, Bâtiment Jean Monnet, A1/062A,
L-2920 Luxembourg, Luxembourg GD
EVENSON, Mr Thomas, Translator
Framatome, Tour Fiat, 92083 Paris La Défense, France

FANCHETTE, Mr André, Translator
Alsthom, 55 avenue Jean Jaurès, 93000 Le Bourget, France
FAULKNER, Ms Jane, Staff Translator
Brixton Estate plc, 12 Babington Road, London NW4 4LD, UK
FAUST, Mr Berthold, Manager, Technical Writing and Translations
Norsk Data Dietz, Solinger Str. 9, D-4330 Mülheim A.D. Ruhr, Federal
Republic of Germany
FEATHER, Dr Peter, Technical Translator
Glaxo Group Research Limited, Greenford Road, Greenford, Middlesex UB6
0HE, UK
FEICHTENBERGER, Mr Klaus
Graz University, A-8111 Judendorf-Strassengel, Austria
FENNER, Mr Andrew, Freelance Translator
21c Grosvenor Road, London E11 2EW, UK
FERNEY, Mr Tony, Translator
Total Compagnie Française des Pétroles, 5 rue Michel-Ange, F-75116 Paris,
France
FERRIS, Mrs Evelyn, German Translator
Fédération Dentaire Internationale, 64 Wimpole Street, London W1M 8AL,
UK
FLEURENT, Mr Claude, Translations Coordinator
May and Baker Limited, Dagenham, Essex RM10 7XS, UK
FORD, Mr Wally, Translator
Department of Trade and Industry, Ebury Bridge House, 2–18 Ebury Bridge
Road, London SW1W 8QD, UK
FØRSUND, Ms Brit, Project Secretary
ADNOM, University of Oslo, PO Box 1003, Blindern, N-0315 Oslo 3,
Norway
FORTUNE, Mrs M.
Ciba-Geigy Pharmaceuticals, Wimblehurst Road, Horsham, Sussex RH12
4AB, UK
FOUCHAUX, Mr Norbert, Reviser
International Labour Office, CH-1211 Geneva 22, Switzerland
FRAME, Mr Ian, Translator
Court of Justice of the European Communities, 141 B rue de la Tour Jacob,
L-1831 Luxembourg, Luxembourg GD
FRANK, Mr Manfred, Chief, Foreign Languages Service
Bundesgesundheitsamt (Federal Health Office), Postfach 33 00 13, D-1000
Berlin 33, Federal Republic of Germany

FREIGANG, Mr Karl-Heinz, Researcher
Universität des Saarlandes, Sonderforschungsbereich 100, SFB 100, Bau 4, D-6600 Saarbrücken 11, Federal Republic of Germany
FREYSER, Drs Jan, Manager
Ink Language Service Limited, Prins Hendriklaan 52, 1075 BE Amsterdam, The Netherlands
FROUD, Mr George, Overseas Relations Engineer (Retired)
Electricity Council, c/o 11 Roundacre, London SW19 6DB, UK
FULTON, Dr Michael, Partner
20th Century Translators and Interpreters, The Chase, Behoes Lane, Woodcote, Reading, Berkshire RG8 0PP, UK
FURTHAUER, D. Dolm Eva, Conference Interpreter/Freelance Translator
Neudeggergasse 14/22, A-1080 Vienna, Austria

GARDES, Ms Jacqueline, Senior Reviser
World Bank, 1818 H Street NW, Washington, DC 20433, USA
GIBBS, Mr David, Manager, Translation Services
Rank Xerox, C&SE, PO Box 17, Bessemer Road, Welwyn Garden City, Hertford-shire AL7 1HE, UK
GILDERSON, Mr Alan, Export Copy Director
Anderson & Lembke, 1 Helsingborg AB, Box 2136, S-250 02 Helsingborg, Sweden
GLEAVE, Mr John, Translator/Interpreter
Alsthom Atlantique, avenue des Trois Chênes, F-90001 Belfort Cedex, France
GRAHAM, Mr Paul, Translation Coordinator
Alsthom Neyrtec, F-38800 Pont-de-Claix, France
GRAISSIN, Mr Jean Baptiste, Engineer
Avions Marcel Dassault/Bréguet Aviation, 85 bd Senard, F-92210 St Cloud, France
GRAY, Mr David, Translations Coordinator
Institut Laue-Langevin, 156X, F-38042 Grenoble Cedex, France
GREAVES, Mr David, Translator
Carle and Montanari Spa, Via Neera 39, 1-20141 Milan, Italy
GREEN-ARMYTAGE, Mr Jonathan, Senior Reporter
Computer Weekly, Quadrant House, The Quadrant, Sutton, Surrey SM2 5AS, UK
GREENWOOD, Mr Malcolm, Translator
Department of Trade and Industry, Room 417, Ebury Bridge House, Ebury Bridge Road, London SW1W 8QD, UK
GRIGO, Dipl. Dolm. Karl-Heinz, Foreign Language Services
Ruhrgas AG, Huttropstr. 60, D-4300 Essen 1, Federal Republic of Germany
GUEDES, Ms Josette, Legal and Technical Translator
42 Whitehall Park, Highgate, London N19 3TN, UK
GUISE, Miss Linda, Translator
Huntingdon Research Centre Limited, Huntingdon, Cambridgeshire PE18 6ES, UK

HABERMANN, Dr F.W.A.
Kernforschungszentrum Karlsruhe GmbH, International Cooperation Projekt Schneller Brüter, PO Box 36 40, D-7500 Karlsruhe, Federal Republic of Germany
HAMER, Dr L.A.A. van den, Head of Department of Small Industry
Ministry of Economic Affairs, Bezuidenhoutseweg 20, 2594 AV The Hague, The Netherlands

HAMILTON, Mr Ian, Acting Chief, Terminology Section
United Nations Office at Geneva, E. 5102 Palais des Nations, CH-1211 Geneva 10, Switzerland

HANNAH, Ms Jean, Research Fellow
University of Reading, Department of Typography and Graphic Communication, 2 Earley Gate, Whiteknights, Reading RG6 2AU, UK

HANSTOCK, Ms Jane, Postgraduate Course Tutor
University of Salford, Department of Modern Languages, Salford M5 4WT, UK

HARDY, Mr Bernard, Manager, Commercial Printing Division
Rank Xerox Research (UK) Ltd, 30 Church Street, Welwyn, Hertfordshire, UK

HARNETT, Ms Julie
Editorial Consultancy & Services, 10 Post Lane, Meadway, Twickenham, Middlesex TW2 6NZ, UK

HART, Mr George, Technical Information Panel Executive
AGARD, 7 rue Ancelle, F-92200 Neuilly-sur-Seine, France

HASSEL, Mr Harro, Managing Director
LOGOS Computer Systems GmbH, 11 Lyonerstr., 6000 Frankfurt 71, Federal Republic of Germany

HAYWARD, Mr Oliver, Head, Translation Branch (LRD)
Foreign & Commonwealth Office/ODA, Room WH MZ 41A, King Charles Street, London SW1A 2AH, UK

HAYWARD, Mr Ron, Promotion Manager
Elsevier Science Publishers, PO Box 330, 1000 AH Amsterdam, The Netherlands

HEADLEY, Mr Neil, Translator
Swiss Reinsurance Company, CH-8022 Zurich, Switzerland

HEFFERNAN, Ms Anne, Translator
Department of Trade and Industry, Room 426, Ebury Bridge House, Ebury Bridge Road, London SW1W 8QD, UK

HEITMANN, Mr Wolfgang
Nixdorf Computers AG, Furstenallee 7, D-4970 Paderborn, Federal Republic of Germany

HELGESEN, Mr Ole Thomas, Section Head
Elf Aquitaine Norge A/S, PO Box 168, N-4001 Stavanger, Norway

HEUKELOM, Dorothea van, Head of Legal Section
Dutch Ministry of Foreign Affairs, Vlaskamp 358, 2592 AK, The Hague, The Netherlands

HEUSS, Dr Wolfgang, Chairman, English Department
Sprachen- und Dolmetscher-Institut München, Amalienstr. 73, D-8000 Munich, Federal Republic of Germany

HINCHCLIFFE, Mr Peter, Translations Unit Head
Health & Safety Executive, Library and Information Services, Harpur Hill, Buxton, Derbyshire SK17 9JN, UK

HOARE, Mr Kenneth, Patents Abstracting Manager
Derwent Publications Limited, Rochdale House, 128 Theobalds Road, London WC1X 8RP, UK

HOBBS, Barbara, Conferences Secretary
Aslib, Information House, 26–27 Boswell Street, London WC1N 3JZ, UK

HOBBS, Ms Irene, Self-employed Translator
4 avenue Bartholomé, F-78370 Plaisir, France

HODGE, Mr Basil, Head of Translation and Minutes Section
CERN (Conseil Européen pour la Recherche Nucléaire), CH-1211 Geneva 23, Switzerland
HOOPER, Dr Raymond, Head of Pharmaceutical Translations
Boehringer Mannheim GmbH, Sandhoferstrasse 116, D-6800 Mannheim 31, Federal Republic of Germany
HOYER, Mrs A.
Nederlandse Philips Bedrijven BV, Building VO-P, PO Box 218, 5600 MD Eindhoven, The Netherlands
HULME, Mrs Anne, Freelance Translator
16 Longford, Market Drayton, Shropshire TF9 3PW, UK
HUNT, Mr David, System Consultant (Computer Translation)
ITT Translations, Great Eastern House, Edinburgh Way, Harlow, Essex CM20 2BN, UK
HUNT, Ms Teresa, Translator
Departments of the Environment and Transport, P3/156, 2 Marsham Street, London SW1P 3EB, UK
HUTCHINS, Mr John, Sub-Librarian
University of East Anglia, University Plain, Norwich NR4 7TJ, UK

IMBERT, Ms Elyane, Systems Support/Training Manager
Weidner Translation (Europe) Limited, Fryern House, 125 Winchester Road, Chandlers Ford, Eastleigh, Hampshire SO5 2DR, UK
INGO, Dr Rune, Professor of Modern Finnish
University of Vaasa (Vaasan korkeakoulu), Raastuvankatu 31, 65100 Vaasa, Finland

JABER, Nadar Mohamed, Principal
Jeddah Translation Bureau, PO Box 3595, Jeddah 21481, Saudi Arabia
JACKSON, Mr Bill, Manager, UK Office, Metals Information
Institute of Metals, 1 Carlton House Terrace, London SW1Y 5DB, UK
JAHR, Ms Mette-Cathrine, Translation Manager
Digital Equipment Organisation A/S, Ammerudveien 22, N-0958 Oslo 9, Norway
JENSEN, Mr Jürgen, Civil Servant
Bundeskanzlaramt, Aachener Str. 8, D-5000 Köln 1, Federal Republic of Germany
JESPERSEN, Sherry, Manager, Professional Development Group
Aslib, Information House, 26–27 Boswell Street, London WC1N 3JZ, UK
JOHNSON, Mr Rod, Senior Lecturer
UMIST, Centre for Computational Linguistics, PO Box 88, Manchester M60 1QD, UK
JONES, Mr Neil, Software Engineer
Digital Equipment Company Limited, Engineering Division, Mailstop REO2-F/M2, PO Box 121, Reading, Berkshire RG2 0TU, UK

KAULBACK, Mr Jalik, Technical Editor
BRGM (Bureau de Recherches Géologiques et Minières), PO Box 1492, Jeddah, Saudi Arabia
KAULBACK, Mrs Sarah, Independent Translator
30 rue de la Bretonnerie, F-45000 Orléans, France
KAYE, Mr Antony, Translator
Technoscript AB, Box 30158, S-104 25 Stockholm, Sweden

KEIL, Mr Gerald C., Computational Linguist
Universität des Saarlandes, Projekt SUSANNAH, Fachrichtung 'Angewandte Sprachwissenschaft' D-6600 Saarbrücken 11, Federal Republic of Germany
KELCH, Dr Hans
BK, Bannscheidtstr. 9, D-5300 Bonn, Federal Republic of Germany
KEMBLE, Ms Helen, Government Authorised Translator (Norway)
Jansbergveien 5, N-0861 Oslo 8, Norway
KEMP, Dr John, Geologist/Translator
Bureau de Recherches Géologiques et Minières, BP 6009, 45060 Orléans Cedex, France
KESSLER, Mr Christian, Computers Management
SOGREAH, 6 rue de Lorraine, F-38130 Echirolles, France
KHOUZAM, Mr Matteo, Conference Interpreter – English/French/Italian
Via Buonarroti 35, I-20145 Milan, Italy
KINGSCOTT, Mr Geoffrey, Director
Praetorius Limited, 5 East Circus Street, Nottingham NG1 5AH, UK
KIRKMAN, Mr Ronald, Chief Publications Branch
International Labour Office, CH-1211 Geneva 22, Switzerland
KNIGHT, Mr David, Managing Director
David Knight & Co. Språkkonsulter AB, Box 363, S-101 24 Stockholm, Sweden
KOBRIN, Mrs Catherine, Editor
International Labour Office, CH-1211 Geneva 22, Switzerland
KOOPMAN, Mr Paul, Head of Reporting Services (IS/2)
Koninklijke/Shell-Laboratorium, Amsterdam, PO Box 3003, 1003 AA Amsterdam, The Netherlands
KRUSE NIELSEN, Mr Allan, Manager of Translation Tools
European Language Services, IBM, 150, Birkerod Kongevej, DK-3460, Birkerod, Denmark

LANNER, Mr Josef, Translator
Lenzing AG, Hamburgerstrasse 9, A-4840 Vöcklabruck, Austria
LARSEN, Chris, Head Programmer
LinguaTech International, 381 West 2230 North, Suite 360, Provo, Utah 84604, USA
LASHMAR, Mrs Nicole, Translator
Shell UK Limited, Shell Centre, London SE1 7NA, UK
LATORRE, José-Maria, Spanish Translator
United Nations Environment Programme (UNEP), PO Box 30552, Nairobi, Kenya
LAUREN, Dr Christer, Professor
University of Vaasa/School of Modern Languages, Rådhusgatan 31, SF-65100 Vaasa, Finland
LAWSON, Ms Veronica, Associate Editor, *Computers and Translation*
30 Half Moon Lane, Herne Hill, London SE24 9HU, UK
LAYTON, Mr Tony, Director, Special Studies Unit
University of Salford, Salford M5 4WT, UK
LE-HONG, Mr Khai, Head of Translation Department
Daimler–Benz Aktiengesellschaft, PO Box 202, D-7000 Stuttgart 60, Federal Republic of Germany
LEFEBURE, Mr Eric, Manager, Translating Services
Bank of England, Threadneedle Street, London EC2R 8AH, UK

LEISSE, Ms Cornelia, Translator
ICI – Pharma, Übersetzungsstelle, Postfach 10 31 09, D-6900 Heidelberg 1, Federal Republic of Germany
L'HUILLIER, Ms Monique, Lecturer in French
Brunel University Language Centre, Uxbridge, Middlesex UB8 3PH, UK
LINSHOFT-STILLER, Mrs Brigitte
CEDEFOP (European Centre for the Development of Vocational Training), 22 Bundesallee, D-1000 Berlin 15, Federal Republic of Germany
LONG, Mr Peter, Head of Translation Section
European Foundation for the Improvement of Living and Working Conditions, Loughlinstown House, Loughlinstown, Co. Dublin, Republic of Ireland
LUTTERKORT, Mrs Erica, Director
European Patent Office, Erhardtstrasse 27, D-8000 Munich 2, Federal Republic of Germany
LYYRA, Ms Mirja-Sisko, Medical Translator
Suomen Kääntäjäin ja Tulkkien Liitto, Pihlajatie 31 A 8, 00270 Helsinki, Finland

McCAFFREY, Dr Arthur, Advanced Development Manager
Digital Equipment Co. Limited, c/o Linda Hempel, Mailstop REO2-F/M2, Engineering Division, PO Box 121, Reading, Berkshire RG2 0TU, UK
McCALLUM, Mr Dugald, Translator
Unilever Research, Port Sunlight Laboratory, Quarry Road East, Bebington, Wirral, Merseyside L63 3JW, UK
McCLUSKEY, Mr Brian, Head of English Translation Division
Commission of the European Communities, Bâtiment Jean Monnet, rue Alcide de Gasperi, L-2920 Luxembourg, Luxembourg GD
McDONALD, Mr Ian, Director
Translation & Languages Consultants (International), 4 Witham Road, Woodhall Spa, Lincolnshire LN10 6RW, UK
McDONALD, Mr Laurence, Head of Translation Services
BP Chemicals Limited, Belgrave House, 76 Buckingham Palace Road, London SW1W 0SU, UK
McGILVRAY, Mr Ian, Freelance Translator
Viale A. Boito 67, 00199 Rome, Italy
McPARTLIN, Mr Chris, Head of Translation Department and Language Laboratory, Bayer AG, Friedrich-Ebert-Str. 217–333, D-5600 Wuppertal 1, Federal Republic of Germany
MAGNUSSON MURRAY, Mrs Ulla, Manager, Translations of Linguistics
ITT Europe Eng. Support Centre, Great Eastern House, Edinburgh Way, Harlow, Essex CM20 2BN, UK
MARQUES, Mr Luis G., Director, Translation and Records Division
UNESCO, 7 Place Fontenoy, 75007 Paris, France
MARSHALL, Mr Peter, Editor
Foreign Broadcast Information Service, Room P, 13 American Embassy, Grosvenor Square, London W1A 1AE, UK
MASION, Mr Bernhard, MT Developer
Computer Gesellschaft Konstanz GmbH, Postfach 11 42, D-7750 Konstanz, Federal Republic of Germany
MASON, Miss Jane, Translation Systems Coordinator
Rank Xerox, C&SE, PO Box 17, Bessemer Road, Welwyn Garden City, Hertfordshire AL7 1HE, UK

MATOZA, Mr Marc
  Automated Language Processing Systems, 3 avenue Beauregard, CH-2035 Corcelles, Switzerland
MAYORCAS-COHEN, Ms Pamela
  Commission of the European Communities, Division 9/C/2, JMO A2/111, Plateau Kirchberg, L-2920 Luxembourg, Luxembourg GD
MEER, Mr Jaap van der, Managing Director
  Ink Language Service Limited, Prins Hendriklaan 52, 1075 BE Amsterdam, The Netherlands
MELBY, Dr Alan, Director of Research and Development
  LinguaTech International, 381 West 2230 North, Suite 360, Provo, Utah 84604, USA
MELING, Mrs Nina, Sr. M. Trans.
  Phillips Petroleum Company Norway, PO Box 220, N-4056 Tananger, Norway
MELIS, Ms Jan, Translator/Reviser
  INIEX, 200 rue du Chéra, B-4000 Liège, Belgium
MIETLE, Mrs Jo-Ann, Freelance Translator
  Løtveitvegen 2, N-5064 Straumsgrend, Norway
MILNE, Mr David, Head of Translations
  AB BOFORS, Box 500, S-691 80 Bofors, Sweden
MOLDEN, Mr Walter, Manager, European Language Services
  IBM, Copenhagen DK-2100, Denmark
MOORE, Mrs F.H., Translator
  Press Centre, 75 Shoe Lane, London EC4, UK
MORRIS, Dr Rose, Head of Lexicology Division
  Human Sciences Research Council, Private Bag X41, Pretoria 0001, South Africa
MOSTERT, Mr Frederick J.A., Translator/Editor
  Merck Sharp & Dohme BV, Postbus 581, 2003PC Haarlem, The Netherlands
MOTA, Mr Valdemar, Manager, Foreign Languages Department
  AB VOLVO, S-405 08 Gothenburg, Sweden
MOULES, Mrs Leonore, Technical Translator
  Mannesmann Demag, 21 Danvers Road, Broughton, near Banbury, Oxon OX15 5DU, UK
MULLER, Drs Catherine, Director
  Taalwerk-Textperts BV, Beatrixlaan 1, PO Box 3019, 3760 DA Soest, The Netherlands
MULLIN, Dr Gill, Research Associate
  Canon (UK) Limited, Canon House, Manor Road, Wallington, Surrey SM6 0AJ, UK
MULLOY, Mrs Verena, Translator
  International Computers Limited, Kings House, 33 Kings Road, Reading, Berkshire RG1 3PX, UK

NAJJAR-BASHI, Miss Homa, Linguist and Translator
  59 Cranley Court, Cranley Road, Guildford, Surrey GU1 2JW, UK
NANCARROW, Mr P.H., Joint Research Director
  Wolfson College, Cambridge CB3 9BB, UK
NAPTHINE, Mrs Anne, Translator
  Shell (UK) Limited, Shell Centre, London SE1 7NA, UK
NAUSTHAUG, Mr Olav, Manager, Translations
  Norsk Data AS, PO Box 25, Bogervo, N-0621 Oslo 6, Norway

NEUKAMM, Siegfried, Dezernatsleiter
    Bundesstelle für Fernmeldestatistik, Wanneystr. 10, D-8035 Gauting 2, Federal Republic of Germany
NEWTON, Mr John, Managing Director
    Weidner Translation (Europe) Limited, Fryern House, 125 Winchester Road, Chandlers Ford, Eastleigh, Hampshire SO5 2DR, UK
NISHIDA, Dr Toyoaki, Assistant Professor
    Kyoto University, Sakyo-ku, Kyoto 606, Japan
NOCK, Mrs Anne, Freelance Translator
    15 Ewell Downs Road, Ewell, Epsom, Surrey KT17 3BT, UK
NORDSTROM, Mr Per-Erik, Head of Translation Department
    Saab-Scania, S-15187 Södertälje, Sweden
NORTHCUT, Mr John D., Systems Officer
    International Civil Aviation Organization, 1000 Sherbrooke Street West, Montreal, Quebec H3A 2R2, Canada

O'CONNOR, Ms Helen, Translator/Information Officer
    Electricity Council (Overseas Branch), 30 Millbank, London SW1P 4RD, UK
O'SHAUGHNESSY, Ms Patricia, Senior Translator
    Bayer UK Limited, Strawberry Hill, Newbury, Berkshire RG13 1JA, UK
OSTLER, Dr Nicholas, Senior Consultant
    Scicon Limited, 49 Berners Street, London W1P 4AQ, UK

PARSONS, Mr Denys, Freelance Editor
    21 Kingsley Place, London N6 5EA, UK
PASQUET, Ms Claudette, Freelance Translator
    48 avenue Jules Ferry, F-92160 Antony, France
PEARCE, Mr David, Translator
    FRAMATEG, Tour Fiat, F-92084 Paris La Défense, France
PENNEY, Miss Jan, Translator
    Shell UK Limited, Shell Centre, London SE1 7NA, UK
PENNINGS, Dr L.J.
    NOBIN, Burg. van Karnebeeklaan 19, 2585 BA The Hague, The Netherlands
PETERS, A.J., Head, Corporate Translation Department
    DSM, PO Box 18, 6160 MD Geleen, The Netherlands
PETTENGELL, Ms Karen, Office Manager
    Weidner Translation (Europe) Limited, Fryern House, 125 Winchester Road, Chandlers Ford, Eastleigh, Hampshire SO5 2DR, UK
PFEILSTUCKER, Mr Marc, Translator
    International Computers, Lovelace Road, Bracknell, Berkshire RG12 4SN, UK
PHILLIPS, Mrs Montserrat, Freelance Translator
    22 Greenfields Drive, Bridgnorth WV16 4RJ, UK
PIACQUADIO, Ann, Credit Controller
    Aslib, Information House, 26–27 Boswell Street, London WC1N 3JZ, UK
PICKEN, Ms Catriona, Freelance Translator and Consultant
    2 Sutherland Square, London SE17 3EQ, UK
PICKNETT, Mrs Jeanne-Marie
    W.S. Atkins Group Consultants, Woodcote Grove, Ashley Road, Epsom, Surrey KT18 5BW, UK
PIGOTT, Mr Ian, Systran Project Leader
    Commission of the European Communities, Bâtiment Jean Monnet B4/24, BP 1907, Luxembourg, Luxembourg GD

POLLHAMMER, Mr G., Senior Lecturer
Leeds Polytechnic, School of International Studies, Beckett Park, Leeds LS6 3QD, UK

RABEN, Prof. Joseph, Director
Paradigm Press Inc., PO Box 1057, Osprey, FL.33559-1057, USA

RAY, Ms Rebecca
Automated Language Processing Systems, 3 avenue Beauregard, CH-2030 Corcelles, Switzerland

RAYNIER, Mr Jean-Louis, Sales Manager
Gachot SA, 26 bis avenue de Paris – BP 14, 95230 Soisy-sous-Montmorency, France

REISENBERGER, Mr Rainer, Managing Director
Arrow Technical Translations Limited, Princes House, Orange Street, Canterbury, Kent CT1 2JA, UK

RERAT, Mme Kipsten, Translator
INRA – CNRZ, Unité Centrale de Documentation, 78350 Jouy-en-Josas, France

RICE, Miss Beryl, Head of Languages Unit
ICI plc, Imperial Chemical House, Millbank, London SW1P 3JF, UK

RIDER, Ms Inger, Editor
Esselte Studium, S-171 76 Solna, Sweden

RIEGER, Mr Hans J., Manager, Translation Department
Hoechst AG, Postfach 800320, D-6230 Hoechst 80, Federal Republic of Germany

RISHWORTH, Mr Ronald, Head of Translation Division
Shell Internationale Petroleum Maatschappij BV, PO Box 162, 2501 AN The Hague, The Netherlands

ROBERTS, Mrs Dawne, Freelance Translator
71 Wensleydale Road, Hampton, Middlesex TW12 2LP, UK

RODRIGUEZ, Carlos, Head, Translation Section
International Organization for Standardization (ISO), 1 rue de Varembe, CH-1211 Geneva 20, Switzerland

ROEBUCK, Miss Michele, Translator
ICI plc, Petrochemicals & Plastics Division, PO Box 90, Wilton, Middlesbrough, Cleveland TS6 8JE, UK

ROLFE, Mr Paul, Senior Library Assistant
Bath University Library, Claverton Down, Bath BA2 7AY, UK

ROLLING, Loll, Head, Multilingual Action Programme
Commission of the European Communities, L-2920 Luxembourg, Luxembourg GD

ROOKE, Mr David
Textnet, 10 St Cross Street, London EC1N 8UB, UK

ROOKE, Mr Robert
Textnet, 10 St Cross Street, London EC1N 8UB, UK

ROSSITER, Miss Angie, Software Nationalisation Coordinator
Rank Xerox Limited, 30 Church Street, Welwyn Garden City, Hertfordshire, AL6 9LX, UK

RUE, Mrs Jacqueline de la, Editor, Translation Department
Bell Telephone Manufacturing Company, Francis Wellesplein 1, B-2018 Antwerp, Belgium

RUTGERS, Mr Bernardo T., Chief, Language Branch
International Civil Aviation Organization, 1000 Sherbrooke Street West, Suite 400, Room 1305, Montreal, Quebec H3A 2R2, Canada
RYDER, Mr John, Technical Translator
AB Volvo, S-405 08 Gothenburg, Sweden

SADLER, Dr Victor, Linguist
BSO/Research, Postbus 8348, NL-3503 RH Utrecht, The Netherlands
SALAMA-CARR, Dr Myriam, Lecturer in French
University of Salford, c/o 91 St Ann's Way, Leeds LS4 2SQ, UK
SANS, Mr René, Member of the Board
APETI (Asoc. Prof. Española de Traductores e Intérpretes), 20 Velayos Street, Dp 5-A, 28035 Madrid, Spain
SAWITZA, Ms Annette, Technical Writer
Norsk Data GmbH, Solinger Str. 9, D-4330 Mülheim/Ruhr, Federal Republic of Germany
SAWYER, Mr Kevin, Translator
Framatome, 10 rue Juliette Récamier, F-69006 Lyons, France
SCHATZ, Ms Hannelore, Secretary/Translator
Girozentrale Vienna, 68 Cornhill, London EC3V 3QE, UK
SCHMITZ, Mr Klaus-Dirk, Researcher
Universität des Saarlandes, Sonderforschungsbereich 100, SFB 100, Bau 4, D-6600 Saarbrücken 11, Federal Republic of Germany
SCHWOB, Mr Kurt, Teacher of Translation
Zurich School of Interpreters, Scheuchzerstr 68, CH-8006 Zurich, Switzerland
SCOTT, Miss F.
Mycrom Information Systems, Unit 13, Horseshoe Park, Pangbourne, Reading, Berkshire RG8 7JW, UK
SECHERESSE, F., Translator
Alsthom, 55 avenue Jean Jaurès, 93000 Le Bourget, France
SENECAL, Ms Brigitte
Shell Recherche SA, Centre de Recherche, F-76530 Grand-Couronne, France
SEREN-ROSSO, Mrs Margaret, Freelance Technical Translator and Writer
'Résidence Les Dauphins', 3 square Regnault/Déf. 6, F-92400 Courbevoie, France
SEVERINI, Dr Alfiero, Linguist–Programmer (Systran)
Informalux SA – Luxembourg, 1A route de Trèves, Findel, L-2632 Luxembourg, Luxembourg GD
SIENY, Dr Mahmoud, Director
Arabic Linguistic Institute, King Saud University, PO Box 4274, Riyadh 11491, Saudi Arabia
SIMPSON, Prof. Ekundayo, Professor of French/Conference Interpreter
University of Lagos (Nigeria), Department of Modern European Languages, Faculty of Arts, Akoka, Nigeria
SIQVELAND, Mr Torgeir M., Sr. Coordinator Translation
Mobil Exploration Norway Inc., PO Box 510, N-4001 Stavanger, Norway
SIVESIND, Ms Linda, Translator/Translation Administrator
Ministry of Foreign Affairs, 7 Juni Pl. 1, Postboks 8114 Dep., N-0032 Oslo, Norway
SKINNER, Ms Hazel, Translator/Interpreter
British Aerospace, 59 Collinswood Road, Stevenage, Hertfordshire SG2 9ES, UK

SLADE, Ms Julie, Technical Translator/Manager
British Telecom, BTRL, Translation Service, Martlesham Heath, Ipswich IP5 7RE, UK
SLEEBOS, Ms Eveline, Freelance Translator and Interpreter
Vlaskamp 374, 2592 AL The Hague, The Netherlands
SMITH, Miss Christine, Librarian
Property Services Agency, C 122, Whitgift Centre, Croydon CR9 3LY, UK
SMITH, Mr David, Translation Program Manager
Digital Equipment Co. Limited, Engineering Division, Mailstop REO2-F/M2, PO Box 121, Reading, Berkshire RG2 OTU, UK
SNELL, Ms Barbara, Translation Consultant
Translation Service, 14 Albion Street, Gloucester GL4 8HX, UK
SOMERS, Dr Harold, Lecturer
UMIST, Centre for Computational Linguistics, PO Box 88, Manchester M60 1QD, UK
STANFORTH, Professor Anthony, Head of Department of Languages
Heriot-Watt University, Chambers Street, Edinburgh EH1 1HX, UK
STANGE, Mr Chris, Head of Translation Department
E. Merck, Frankfurterstr. 250, D-6100 Darmstadt, Federal Republic of Germany
STANLEY, Mr Bob, Managing Director
Interlingua TTI Limited, 15–19 Kingsway, London WC2B 6UU, UK
STENGEL, Mr Thomas, Translator
Alsthom, 38 avenue Kléber, F-95795 Paris Cedex 16, France
STENTIFORD, Dr Fred, Head of Group
British Telecom, BT Research Laboratories, Martlesham Heath, Ipswich IP5 7RE, UK
STEYN, Cees van, Management Consultant
Van de Bunt Management Consultants, PO Box 7960, 1008 AD Amsterdam, The Netherlands
STOLKE, Mr Nicholas
Automated Language Processing Systems, 3 avenue Beauregard, CH-2035 Corcelles, Switzerland
STOLL, C-H, General Manager
Systran Institut/ECAT, 9–11 rue Jean Pierre Sauvage, L-2514 Luxembourg, Luxembourg GD
STOWELL, Mr John, Senior Translator
Boehringer Ingelheim Limited, Southern Industrial Estate, Bracknell, Berkshire RG12 4YS, UK
SUMMERS, Dr Richard, Chief Translator
Departments of Environment and Transport, Room P3/156, 2 Marsham Street, London SW1P 3EB, UK
SUTHERLAND, Mr Gray, Senior Translator
HQ AFCENT, BFPO 28
SUTHERLAND, Mr Roderick, Translation Manager
Volvo Car Corporation, Department 52381, PVP, S-405 08 Torslanda, Sweden
SUTTON, Mr Patrick, Translator
Department of Health and Social Security, Room A311, Alexander Fleming House, Elephant and Castle, London SE1 6BY, UK
SWEENEY, Ms Bernice, Manager – Education and Training
ECHO (European Commission Host Organisation), 177 route d'Esch, L-1471 Luxembourg, Luxembourg GD

TERSTALL, Rina, Dictionary Editor
Elsevier Science Publishers, PO Box 330, 1000 AH Amsterdam, The Netherlands

THOMAS, Mrs Patricia, Research Officer
University of Surrey, Department of Linguistic & International Studies, Guildford, Surrey GU2 5XH, UK

THOMAS, Mr Peter, Translator
Bank of Norway, Utrednings og Informasjonsavdelingen, Norges Bank, Bankplassen 2, N-0151 Oslo 1, Norway

THOUIN, Professor Benoît, Programme Coordinator and President
CLC Limited, University of Ottawa, PO Box 420, Station A, Hull, Quebec J8Y 6P2, Canada

TORSVIK, Ms Anne, Senior Translation Editor
Digital Equipment Corporation A/S, Ammerudveien 22, N-0958 Oslo 9, Norway

TOUBRO, Ms Charlotte, Research Assistant
Eurotra-DK, University of Copenhagen, Eurotra-DK, Njalsgade 80, DK-2300 Copenhagen S, Denmark

TRABULSI, Mr Sami, Head of Department
Gachot SA, 26 bis avenue de Paris – BP 14, F-95230 Soisy-sous-Montmorency, France

TROJANUS, Mr Karl-Heinz, Translator
NATO, 11 Beim Weisenstein, D-6022 Saarbrücken-Dudweiler, Federal Republic of Germany

TYBULEWICZ, Mr Albin, Scientific Editor/Translator
2 Oak Dene, West Ealing, London W13 8AW, UK

URLINGS, Lou
Van de Bunt Management Consultants, PO Box 7960, 1008 AD Amsterdam, The Netherlands

VALLARIO, Dott. Milvia
Aeritalia Gra Dasv, Corso Marche 41, 1-10146 Turin, Italy

VALLINI, Mr Vittorio, Technical Publication Automation
Aeritalia Gra Dasv, Corso Marche 41, 1-10146 Turin, Italy

VAN DER LAAN, Mr Herman, Management Consultant
International Labour Office, CH-1211 Geneva 22, Switzerland

VERMEYEN, Karel, Translator
Lexitel SA, 119 Chaussée St Pierre, B-1040 Brussels, Belgium

VERRINDER, Mr Jeremy, Dean, Faculty of Languages
Polytechnic of Central London, Euston Centre, London NW1 3ET, UK

VIGNAUD, Mrs Yvonne, Chairman and Managing Director
Alpha International Translations Limited, 74 Maida Vale, London W9 1PR, UK

VOIGT, Dr Walter, Publisher
Langenscheidt Publishers, Postfach 40 11 20, D-8000 Munich 40, Federal Republic of Germany

VROOMEN, Dr W.A.M. de
Nobin, Burg. van Karnebeeklaan 19, 2585 BA The Hague, The Netherlands

WAGNER, Mrs Emma, Reviser
Commission of the European Communities, PO Box 1907, Bâtiment Jean Monnet, Luxembourg, Luxembourg GD

WALL, Miss Shelagh, Translator
    Department of Trade and Industry, Ebury Bridge House, 2–18 Ebury Bridge Road, London SW1W 8QD, UK
WEEKS, David, Self-employed Translator
    Clare Cottage, Hale Road, Farnham, Surrey GU9 9QH, UK
WHITMORE, Mr Russell, Deputy Head of Translations Section
    Central Electricity Generating Board, Sudbury House, 15 Newgate Street, London EC1A 7AU, UK
WHITTARD, Mrs Ruth, Translator
    Mothercare (UK) Limited, Cherry Tree Road, Watford, Hertfordshire WD2 5SH, UK
WIERTZ, Mrs Jolien, Office Organisation Consultant
    Philips International, BV Corporation 08E Department, Postbox 218, 5600 MD Eindhoven, The Netherlands
WILLIAMSON, Ms Elizabeth, Freelance Translator
    18 Crets-de-Champel, CH-1206 Geneva, Switzerland
WILMS, Mr Franz-Josef M., Scientific Research Assistant
    Universität des Saarlandes, Projekt SUSANNAH, Fachrichtung 'Angewandte Sprachwissenschaft', D-6600 Saarbrucken 11, Federal Republic of Germany
WILSON, Mrs Barbara, Senior Translator
    Foreign and Commonwealth Office/ODA, Room WH MZ42, Whitehall, London SW1A 2AH, UK
WINTER, Jutta, Translator, Research Assistant in MT Project
    IAI – EUROTRA-D Project, Martin-Luther-Str. 14, D-6600 Saarbrücken, Federal Republic of Germany
WIRZENIUS, Mrs Pirkko, Secretary and Technical Translator
    KONE Corporation, KLG Research Centre, PO Box 6, SF-05801 Hyvinkää, Finland
WOOD, Mr Derek, Freelance Translator
    4 Mansfield Close, West Parley, Wimbourne, Dorset BH22 8QP, UK
WOODHALL, Mr Michael
    Manchester Business School, Language Learning Centre, Booth Street West, Manchester M15 6PB, UK

ZEGERS, Mr Cornelis, Translation Coordinator
    Texas Instruments, BP 5, F-06270 Villeneuve-Loubet, France
ZEITLER, Ms Christine, Leiterin Übersetzungen
    c/o BMW AG, Postfach 40 02 40, D-8000 Munich 40, Federal Republic of Germany
ZENTNER, Miss Sonja, Chief Translator
    HM Customs and Excise, King's Beam House (R 257), Mark Lane, London EC3R 7HE, UK